The
Ultimate
Cake Decorator

The
Ultimate
Cake
Decorator

Janice Murfitt and Louise Pickford

HERMES
HOUSE

This edition published in 1998 by Hermes House

Hermes House is an imprint of
Anness Publishing Limited
Hermes House
88-89 Blackfriars Road
London SE1 8HA

© Anness Publishing Limited 1992, 1995

Published in the USA by Hermes House
Anness Publishing Inc., 27 West 20th Street, New York, NY 10011;
(800) 354-9657

A CIP catalogue record for this book is available from the British Library.

ISBN 1 84038 060 8

Publisher: Joanna Lorenz
Project Editor: Judith Simons
Art Director: Peter Bridgewater
Designer: James Lawrence
Photography: David Armstrong

Printed in Singapore by Star Standard Industries Pte. Ltd.

1 3 5 7 9 10 8 6 4 2

Measurements

Three sets of equivalent measurements have been provided in the
recipes here, in the following order: Metric, Imperial and American.
The golden rule is never to mix the units of measure within a recipe.
The conversions are approximate, but accurate enough to
ensure successful results.

CONTENTS

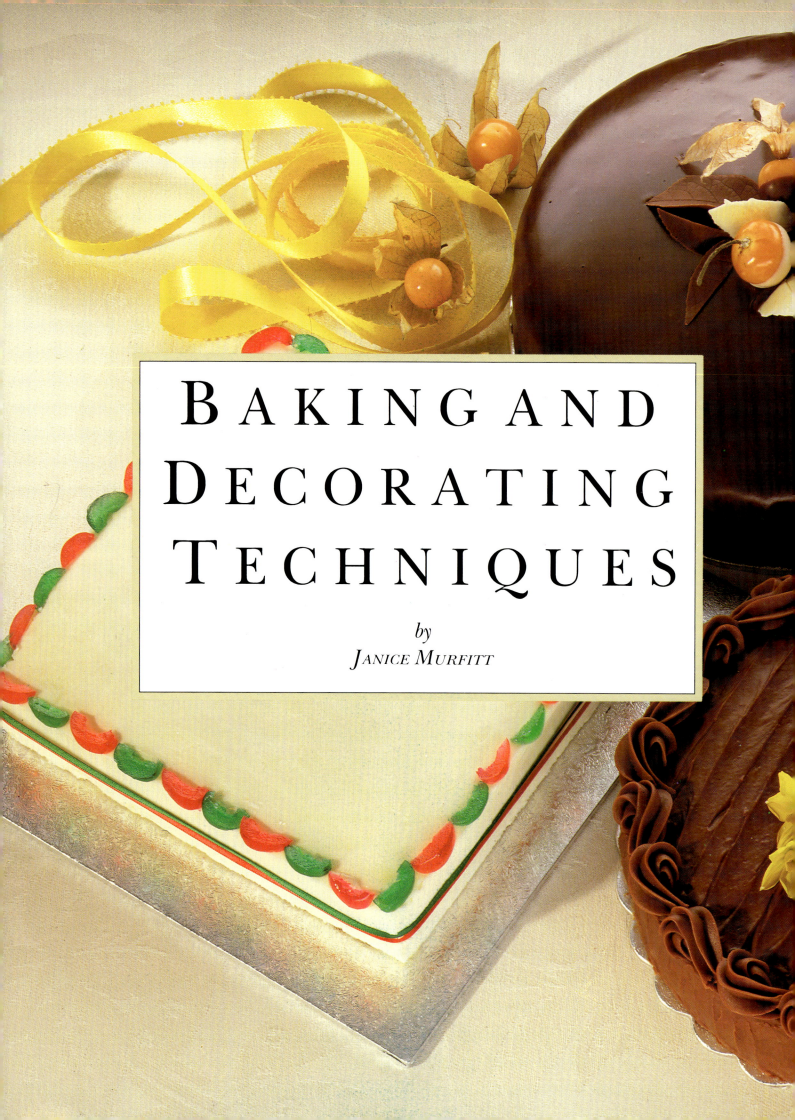

BAKING AND DECORATING TECHNIQUES

by

Janice Murfitt

INTRODUCTION

Baking and Decorating Techniques covers all aspects of cake making, icing and decorating and has been carefully planned to take you step by step through all the stages and methods involved. Beginning with the basics, there are tried and tested recipes for a wide variety of classic sponge and fruit cakes and simple icings and frostings for quick-and-easy baking. There are also recipes for the classic cake coverings — marzipan, sugarpaste (fondant) and royal icing — plus step-by-step guides to covering square and round cakes.

When it comes to the final decoration on a cake, this is where your own creative skills and imagination can be used to full effect.

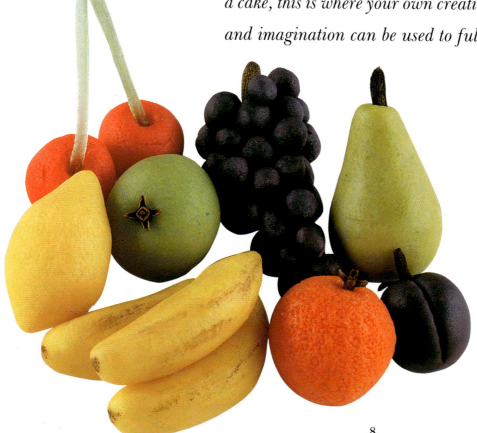

There are many techniques included here from simple bought decorations, such as coloured ribbons and flowers, and sweets (candies), nuts and crystallized fruits, to chocolate run-outs, curls and cut-outs. Marzipan and sugarpaste (fondant) can be coloured and moulded or modelled into fruit and flower shapes, used for cut-out flowers, frills and abstract decorations, and for crimped and embossed designs. Finally, royal icing, perhaps the most difficult medium to work with, can be piped to produce the daintiest lace pieces, sugar flowers, run-outs and beautiful borders. Follow the detailed illustrated step-by-step guides to perfect cake making and decorating to create a host of varied finishes, from the simple to the lavish.

BAKING TECHNIQUES

Cake-making Equipment

To obtain the very best results when making cakes, it is necessary to have a selection of good equipment. Start with the basic items that are needed immediately, then gradually add to your collection as your skills progress. Always buy good quality equipment, and with care it will not need replacing.

1 Cooling rack
2 Scissors
3 Cakeboards
4 Electric hand mixer
5 Wire whisk
6 Scales
7 Cake boxes
8 Measuring jug
9 Cutters
10 Ruler
11 Mixing bowls
12 Greaseproof (wax) paper
13 Baking parchment
14 Baking sheets
15 Pastry brushes

16 Cling film (plastic wrap)
17 Plastic spatula
18 Wooden spoon
19 Baking tins (pans)
20 Knife
21 Palette knife (spatula)
22 Cranked-handle palette knife (spatula)
23 Pencils
24 Standard measuring spoons
25 Standard measuring cups

GENERAL EQUIPMENT

The following items will be needed for making basic cakes and icings and for simple cake decorating:

SCALES – accurate scales for weighing all cake ingredients are essential. Without them, good results cannot be achieved. Choose scales with separate weights for the most accurate results.

MEASURING JUG – with metric, imperial and cup measurements for accurate measuring of liquids in millilitres, fluid ounces or pints, or dry and liquid ingredients in cup sizes.

STANDARD MEASURING SPOONS – for spoon measurements which are constantly accurate for dry and liquid ingredients; general spoons vary in size, causing inaccurate measurement.

STANDARD MEASURING CUPS – like the spoons, these give a constantly accurate measurement for dry ingredients and liquids.

WOODEN SPOONS – a selection of wooden spoons with handles of varying lengths, suitable for beating large or small quantities of mixture.

WHISKS – a small hand rotary whisk or a wire whisk are necessary for whisking cream, egg whites or light mixtures to give a smooth consistency.

ELECTRIC HAND MIXERS – invaluable for whisking mixtures over hot water, such as whisked sponge cake or cooked meringues.

ELECTRIC FOOD MIXERS – these more efficient mixers are necessary when making large quantities of cake mixtures or icings for wedding cakes or special occasions. Care must be taken when using not to over-mix.

FOOD PROCESSORS – ideal for chopping ingredients quickly, beating butter icing or for cake mixtures. Care must be taken not to over-process mixtures.

PLASTIC OR WOODEN MIXING SPATULAS – these come in many shapes and sizes, usually made with a flexible plastic blade. Essential for folding ingredients thoroughly into lightly-whipped mixtures or cake batters, and for removing all the mixture from the bowl.

BOWLS – a selection of small, medium and large heatproof bowls in glass or china, with smooth rounded insides for thorough, even mixing when using a wooden spoon or an electric mixer.

TINS (PANS) AND MOULDS – always choose the best quality tins (pans) for baking. The thickness of the metal prevents overcooking and ensures the tins (pans) retain their shape without bending or warping.

BAKING SHEETS – choose heavy-duty baking sheets with flat edges which will not warp in the oven. These are necessary for baking meringues, pastry or sponge cake layers. Baking sheets which have sides are ideal for standing cake tins (pans) on in the oven.

COOLING RACKS – obtainable in different sizes, round or oblong, with wide or narrow mesh. It is advisable to have a selection.

PAPERS – greaseproof (waxed) paper, baking parchment, run-out silk and rice papers all have their own use. Greaseproof (wax) paper is suitable for lining tins; finer waxed paper and run-out silk, if available, is flexible and ideal for icing run-outs and piped decorations; baking parchment is ideal for meringues, spreading melted chocolate, drying moulded or cut-out sugar decorations; rice paper is for biscuits, macaroons and meringue mixture.

GLAZING BRUSHES – small and medium brushes are useful for brushing tins and moulds with melted fat or oil. A larger size is required for brushing cakes with glaze.

CUTTERS – a set of plain round and fluted cutters is always useful; fancy biscuit (cookie) cutters are available in many sizes and you will find endless uses for them.

KNIVES – a selection of small, medium and large knives are necessary for preparing ingredients and for cutting cakes into layers.

METAL PALETTE KNIVES (SPATULAS) – small, medium and large straight palette knives (spatulas) with flexible blades are used for loosening cakes from tins, and for applying, spreading and smoothing icing. A small cranked-handle palette knife (spatula) is ideal for lifting and transferring small and fragile icing decorations.

RULER, SCISSORS AND PENCIL – always needed when making cakes.

CAKEBOARDS – available in many different shapes and sizes, the most popular being rounds and squares. Use thick cakeboards for large iced (frosted) cakes and wedding cakes, and the thin cakeboards for light cakes with butter or cream icing (frosting).

BOXES – cake boxes are invaluable when making celebration cakes; once they have been made and placed on a cakeboard, they can be stored in boxes to keep them clean, dry and free from damage.

Cake Tins (Pans)

It is so important to have the correct size and shaped tin (pan) for the recipe you are following in order to get the best results. If the tin (pan) size or shape is incorrect, it will not only affect the size and depth of the cake, but also the cooking time, texture and appearance.

Always measure a cake tin (pan) across the base, not the top, to give an accurate measurement.

CHOOSING CAKE TINS (PANS)

The quality of cake tins (pans) is just as important, especially for cakes that require long, slow cooking. They should always be made of the best quality metal and have a fixed base which will not distort during cooking, or bend easily during handling or storing. Good cake tins (pans) are an investment; they only need to be purchased once if they are looked after properly.

Always line cake tins (pans) with greaseproof (wax) paper whenever possible, unless the recipe states otherwise; this will prevent marking or discolouring of the tin (pan). Wash and dry the tin (pan) thoroughly and store in a warm place to prevent rusting.

HIRING CAKE TINS (PANS)

Unusual-shaped cake tins (pans) are fun to use, especially when making a celebration cake. Rather than incurring the expense of a specially-shaped tin (pan) which you may only use once, it may be better to hire one.

These tins (pans) come in a variety of shapes and sizes and are available for hire through many kitchen shops, cake-icing specialists or bakeries. They normally require a deposit for the tin (pan), then a small hire fee which is charged at a daily rate.

Lining Cake Tins (Pans)

Cake tins (pans) are lined in different ways, depending on the type of cake you are making. Sometimes tins (pans) are only lightly greased and floured, as when making a light whisked sponge cake mixture. In this way the shape holds to the sides of the tin (pan) during cooking; if paper-lined, it would pull away, producing a misshapen cake.

Most cakes, however, are baked in tins (pans) lined with greaseproof (wax) paper. Sometimes only the base is covered for a cake requiring short-term cooking. Both the base and sides are lined when cakes need longer cooking, or for richer cake mixtures which may stick to the tin (pan), causing difficulty when turning out. Swiss (jelly) roll tins (pans) have to be lined neatly with one piece of paper so the cake can be turned out of the tin (pan) quickly to form into a roll. Cakes which need long-term cooking, such as fruit cakes, require a double thickness of paper inside the tin (pan) and the protection of double thickness brown paper around the outside so that the cake cooks evenly throughout.

Generally cake tins (pans) are brushed with melted vegetable fat or oil and lined with single or double thickness greaseproof (wax) paper. Non-stick baking parchment paper, which is slightly thicker, may also be used, especially if mixtures need to be turned out quickly.

Lining a Sandwich Tin (Shallow Cake Pan)

1 Place the tin (pan) over a piece of greaseproof (wax) paper. Using a pencil, draw around the outside of the tin (pan). Cut out the shape using a pair of sharp scissors.

2 Brush the tin (pan) lightly with melted vegetable fat or oil and fit the greaseproof (wax) paper shape over the base of the tin (pan). Brush the paper with melted white fat or oil.

MIXING CAKES SUCCESSFULLY

There are a few simple guidelines which must be followed to achieve the best results when making any cake.

- Unlike many recipes, those for cakes must be followed accurately. Measure all the ingredients carefully with scales or measuring cups, spoons and a measuring jug. Do not be tempted to add a little extra of any ingredient as this will upset the balance.
- Always make sure you have the correct shape and size of tin (pan) for the recipe, otherwise this will affect the depth of the cake, the cooking time and the texture.
- Make sure the tin (pan) is properly prepared and lined for cooking the recipe you have chosen to make.
- Check that you have all the necessary ingredients that are stated in the recipe, and that they are at the right temperature.
- Eggs should be size 3, unless otherwise stated. Farm eggs impart a wonderful flavour, but unless they are graded they may be too large for cakes, making the mixture slack.
- Ensure soft margarine is kept chilled in the refrigerator to maintain the right consistency, and leave butter out to become room temperature and soft for creaming.
- Sift all dry ingredients to help aerate the mixture and to disperse lumps.
- When making cakes by hand, beat well with a wooden spoon until the mixture is light and glossy; scrape down the mixture during beating with a plastic mixing spatula to ensure even mixing.
- If a cake is being made in a food processor or an electric mixer, be very careful not to overprocess or overbeat. This will cause the mixture to collapse and dip in the middle during baking. Remember to scrape down the batter with a plastic spatula during mixing, and to follow the manufacturer's instructions for the best results.
- If ingredients have to be folded into a mixture, use a plastic spatula with a flexible blade to cut through the mixture, turning it over and at the same time moving the bowl. Do not be tempted to stir, or be heavy-handed with, the mixture or it will lose air and become heavy.
- Level mixtures in the tin (pan) before baking, to ensure the cake top is flat when baked.
- Do check that your oven is at the correct temperature before cooking the cake.
- Test the cake before the stated cooking time as this is only a guide, and test the cake again before removing it from the oven.

COOKING CAKES SUCCESSFULLY

Many problems arise when cooking cakes, mainly because ovens do vary. Factors affecting cooking results include the heat source. Some ovens are hot, others are slow, others are fan-assisted. Recipes always give cooking times, but you must remember these times are simply a guide. At the same time, the guidelines below assume the recipes and tin (pan) sizes have been followed as advised.

- Do check that your oven is preheated to the temperature stated in the recipe. Failure to do so will affect the rising of the cake and the cooking time.
- If the cake appears to be cooked before the given time, it may indicate that the oven is hot; conversely, if it takes longer to cook, it means the oven is slow.

- A good test is to cook a homemade two-egg quick mix cake in a 20 cm/8 in sandwich tin (shallow cake pan) for about 35–40 minutes at 160°C/325°F/Gas 3. The cake should appear level and lightly browned. If the cake is cooked before the time, adjust the setting lower in the future, or higher for a cake which takes longer.
- The temperature of the cake mixture can cause the cooking time to vary. If conditions are cold, the mixture will be cold and take longer to cook; in the same way, if it is warm cooking time will be slightly quicker.
- The surface of the cake should be evenly browned and level; if the cake is overcooked on one side or risen to one side, the heating of the oven is uneven or the oven shelf is not level.

Lining a Swiss (Jelly) Roll Tin

1 Place the tin (pan) in the centre of a piece of greaseproof (wax) paper, 2.5 cm/1 in larger all round than the tin (pan). Cut from the corner of the paper to the corner of the tin (pan), using a pair of sharp scissors.

2 Lightly brush the tin (pan) with melted vegetable fat or oil and fit the paper into the tin (pan), neatly pressing into the corners. Brush the paper lightly with melted vegetable fat or oil.

Lining a Deep Cake Tin (Pan)

1 Place the tin (pan) on a double thickness of greaseproof (wax) paper or baking parchment. Draw around the base with a pencil. Cut out the marked shape with a pair of scissors.

2 Cut a strip of double thickness greaseproof (wax) paper or baking parchment long enough to wrap around the outside of the tin (pan), leaving a small overlap. It should stand 2.5 cm/1 in above the top of the tin (pan).

3 Brush the base and sides of the tin (pan) with melted vegetable fat or oil. Place the double strip of paper inside the tin (pan), pressing well against the sides and making sharp creases if it must fit into corners. Place the cut-out shape in the base of the tin and press it flat.

4 Brush the base and side papers well with melted vegetable fat or oil. Place a strip of double thickness brown paper around the outside of the tin (pan) and tie securely with string.

Line a baking (cookie) sheet with three or four layers of brown paper and stand the tin (pan) on top.

Testing Cakes

• Always check the cake five or ten minutes before the given cooking time is completed, just in case the oven is a little fast. It is always better to slightly under-cook a cake, since the mixture continues to cook in the tin (pan) after removing it from the oven.

• Always test the cake immediately before removing it from the oven, just in case it is not ready at the advised time. This could be due to a slow oven.

• For all cakes – other than fruit cakes – test by pressing very lightly on the centre of the cake with the fingers; if it springs back, the cake is cooked. Otherwise your fingers will leave a slight depression, indicating the cake needs extra cooking time. Retest at five-minute intervals.

• Fruit cakes are best tested using a warmed skewer inserted into the centre

of the cake. If the skewer comes out clean, the cake is ready. Otherwise return the cake to the oven and retest at ten-minute intervals.

Storing Cakes

Everyday cakes, sponges and meringues may be kept in an airtight container or simply wrapped in cling film (plastic wrap) or foil; this will ensure they keep moist and fresh with the exclusion of the air. Store the cakes in a cool, dry place for up to a week; meringues will store for up to one month. Avoid warm, moist conditions as this will encourage mould growth.

To store fruit cakes, leave the lining paper on the cakes. This seals onto the surface during cooking and keeps the cakes moist and fresh. Wrap the cakes in a double layer of foil and keep in a cool

place. Never seal a fruit cake in an airtight container for long periods of time as this may encourage mould growth.

Rich, heavy fruit cakes keep well because of their high fruit content; although they are moist and full of flavour, they are at their best when they are first made. Such cakes do mature with keeping, but most should be consumed within three months. If you are going to keep a fruit cake for several months before marzipanning or icing it, pour over alcohol a little at a time at monthly intervals, turning the cake each time.

Light fruit cakes are stored in the same way as their rich cousins, but since they have less fruit in them, their keeping qualities are not so good. These cakes are at their best when first made, or eaten within one month of making.

For longterm storage, fruit cakes are better frozen in their double wrapping and foil.

Once the cakes have been marzipanned and iced, they will keep longer. But iced cakes must be stored in cardboard boxes in a warm, dry atmosphere, to maintain them dust-free and in good condition. Damp and cold are the worst conditions, causing the icing to stain and colourings to run.

Freeze a decorated celebration cake in the cake box, ensuring the lid is sealed with tape. Take the cake out of its box and defrost it slowly in a cool, dry place. When the cake has thawed, transfer to a warm, dry place to ensure the icing dries completely. Wedding cakes which have been kept for a long time may need re-icing and decorating.

CALCULATING QUANTITIES AND CUTTING CAKES

To work out the number of servings from a round or square cake is extremely simple and the final total depends on whether you require just a small finger of cake or a more substantial slice.

Whether the cake is round or square, cut across the cake from edge to edge into about 2.5 cm/1 in slices, thinner if desired. (Do not cut a round cake into wedges.) Cut each slice into 4 cm/1½ in pieces or thereabouts.

Using these guidelines, it should be easy to calculate the number of cake slices you can cut from any given size

cake. A square cake is larger than a round cake of the same proportions and will yield more slices. On a round cake the slices become smaller at the curved edges, and the first and last slice of the cake is mainly marzipan and icing. Always keep this in mind when calculating the servings.

Example
According to the measurements above a 20 cm/8 in square cake will yield about 40 slices and a 20 cm/8 in round cake will yield about 35 slices.

BASIC CAKE RECIPES

A quick mix sponge cake is light and fluffy; ideal for this springtime cake decorated with lemon butter icing and marzipan flowers.

Quick Mix Sponge Cake

This is a quick-and-easy reliable recipe for making everyday cakes in various sizes, shapes and flavours.

INGREDIENTS	2-EGG QUANTITY	3-EGG QUANTITY	4-EGG QUANTITY
● Self-raising flour	125 g/4 oz/1 cup	175 g/6 oz/1½ cups	225 g/8 oz/2 cups
● Baking powder	5 ml/1 tsp/1 tsp	7.5 ml/1½ tsp/1½ tsp	10 ml/2 tsp/2 tsp
● Caster (superfine) sugar	125 g/4 oz/½ cup	175 g/6 oz/¾ cup	225 g/8 oz/1 cup
● Soft margarine	125 g/4 oz/½ cup	175 g/6 oz/¾ cup	225 g/8 oz/1 cup
● Eggs	2	3	4

1 Preheat the oven to 170°C/325°F/Gas 3. Prepare the tin (pan) according to the recipe.

2 Sift the flour and baking powder into a bowl. Add sugar, margarine and eggs. Mix together with a wooden spoon, then beat for 1–2 minutes until smooth and glossy.

3 Stir in chosen flavourings and beat until evenly blended.

4 Pour into prepared tin (pan), level the top and bake as required.

CHOICE OF FLAVOURINGS

The following amounts are for a 2-egg quantity cake. Increase the suggested flavourings to suit the quantity being made.

Citrus – 10 ml/2 tsp/2 tsp finely grated orange, lemon or lime rind
Chocolate – add 15 ml/1 tbsp/1 tbsp cocoa blended with 15 ml/1 tbsp/1 tbsp boiling water, or 25 g/1 oz/scant ¼ cup chocolate dots, melted
Coffee – 10 ml/2 tsp/2 tsp coffee granules blended with 5 ml/1 tsp/1 tsp boiling water
Nuts – replace 25 g/1 oz/2 tbsp flour with finely ground nuts

Whisked Sponge Cake

This light sponge can be used for making Swiss rolls, cakes or gateaux.

Airy whisked sponge cake is the classic base for swiss rolls; here incorporating a cream and raspberry filling.

INGREDIENTS	2-EGG QUANTITY	3-EGG QUANTITY	4-EGG QUANTITY
• Eggs	2	3	4
• Caster (superfine) sugar	50 g/2 oz/¼ cup	75 g/3 oz/⅓ cup	125 g/4 oz/½ cup
• Plain (all-purpose) flour	50 g/2 oz/½ cup	75 g/3 oz/¾ cup	125 g/4 oz/1 cup

1 Preheat the oven to 180°C/350°F/Gas 4. Prepare the tin (pan) according to the recipe.

2 Whisk together the eggs and sugar in a heatproof bowl until thoroughly blended. Place the bowl over a saucepan of simmering water and whisk until thick and pale. Remove the bowl from the saucepan and continue whisking until the mixture is cool and leaves a thick trail on the surface when the beaters are lifted.

3 Sift the flour onto the surface, add any desired flavourings and, using a plastic spatula, carefully fold the flour into the mixture until smooth.

4 Pour into a prepared tin (pan), tilt to level and bake as required.

TO MAKE A SWISS (JELLY) ROLL

1 *Sprinkle a sheet of greaseproof (wax) paper liberally with caster sugar. Turn the baked cake upside down onto the paper to release. Quickly remove the lining paper.*

2 *Trim off the edges of the cake for an even rectangular outline. Spread the cake thickly with approximately 225 g/8 oz/½ lb warmed jam.*

3 *Fold the paper over from the back to start the roll, then pull the paper gradually until the roll is complete.*

CHOICE OF FLAVOURINGS

The following amounts are for a 2-egg quantity cake. Increase the suggested flavourings to suit the quantity being made.

Citrus – 10 ml/2 tsp/2 tsp finely grated orange, lemon, lime rind
Chocolate – replace 15 ml/1 tbsp/1 tbsp cocoa powder for flour, or add 25 g/1 oz/1 square plain (semisweet) chocolate, melted
Coffee – 10 ml/2 tsp/2 tsp coffee granules blended with 5 ml/1 tsp/1 tsp boiling water
Nuts – replace 25 g/1 oz/2 tbsp flour with the same proportion of finely ground nuts.

Madeira Cake

A good, plain cake which can be made as an alternative to a light or rich fruit cake. It is firm and moist, can be flavoured to taste, and makes a good base for icing and decorating.

A madeira cake is traditionally used for decorative novelty cakes, as it provides a firm and lasting sponge base.

MADEIRA CAKE CHART

Cake Tin Sizes	15 cm/6 in Square	18 cm/7 in Square	20 cm/8 in Square	23 cm/9 in Square	25 cm/10 in Square	28 cm/11 in Square	30 cm/12 in Square
	18 cm/7 in Round	20 cm/8 in Round	23 cm/9 in Round	25 cm/10 in Round	28 cm/11 in Round	30 cm/12 in Round	33 cm/13 in Round
INGREDIENTS							
Plain (all-purpose) flour	225 g/ 8 oz/ 2 cups	350 g/ 12 oz/ 3 cups	450 g/ 1 lb/ 4 cups	500 g/ 1 lb 2 oz/ 4½ cups	575 g/ 1¼ lb/ 5 cups	675 g/ 1½ lb/ 6 cups	900 g/ 2 lb/ 8 cups
Baking powder	5 ml/ 1 tsp/ 1 tsp	7.5 ml/ 1½ tsp/ 1½ tsp	10 ml/ 2 tsp/ 2 tsp	12.5 ml/ 2½ tsp/ 2½ tsp	15 ml/ 3 tsp/ 3 tsp	17.5 ml/ 3½ tsp/ 3½ tsp	20 ml/ 4 tsp/ 4 tsp
Caster (superfine) sugar	175 g/ 6 oz/ ¾ cup	275 g/ 10 oz/ 1¼ cups	400 g/ 14 oz/ 1¾ cups	450 g/ 1 lb/ 2 cups	500 g/ 1 lb 2 oz/ 2¼ cups	625 g/ 1 lb 6 oz/ 2¾ cups	725 g/ 1 lb 10 oz/ 3¼ cups
Soft margarine	175 g/ 6 oz/ ¾ cup	275 g/ 10 oz/ 1¼ cups	400 g/ 14 oz/ 1¾ cups	450 g/ 1 lb/ 2 cups	500 g/ 1 lb 2 oz/ 2¼ cups	625 g/ 1 lb 6 oz/ 2¾ cups	725 g/ 1 lb 10 oz/ 3¼ cups
Size 3 eggs	3	5	7	8	10	12	13
Milk	30 ml/ 2 tbsp/ 2 tbsp	45 ml/ 3 tbsp/ 3 tbsp	55 ml/ 3½ tbsp/ 3½ tbsp	60 ml/ 4 tbsp/ 4 tbsp	70 ml/ 4½ tbsp/ 4½ tbsp	75 ml/ 5 tbsp/ 5 tbsp	85 ml/ 5½ tbsp/ 5½ tbsp
Approx. Cooking Time	1¼–1½ hours	1½–1¾ hours	1¾–2 hours	1¾–2 hours	2–2¼ hours	2¼–2½ hours	2½–2¾ hours

1 Preheat the oven to 170°C/325°F/Gas 3. Grease and line a deep cake tin (pan) (see Lining Cake Tins [Pans]).

2 Sift flour and baking powder into a mixing bowl. Add sugar, margarine, eggs and milk. Mix together with a wooden spoon, then beat for 1–2 minutes until smooth and glossy. Alternatively, use an electric mixer and beat for 1 minute only.

3 Add any flavourings desired and mix until well blended.

The following amounts are for a 3-egg quantity cake. Increase the suggested flavourings to suit the quantities being made.
Cherry – 175 g/6 oz/1 scant cup glacé cherries, halved
Citrus – replace milk with lemon, orange or lime juice and 5 ml/1 tsp/1 tsp of grated lemon, orange or lime rind
Coconut – 50 g/2 oz/1 cup desiccated (shredded) coconut
Nuts – replace 125 g/4 oz/1 cup flour with ground almonds, hazelnuts, walnuts or pecan nuts

4 Place the mixture into the prepared tin (pan) and spread evenly. Give the tin (pan) a sharp tap to remove any air pockets. Make a depression in the centre of the mixture to ensure a level surface.

5 Bake the cake in the centre of the oven. Follow the chart cooking times, according to the size of the cake. It is cooked when the cake springs back when lightly pressed in the centre.

STORING

Leave the cake to cool in the tin (pan), then remove and cool completely on a wire rack. Wrap in plastic wrap or foil and store in a cool place until required.

Rich Fruit Cake

This recipe makes a very moist rich cake suitable for any celebration. The cake can be made in stages, especially if time is short or if you are making more than one. It is easiest if the fruit is prepared and soaked overnight and the cake made the following day. Once the mixture is in the tin (pan), the surface may be covered with cling film (plastic wrap) and the cake stored in a cool place overnight if cooking is not possible on the day. The quantities have been carefully worked out so that the depth of each cake is the same. This is important when making several tiers for a wedding cake.

A classic rich fruit cake is traditionally used for christening cakes, as in the base for this delightful creation for a baby girl.

1 *Into a large mixing bowl place the raisins, sultanas (golden raisins), currants, glacé cherries, mixed (candied) peel, flaked almonds, lemon rind and juice, brandy or sherry. Mix all the ingredients together until well blended, then cover the bowl with cling film (plastic wrap). Leave for several hours or overnight if required.*

2 *Pre-heat the oven to 140°C/275°F/Gas 1 and prepare a deep cake tin (see Lining Cake Tins [Pans]). Sift the flour and mixed spice into another mixing bowl. Add the ground almonds, sugar, butter, treacle (or molasses) and eggs. Mix together with a wooden spoon, then beat for 1–2 minutes until smooth and glossy. Alternatively, beat for 1 minute using an electric mixer.*

3 *Gradually add mixed fruit and fold into cake mixture using a plastic or wooden spatula until all the fruit has been evenly blended.*

4 *Spoon the mixture into the prepared tin (pan) and spread evenly. Give the container a few sharp bangs to level the mixture and to remove any air pockets. Smooth the surface with the back of a metal spoon, making a slight depression in the centre. The cake surface may be covered with cling film (plastic wrap) and left overnight in a cool place if required.*

5 *Bake the cake in the centre of the oven following the chart cooking time as a guide. Test the cake to see if it is cooked 30 minutes before the end of the cooking time. The cake should feel firm and, when a fine skewer is inserted into the centre, it should come out quite clean. If the cake is not cooked, retest it at 15-minute intervals. Remove the cake from the oven and allow it to cool in the tin (pan).*

6 *Turn the cake out of the tin (pan) but do not remove the lining paper as it helps to keep the moisture in. Spoon half quantity of brandy or sherry used in each cake over the top of the cooked cake and wrap in a double thickness of foil.*

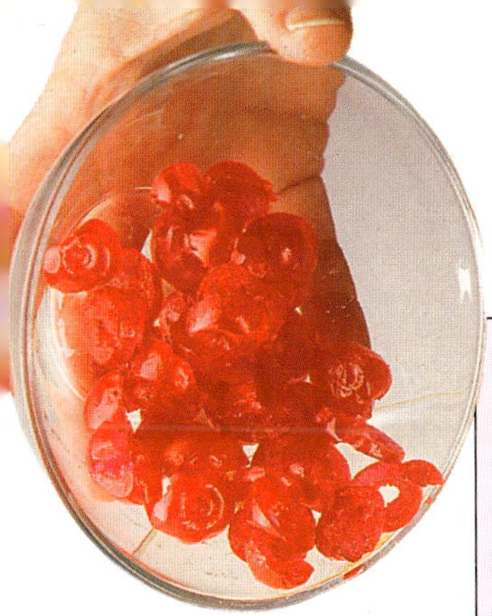

RICH FRUIT CAKE CHART

Cake Tin Sizes	12 cm/5 in Square / 15 cm/6 in Round	15 cm/6 in Square / 18 cm/7 in Round	18 cm/7 in Square / 20 cm/8 in Round	20 cm/8 in Square / 23 cm/9 in Round	23 cm/9 in Square / 25 cm/10 in Round	25 cm/10 in Square / 28 cm/11 in Round	28 cm/11 in Square / 30 cm/12 in Round	30 cm/12 in Square / 33 cm/13 in Round
INGREDIENTS								
Raisins	200 g/ 7 oz/ 1⅓ cups	250 g/ 9 oz/ 1¾ cups	325 g/ 11 oz/ 2 cups	375 g/ 13 oz/ 2½ cups	425 g/ 15 oz/ 2⅔ cups	575 g/ 1¼ lb/ 3¾ cups	675 g/ 1½ lb/ 4½ cups	800 g/ 1¾ lb/ 5¼ cups
Sultanas (golden raisins)	125 g/ 4 oz/ ¾ cup	175 g/ 6 oz/ 1¼ cups	225 g/ 8 oz/ 1½ cups	275 g/ 10 oz/ 1⅔ cups	350 g/ 12 oz/ 2¼ cups	475 g/ 1 lb 1 oz/ 3¼ cups	600 g/ 1 lb 5 oz/ 4 cups	675 g/ 1½ lb/ 4½ cups
Currants	75 g/ 3 oz/ ⅔ cup	125 g/ 4 oz/ ¾ cup	175 g/ 6 oz/ 1¼ cups	225 g/ 8 oz/ 1⅔ cups	275 g/ 10 oz/ 2 cups	400 g/ 14 oz/ 3 cups	475 g/ 1 lb 1 oz/ 3½ cups	575 g/ 1¼ lb/ 4 cups
Glacé cherries, halved	75 g/ 3 oz/ ½ cup	75 g/ 3 oz/ ½ cup	150 g/ 5 oz/ 1 cup	175 g/ 6 oz/ 1 cup	200 g/ 7 oz/ 1⅓ cups	225 g/ 8 oz/ 1½ cups	275 g/ 10 oz/ 1⅔ cups	350 g/ 12 oz/ 2¼ cups
Mixed peel	25 g/ 1 oz/ ¼ cup	40 g/ 1½ oz/ ⅓ cup	50 g/ 2 oz/ ⅓ cup	75 g/ 3 oz/ ½ cup	125 g/ 4 oz/ ¾ cup	175 g/ 6 oz/ 1 cup	225 g/ 8 oz/ 1½ cups	275 g/ 10 oz/ 1⅔ cups
Flaked almonds	25 g/ 1 oz/ ¼ cup	40 g/ 1½ oz/ ⅓ cup	50 g/ 2 oz/ ½ cup	75 g/ 3 oz/ ¾ cup	125 g/ 4 oz/ 1 cup	175 g/ 6 oz/ 1⅔ cup	225 g/ 8 oz/ 2¼ cups	275 g/ 10 oz/ 2¾ cups
Lemon rind, coarsely grated	5 ml/ 1 tsp/ 1 tsp	7.5 ml/ 1½ tsp/ 1½ tsp	10 ml/ 2 tsp/ 2 tsp	12 ml/ 2½ tsp/ 2½ tsp	15 ml/ ½ fl oz/ 1 tbsp	25 ml/ 1½ tbsp/ 1½ tbsp	25 ml/ 1½ tbsp/ 1½ tbsp	30 ml/ 2 tbsp/ 2 tbsp
Lemon juice	15 ml/ 1 tbsp/ 1 tbsp	25 ml/ 1½ tbsp/ 1½ tbsp	30 ml/ 2 tbsp/ 2 tbsp	40 ml/ 2½ tbsp/ 2½ tbsp	45 ml/ 3 tbsp/ 3 tbsp	60 ml/ 4 tbsp/ 4 tbsp	75 ml/ 5 tbsp/ 5 tbsp	90 ml/ 6 tbsp/ 6 tbsp
Brandy or sherry	15 ml/ 1 tbsp/ 1 tbsp	30 ml/ 2 tbsp/ 2 tbsp	45 ml/ 3 tbsp/ 3 tbsp	60 ml/ 4 tbsp/ 4 tbsp	75 ml/ 5 tbsp/ 5 tbsp	90 ml/ 6 tbsp/ 6 tbsp	105 ml/ 7 tbsp/ 7 tbsp	120 ml/ 8 tbsp/ ½ cup
Plain (all-purpose) flour	175 g/ 6 oz/ 1½ cups	200 g/ 7 oz/ 1¾ cups	250 g/ 9 oz/ 2¼ cups	325 g/ 11 oz/ 2¾ cups	400 g/ 14 oz/ 3½ cups	500 g/ 1 lb 2 oz/ 4½ cups	625 g/ 1 lb 6 oz/ 5½ cups	725 g/ 1 lb 10 oz/ 6½ cups
Ground mixed spice	5 ml/ 1 tsp/ 1 tsp	7.5 ml/ 1½ tsp/ 1½ tsp	12 ml/ 2½ tsp/ 2½ tsp	15 ml/ 1 tbsp/ 1 tbsp	18 ml/ 1¼ tbsp/ 1¼ tbsp	25 ml/ 1½ tbsp/ 1½ tbsp	30 ml/ 2 tbsp/ 2 tbsp	70 ml/ 3½ tbsp/ 3½ tbsp
Ground almonds	25 g/ 1 oz/ ¼ cup	40 g/ 1½ oz/ ⅓ cup	65 g/ 2½ oz/ ⅔ cup	125 g/ 4 oz/ 1¼ cups	150 g/ 5 oz/ 1⅓ cups	225 g/ 8 oz/ 2¼ cups	275 g/ 10 oz/ 2¾ cups	350 g/ 12 oz/ 3⅓ cups
Dark brown sugar	125 g/ 4 oz/ ¾ cup	150 g/ 5 oz/ 1 cup	200 g/ 7 oz/ 1⅓ cups	250 g/ 9 oz/ 1⅔ cups	350 g/ 12 oz/ 2¼ cups	475 g/ 1 lb 1 oz/ 3⅓ cups	575 g/ 1¼ lb/ 3¾ cups	650 g/ 1 lb 7 oz/ 4½ cups
Butter, softened	125 g/ 4 oz/ ½ cup	150 g/ 5 oz/ ⅔ cup	200 g/ 7 oz/ 1 cup	250 g/ 9 oz/ 1¼ cups	350 g/ 12 oz/ 1½ cups	475 g/ 1 lb 1 oz/ 2¼ cups	575 g/ 1¼ lb/ 2½ cups	650 g/ 1 lb 7 oz/ 3 cups
Black treacle (or molasses)	10 ml/ ½ tbsp/ ½ tbsp	15 ml/ 1 tbsp/ 1 tbsp	25 ml/ 1½ tbsp/ 1½ tbsp	30 ml/ 2 tbsp/ 2 tbsp	40 ml/ 2½ tbsp/ 2½ tbsp	45 ml/ 3 tbsp/ 3 tbsp	55 ml/ 3½ tbsp/ 3½ tbsp	60 ml/ 4 tbsp/ 4 tbsp
Eggs	2	3	4	5	6	7	8	10
Approx. Cooking Time	2¼–2½ hours	2½–2¾ hours	3–3½ hours	3¼–3¾ hours	3¾–4¼ hours	4–4½ hours	4½–5¼ hours	5¼–5¾ hours

STORING

Store the cake in a cool, dry place on its base with the top uppermost for a week. Unwrap the cake and spoon over the remaining brandy or sherry. Rewrap well and invert the cake. Store it upside down, so the brandy or sherry moistens the top and helps to keep it flat.

The cake will store well for up to 3 months. If it is going to be stored for this length of time, add the brandy or sherry a little at a time at monthly intervals.

Light Fruit Cake

This is a very light moist fruit cake, which can be made to replace the rich version, if required. As there is less fruit in the cake, it has a tendency to dome during cooking, so ensure a deep depression is made in the centre. It will keep for up to one month once it has been marzipanned and iced.

A light fruit teatime cake, simply topped with candied fruits and nuts, and glazed.

1 Preheat the oven to 140°C/275°F/Gas 1. Grease and line a deep cake tin (pan) (see Lining Cake Tins [Pans]).

2 Place the mixed dried fruit, peel, ginger, apricots, orange rind, juice and sherry in a large mixing bowl. Mix all the ingredients together until well blended.

3 Sift the flour, mixed spice and sugar into another mixing bowl, add the butter or margarine, and eggs. Mix together with a wooden spoon, then beat for 1–2 minutes until smooth and glossy. Alternatively, beat for 1 minute using an electric mixer.

4 Gradually add the mixed fruit and fold into the cake mixture, using a plastic spatula, until all the fruit is evenly mixed.

STORING

Remove the cake from oven and leave to cool in the tin (pan). Wrap in foil and store in a cool place for up to 4 weeks.

5 Spoon the mixture into the prepared cake tin (pan) and spread evenly. Give the tin (pan) a few sharp bangs to level the mixture and remove any air pockets. Smooth the surface with the back of a metal spoon, making a fairly deep depression in the centre.

6 Bake the cake in the centre of the oven. Use the chart cooking times as a guide, according to the size of cake you are making. Test the cake 15 minutes before the end of the given cooking time. If cooked, the cake should feel firm and when a fine skewer is inserted into the centre, it should come out quite clean. If the cake is not cooked, retest at 15 minute intervals.

LIGHT FRUIT CAKE CHART

Cake Tin Sizes	12 cm/5 in Square / 15 cm/6 in Round	15 cm/6 in Square / 18 cm/7 in Round	18 cm/7 in Square / 20 cm/8 in Round	20 cm/8 in Square / 23 cm/9 in Round	23 cm/9 in Square / 25 cm/10 in Round	25 cm/10 in Square / 28 cm/11 in Round	28 cm/11 in Square / 30 cm/12 in Round	30 cm/12 in Square / 33 cm/13 in Round
INGREDIENTS								
Mixed dried fruit	275 g/ 10 oz/ 1⅔ cups	400 g/ 14 oz/ 1⅔ cups	450 g/ 1 lb/ 3 cups	675 g/ 1½ lb/ 4½ cups	900 g/ 2 lb/ 6 cups	1.1 kg/ 2½ lb/ 7½ cups	1.5 kg/ 3¼ lb/ 9¾ cups	1.8 kg/ 4 lb/ 12 cups
Mixed cut peel	25 g/ 1 oz/ ¼ cup	25 g/ 1 oz/ ¼ cup	25 g/ 1 oz/ ¼ cup	25 g/ 1 oz/ ¼ cup	50 g/ 2 oz/ ⅓ cup	75 g/ 3 oz/ ½ cup	150 g/ 5 oz/ 1 cup	175 g/ 6 oz/ 1 cup
Stem (preserved) ginger, chopped	25 g/ 1 oz/ ¼ cup	25 g/ 1 oz/ ¼ cup	50 g/ 2 oz/ ⅓ cup	75 g/ 3 oz/ ½ cup	125 g/ 4 oz/ ¾ cup	150 g/ 5 oz/ 1 cup	200 g/ 7 oz/ 1¼ cups	225 g/ 8 oz/ 1½ cups
Dried apricots	25 g/ 1 oz/ ¼ cup	25 g/ 1 oz/ ¼ cup	50 g/ 2 oz/ ½ cup	75 g/ 3 oz/ ¾ cup	125 g/ 4 oz/ 1 cup	150 g/ 5 oz/ 1¼ cups	175 g/ 6 oz/ 1½ cups	225 g/ 8 oz/ 2 cups
Orange rind, coarsely grated	5 ml/ 1 tsp/ 1 tsp	7.5 ml/ 1½ tsp/ 1½ tsp	10 ml/ 2 tsp/ 2 tsp	15 ml/ 1 tbsp/ 1 tbsp	20 ml/ 4 tsp/ 4 tsp	25 ml/ 5 tsp/ 5 tsp	30 ml/ 2 tbsp/ 2 tbsp	40 ml/ 8 tsp/ 8 tsp
Orange juice	15 ml/ 1 tbsp/ 1 tbsp	25 ml/ 1½ tbsp/ 1½ tbsp	30 ml/ 2 tbsp/ 2 tbsp	40 ml/ 2½ tbsp/ 2½ tbsp	45 ml/ 3 tbsp/ 3 tbsp	55 ml/ 3½ tbsp/ 3½ tbsp	70 ml/ 4½ tbsp/ 4½ tbsp	75 ml/ 5 tbsp/ 5 tbsp
Sherry	15 ml/ 1 tbsp/ 1 tbsp	20 ml/ 1½ tbsp/ 1½ tbsp	30 ml/ 2 tbsp/ 2 tbsp	40 ml/ 2½ tbsp/ 2½ tbsp	45 ml/ 3 tbsp/ 3 tbsp	55 ml/ 3½ tbsp/ 3½ tbsp	70 ml/ 4½ tbsp/ 4½ tbsp	85 ml/ 5½ tbsp/ 5½ tbsp
Plain (all-purpose) flour	225 g/ 8 oz/ 2 cups	275 g/ 10 oz/ 2½ cups	350 g/ 12 oz/ 3 cups	450 g/ 1 lb/ 4 cups	575 g/ 1¼ lb/ 5 cups	675 g/ 1½ lb/ 7 cups	900 g/ 2 lb/ 7 cups	1.1 kg/ 2½ lb/ 9 cups
Ground mixed spice	5 ml/ 1 tsp/ 1 tsp	7.5 ml/ 1½ tsp/ 1½ tsp	10 ml/ 2 tsp/ 2 tsp	15 ml/ 1 tbsp/ 1 tbsp	20 ml/ 4 tsp/ 4 tsp	25 ml/ 5 tsp/ 5 tsp	30 ml/ 2 tbsp/ 2 tbsp	40 ml/ 8 tsp/ 8 tsp
Light soft brown sugar	175 g/ 6 oz/ 1 cup	225 g/ 8 oz/ 1 cup	275 g/ 10 oz/ 1⅔ cups	400 g/ 14 oz/ 2½ cups	475 g/ 1 lb 1 oz/ 3¼ cups	575 g/ 1¼ lb/ 3¾ cups	775 g/ 1 lb 11 oz/ 5 cups	975 g/ 2 lb 2 oz/ 6⅓ cups
Butter or margarine, softened	175 g/ 6 oz/ ¾ cup	225 g/ 8 oz/ 1 cup	275 g/ 10 oz/ 1¼ cups	400 g/ 14 oz/ 1¾ cups	475 g/ 1 lb 1 oz/ 2¼ cups	575 g/ 1¼ lb/ 2½ cups	775 g/ 1 lb 11 oz/ 3¼ cups	975 g/ 2 lb 2 oz/ 4¼ cups
Size 3 eggs	3	4	4	5	6	7	9	11
Approx. Cooking Time	2¼–2½ hours	2½–2¾ hours	2¾–3¼ hours	3¼–3¾ hours	3½–4 hours	4–4½ hours	4½–4¾ hours	5–5½ hours

Genoese Sponge Cake

This whisked sponge cake has a firmer texture due to the addition of butter and is suitable for cutting into layers for gateaux, or as a base for a celebration cake.

INGREDIENTS

- *4 eggs*
- *125 g/4 oz/½ cup caster (superfine) sugar*
- *75 g/3 oz/⅓ cup + 3 tsp unsalted butter, melted and cooled slightly*
- *75 g/3 oz/¾ cup + 6 tsp plain (all-purpose) flour*

Genoese sponge is the classic whisked sponge, suitable for plain and highly fancy cakes; here it is deliciously decorated with apricots and praline-coated nuts.

1 *Preheat the oven to 180°C/350°F/Gas 4. Prepare the tin (pan) according to the recipe.*

2 *Whisk eggs and caster (superfine) sugar together in a heatproof bowl until thoroughly blended. Place the bowl over a saucepan of simmering water and whisk the mixture until thick and pale.*

3 *Remove the bowl from the saucepan and continue whisking until the mixture is cool and leaves a thick trail on the surface when beaters are lifted.*

CHOICE OF FLAVOURINGS

Citrus – 10 ml/2 tsp/2 tsp finely grated orange, lemon or lime rind
Chocolate – 50 g/2 oz/2 squares plain (semisweet) chocolate, melted
Coffee – 10 ml/2 tsp/2 tsp coffee granules, dissolved in 5 ml/1 tsp/1 tsp boiling water

4 *Pour the butter carefully into the mixture, leaving any sediment behind.*

5 *Sift flour over surface and, using a plastic spatula, carefully fold the flour, butter and any flavourings into the mixture until smooth and evenly blended.*
Place the mixture into the prepared tin (pan), tilt to level and bake as required.

SIMPLE ICINGS (FROSTINGS)

Special Equipment for Icing

Before embarking on any form of cake icing or decorating, it is necessary to have a selection of icing equipment to achieve good results.

1 Straight edge
2 Turntable
3 Fine nozzles in various sizes and designs
4 Acrylic rolling pin
5 Acrylic dowels
6 Large nozzles in various designs
7 Greaseproof (wax) paper piping bags
8 Cake pillars
9 Florists' wire
10 Flower cutters
11 Stamens
12 Florists' tape
13 Acrylic rolling board

14 Brushes
15 Smoother for sugarpaste (fondant) covered cakes
16 Biscuit (cookie) and aspic cutters
17 Patterned and plain side scrapers
18 Nozzle brush
19 Nylon piping bags
20 Flower nail

TURNTABLE – the most essential piece of equipment for easy movement of cakes while icing and decorating. Although expensive, it will last for ever and is obtainable from most kitchen shops or cake-icing specialists. The turntable should revolve smoothly for applying royal icing to a round cake.

STRAIGHT EDGE – made from metal, stainless steel is the best. It is rigid and will not scratch or bend when using it to level the top of a cake to obtain flat, smooth royal icing.

SIDE SCRAPER – made from plastic or stainless steel and used for smoothing the icing on the sides of a cake. The plastic ones are more flexible and easier to use.

PATTERNED SIDE SCRAPERS – come in a variety of designs and are ideal for finishing the sides of an iced cake in many different patterns.

MUSLIN (CHEESECLOTH) – ideal for covering a bowl of royal icing to prevent a skin forming. As it is white it will not impart any colour.

BRUSHES – fine artists' brushes, available from cake-icing specialists, have many uses for painting flowers and plaques with food colouring; also useful when making icing run-outs.

FLOWER NAIL – can be homemade from a cork and nail. Otherwise buy one from a kitchen shop or a cake-icing specialist. It is invaluable for piping flowers.

SMALL BISCUIT (COOKIE) OR ASPIC CUTTERS – these are used for cutting out various shapes from sugarpaste, marzipan, chocolate or fruit rinds to use as decorations. They also come as numbers and letters. Tiny cutters are available for making cut-out flowers from sugarpaste.

TWEEZERS – these are indispensable for delicate work; buy a pair with rounded ends.

STAMENS – can be found in different colours and finishes from cake-decorating specialists. They are used in the centre of moulded and cut-out sugar flowers.

DOWEL – different sizes of wooden dowel are useful for placing leaves and petals over to dry, giving them a more realistic shape. Acrylic dowels are also used to support the tiers of a cake covered in sugarpaste.

FLORISTS' WIRE AND TAPE – these come in various gauges and colours and are available from cake-icing specialists. Use to wire sugar flowers onto stems, or to bind stems together to form a flower spray.

PIPING BAGS – made in a variety of materials; the nylon ones are soft and flexible for cream, meringue and icing.

Use a nylon piping bag and a large star-shaped nozzle to pipe a decorative border with fresh cream.

Available in small, medium and large sizes, to be fitted with various sizes of nozzles. Greaseproof (wax) paper piping bags can be made easily and used with a variety of straight-sided nozzles, or even without a nozzle.

LARGE NOZZLES – buy a simple selection of small to medium star metal meringue nozzles. These will fit the nylon piping bags and also large homemade greaseproof (wax) paper piping bags. They are ideal for piping cream, meringues and butter icing.

FINE NOZZLES – straight-sided metal nozzles are the best type to buy as they fit into homemade greaseproof (wax) paper piping bags. They are available in many different designs and sizes.

NOZZLE BRUSH – essential for cleaning nozzles without bending or misshaping the ends.

ICING SYRINGES – usually available as a set, with a selection of nozzles, and are ideal for simple piping.

ACRYLIC ROLLING PIN AND BOARD – non-stick, they are ideal for rolling out small pieces of sugarpaste or marzipan decorations.

CAKE PILLARS – these are available in plastic rounds, squares and octagonals, usually with a hole through the centre to cover the acrylic sticks used to support a wedding cake covered with sugarpaste. Plaster pillars have a clean, crisp finish for royal-iced wedding cakes.

Butter Icing

This most popular and well-known icing is made quickly with butter and icing (confectioners) sugar. Add your choice of flavourings and colourings to vary the cake.

INGREDIENTS

Makes 450 g/1 lb/1 lb
- 125 g/4 oz/½ cup unsalted butter, softened
- 225 g/8 oz/2 cups icing (confectioners) sugar, sifted
- 10 ml/2 tsp/2 tsp milk
- 5 ml/1 tsp/1 tsp vanilla essence (extract)

Butter icing is a quick and attractive topping for a cake.

1 Place the butter in a bowl. Using a wooden spoon or an electric mixer, beat until light and fluffy.

2 Stir in the icing (confectioners) sugar, milk and vanilla essence (extract), and/or flavourings until evenly mixed, then beat well until light and smooth.

3 Spread the icing over the cake with a metal palette knife (spatula).

CHOICE OF FLAVOURINGS

Citrus – replace milk and vanilla essence (extract) with orange, lemon or lime juice and 10 ml/2 tsp/2 tsp finely grated orange, lemon or lime rind. Omit the rind if the icing is to be piped.

Chocolate – 15 ml/1 tbsp/1 tbsp cocoa powder blended with 15 ml/1 tbsp/1 tbsp boiling water, cooled
Coffee – 10 ml/2 tsp/2 tsp coffee granules blended with 15 ml/1 tbsp/1 tbsp boiling water, cooled

Crème au Beurre

This icing takes a little more time to make, but it is well worth it. The rich, smooth, light texture makes it suitable for spreading, filling or piping onto special cakes and gateaux. Use it as soon as it is made for best results, or keep it at room temperature for a few hours. Do not reheat or it will curdle.

INGREDIENTS

Makes 350 g/12 oz/³⁄₄ lb
- 60 ml/4 tbsp/4 tbsp water
- 75 g/3 oz/¹⁄₃ cup caster (superfine) sugar
- 2 egg yolks
- 150 g/5 oz/²⁄₃ cup unsalted butter, softened

Creme au beurre is a sophisticated filling and topping for a cake.

1 *Place the water in a small saucepan, bring to boil, remove the saucepan from the heat and stir in the sugar. Heat gently until the sugar has completely dissolved. Remove the spoon.*

2 *Boil rapidly until mixture becomes syrupy, or until the 'thread' stage is reached. To test, remove the pan from heat, place a little syrup on the back of a dry teaspoon. Press a second teaspoon onto the syrup and gently pull apart. The syrup should form a fine thread. If not, return the saucepan to heat, boil rapidly and retest a minute later.*

3 *Whisk the egg yolks together in a bowl. Continue whisking while slowly adding the sugar syrup in a steady stream. Whisk until mixture becomes thick, pale and cool, and leaves a trail on surface when the beaters are lifted.*

CHOICE OF FLAVOURINGS

Citrus – replace water with orange, lemon or lime juice and 10 ml/2 tsp/2 tsp finely grated orange, lemon or lime rind

4 *Beat the butter in a separate bowl until light and fluffy. Add the egg mixture gradually, beating well after each addition, until thick and fluffy.*

Fold in the chosen flavouring, using a spatula, until evenly blended.

Chocolate – 50 g/2 oz/2 squares plain (semisweet) chocolate, melted
Coffee – 10 ml/2 tsp/2 tsp coffee granules, dissolved in 5 ml/1 tsp/1 tsp boiling water, cooled

American Frosting

A light marshmallow icing which crisps on the outside when left to dry, this versatile frosting may be swirled or peaked into a soft coating.

INGREDIENTS

Makes 350 g/12 oz/³⁄₄ lb
- 1 egg white
- 30 ml/2 tbsp/2 tbsp water
- 15 ml/1 tbsp/1 tbsp golden syrup (light corn syrup)
- 5 ml/1 tsp/1 tsp cream of tartar
- 175 g/6 oz/1 cup icing (confectioners) sugar, sifted

American frosting makes a light, fluffy yet crisp topping, its soft white contrasting well with chocolate caraque.

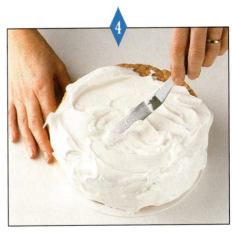

1 Place the egg white, water, golden syrup (light corn syrup) and cream of tartar in a heatproof bowl. Whisk together until thoroughly blended.

2 Stir the icing (confectioners) sugar into the mixture and place the bowl over a saucepan of simmering water. Whisk until the mixture becomes thick and white.

3 Remove the bowl from the saucepan and continue to whisk the frosting until cool and thick, and the mixture stands up in soft peaks.

4 Use immediately to fill or cover cakes.

Glacé Icing

An instant icing for quickly finishing the tops of large or small cakes, this is also used to make feathered icing by introducing a second, coloured, icing to obtain the feathered design.

INGREDIENTS

Makes 350 g/12 oz/³⁄₄ lb
- 225 g/8 oz/1¹⁄₂ cups icing (confectioners) sugar
- 30–45 ml/2–3 tbsp/2–3 tbsp hot water
- food colouring (optional)

1 Sift the icing (confectioners) sugar into a bowl. Using a wooden spoon, gradually stir in enough water to obtain the consistency of thick cream.

2 Beat until white and smooth, and the icing thickly coats the back of a wooden spoon. Colour with a few drops of food colouring if desired.

3 Use immediately to cover the top of the cake.

CHOICE OF FLAVOURINGS

Citrus – replace the water with orange, lemon or lime juice
Chocolate – sift 10 ml/2 tsp/2 tsp cocoa powder with the icing (confectioners) sugar
Coffee – replace the water with strong, liquid coffee

FEATHER ICING

1 Colour one-third glacé icing a pale shade with food colouring. Place in a greaseproof (wax) paper piping bag. Snip off point.
2 Quickly spread the cake surface evenly and smoothly with white glacé icing. Immediately pipe coloured lines of icing, evenly spaced, on top of the white icing.
3 Draw a cocktail stick lightly across the lines of icing in alternate directions, evenly spaced, to form a feather pattern (see above).

COBWEB ICING

1 Pipe circles of glacé icing over the top of the cake and draw a cocktail stick from centre to edge in one direction to make a cobweb design.
2 To vary the pattern, pipe dots of icing evenly over the surface of the cake. Draw a cocktail stick through the dots to make another design.

Butterscotch Frosting

This is a richly-flavoured frosting, using brown sugar and treacle (molasses). It is useful for coating any sponge cake to impart a smooth or swirled finish.

INGREDIENTS

Makes 675 g/1½ lb/1½ lb
- 75 g/3 oz/⅓ cup unsalted butter
- 45 ml/3 tbsp/3 tbsp milk
- 25 g/1 oz/2 tbsp soft light brown sugar
- 15 ml/1 tbsp/1 tbsp black treacle (or molasses)
- 350 g/12 oz/2¼ cups icing (confectioners) sugar, sifted

Butterscotch frosting is deliciously caramel-flavoured and an unusual alternative for coating a cake.

1 Place the butter, milk, sugar and treacle (or molasses) in a heatproof bowl over a saucepan of simmering water. Stir occasionally, using a wooden spoon, until the butter and sugar have melted.

2 Remove the bowl from the saucepan. Stir in the icing (confectioners) sugar, then beat until smooth and glossy.

3 Pour immediately over the cake for a smooth finish, or allow to cool for a thicker spreading consistency.

CHOICE OF FLAVOURINGS

Citrus – replace treacle (molasses) with golden syrup (light corn syrup) and add 10 ml/2 tsp/2 tsp of finely grated orange, lemon or lime rind
Chocolate – sift 15 ml/1 tbsp/1 tbsp cocoa powder with icing (confectioners) sugar
Coffee – replace the treacle (molasses) with 15 ml/1 tbsp/1 tbsp coffee granules

Chocolate Fudge Icing

A rich glossy icing which sets like chocolate fudge, it is versatile enough to smoothly coat, swirl or pipe, depending on the temperature of the icing when it is used.

INGREDIENTS

Makes 450 g/1 lb/1 lb
- *125 g/4 oz/4 squares plain (semisweet) chocolate*
- *50 g/2 oz/¼ cup unsalted butter*
- *1 egg, beaten*
- *175 g/6 oz/1 cup icing (confectioners) sugar, sifted*

Chocolate fudge icing is smooth and sumptuous, with a rich dark colour that contrasts beautifully with fresh flowers in a simple but effective decoration.

1 *Place the chocolate and butter in a heatproof bowl over a saucepan of hot water.*

2 *Stir occasionally with a wooden spoon until melted. Add the egg and beat until smooth.*

3 *Remove the bowl from the saucepan and stir in the icing (confectioners) sugar, then beat until smooth and glossy.*

4 *Pour immediately over the cake for a smooth finish, or leave to cool for a thicker spreading or piping consistency as here.*

Glossy Chocolate Icing

A rich smooth glossy icing, this can be made with plain (semisweet) or milk chocolate.

INGREDIENTS

Makes 350 g/12 oz/¾ lb
- *175 g/6 oz/6 squares plain (semi-sweet) chocolate*
- *150 ml/¼ pt/⅔ cup single (light) cream*

Glossy chocolate icing is the perfect setting for chocolate-dipped fruits and chocolate leaves.

1 *Break up the chocolate into small pieces and place in a medium-sized saucepan with the cream.*

2 *Heat gently, stirring occasionally, until the chocolate has melted and the mixture is smooth.*

3 *Allow the icing to cool until it is thick enough to coat the back of a wooden spoon. Use it at this stage for a smooth glossy icing as here, or allow it to thicken to obtain a swirled pattern icing.*

Meringue Frosting

A lightly-whisked meringue cooked over hot water and combined with softly beaten butter, this icing may be flavoured with the suggested flavourings, and should be used directly it is made.

INGREDIENTS

Makes 450 g/1 lb/1 lb
- *2 egg whites*
- *125 g/4 oz/3/4 cup icing (confectioners) sugar, sifted*
- *150 g/5 oz/2/3 cup unsalted butter, softened*

Meringue frosting creates a fluffy coating for cakes that can be spread or peaked to create a variety of effects.

1 *Whisk egg whites in a clean, heatproof bowl, add the icing (confectioners) sugar and gently whisk to mix well.*

2 *Place the bowl over a saucepan of simmering water and whisk until thick and white. Remove the bowl from the saucepan, continue to whisk until it is cool and the meringue stands up in soft peaks.*

CHOICE OF FLAVOURINGS

Fold in the chosen flavourings, using a spatula, until evenly blended.

Citrus – 10 ml/2 tsp/2 tsp finely grated orange, lemon or lime rind
Chocolate – 50 g/2 oz/2 squares plain (semisweet) chocolate, melted
Coffee – 10 ml/2 tsp/2 tsp coffee granules blended with 5 ml/1 tsp/1 tsp boiling water, cooled

3 *Beat the butter in a separate bowl until light and fluffy. Add the meringue gradually, beating well after each addition, until thick and fluffy. Use immediately for coating, filling and piping cakes.*

MARZIPAN

Marzipan is a pliable paste made from ground almonds and a mixture of sugars. The consistency, texture and colour varies, depending upon how the paste is made, but the end result is used for covering cakes to give a smooth, flat surface before applying royal icing or sugarpaste.

Homemade marzipan has a much richer taste than the commercial variety and can be easily made in manageable quantities. Do take care not to overknead or handle the marzipan too much when making it, as this encourages the oils from the ground almonds to flow. They will eventually seep through the iced surface of the cake, causing staining.

Ready-made marzipan is available in white and yellow varieties. Use the white marzipan for all cakes as it is the most

Marzipan is the classic covering for the traditional Easter Simnel cake, which contains a central layer of marzipan as well as marzipan decoration.

popular and reliable type to use, especially when cakes are being iced in pastel shades or in white. The yellow marzipan has added food colouring but may be used for covering rich fruit cakes. Use with care, however, the yellow colour can show through if the icing is thinly applied, or may cause yellow staining. This marzipan does not take food colourings as well as white marzipan when used for modelling work.

Always use fresh, pliable marzipan to obtain the best results, especially for covering a cake. Be sure to dry the marzipanned cake before applying the icing. Set marzipan ensures a good cake shape during icing and prevents any moisture seeping through from the cake and staining the iced surface.

Always store the marzipanned cake on a clean cakeboard in a cake box in a warm, dry room.

Homemade Marzipan

INGREDIENTS

Makes 450 g/1 lb/1 lb

- 225 g/8 oz/2¼ cups ground almonds
- 125 g/4 oz/½ cup caster (superfine) sugar
- 125 g/4 oz/¾ cup icing (confectioners) sugar, sieved (sifted)
- 5 ml/1 tsp/1 tsp lemon juice
- few drops almond flavouring
- 1 (size 4) egg, or 1 (size 2) egg white

Marzipan is extremely versatile; here it has been used in place of icing for this unusual Christmas cake.

1 Place the ground almonds, caster (superfine) and icing (confectioners) sugars into a bowl. Stir until evenly mixed.

2 Make a 'well' in the centre and add the lemon juice, almond flavouring and enough egg or egg white to mix to a soft but firm dough, using a wooden spoon.

3 Form the marzipan into a ball. Lightly dust a surface with icing (confectioners) sugar and knead the marzipan until smooth and free from cracks.

4 Wrap in cling film (plastic wrap) or store in a polythene (polyethylene) bag until ready for use. Tint with food colouring if required, and use for moulding shapes or covering cakes.

MARZIPAN CHART

Cake Tin Sizes	12 cm/5 in Square	15 cm/6 in Square	18 cm/7 in Square	20 cm/8 in Square	23 cm/9 in Square	25 cm/10 in Square	28 cm/11 in Square	30 cm/12 in Square
	15 cm/6 in Round	18 cm/7 in Round	20 cm/8 in Round	23 cm/9 in Round	25 cm/10 in Round	28 cm/11 in Round	30 cm/12 in Round	33 cm/13 in Round
QUANTITIES								
Apricot glaze	25 ml/ 1½ tbsp/ 1½ tbsp	30 ml/ 2 tbsp/ 2 tbsp	40 ml/ 2½ tbsp/ 2½ tbsp	45 ml/ 3 tbsp/ 3 tbsp	55 ml/ 3½ tbsp/ 3½ tbsp	60 ml/ 4 tbsp/ 4 tbsp	75 ml/ 4½ tbsp/ 4½ tbsp	75 ml/ 5 tbsp/ 5 tbsp
Marzipan	450 g/ 1 lb/ 1 lb	675 g/ 1½ lb/ 1½ lb	800 g/ 1¾ lb/ 1¾ lb	900 g/ 2 lb/ 2 lb	1.1 kg/ 2½ lb/ 2½ lb	1.5 kg/ 3¼ lb/ 3¼ lb	1.8 kg/ 4 lb/ 4 lb	1.9 kg/ 4¼ lb/ 4¼ lb

How to Marzipan a Cake for Royal Icing

1 Unwrap the cake and remove the lining paper. Place the cake on a cakeboard and roll the top with a rolling pin to flatten slightly.

2 Brush the top of the cake with apricot glaze. Lightly dust a surface with icing (confectioners) sugar.

3 Using two-thirds of the marzipan, knead it into a round. Roll out to a 5 mm/¼ in thickness to match the shape of the top of the cake, allowing an extra 2 cm/¾ in all around. Make sure the marzipan moves freely before inverting the cake onto the centre of the marzipan.

4 Trim off the excess marzipan to within 1 cm/½ in of the cake. Using a small flexible metal palette knife (spatula), push the marzipan level to the side of the cake, until all the marzipan is neat around the edge of the cake.

5 Invert the cake and place in the centre of the cakeboard. Brush the sides with apricot glaze. Knead the trimmings together, taking care not to include any crumbs from the cake.

6 Measure and cut a piece of string the length of the side of the cake. Measure and cut another piece of string the depth of the side of the cake from the board to the top.

7 Roll out the marzipan to 5 mm/¼ in thickness. Cut out one side piece for a round cake and four pieces for a square cake, to match the measured string. Knead the trimmings together and re-roll.

8 Carefully fit the marzipan onto the side of the cake and smooth the joins with a metal palette knife (spatula). Leave in a warm, dry place for at least 24 hours before icing.

How to Marzipan a Cake for Sugarpaste (Fondant Icing)

APRICOT GLAZE

It is always a good idea to make a large quantity of apricot glaze, especially when making celebration cakes. Use for brushing the cakes before applying the marzipan, or for glazing fruits on gateaux and cakes.

INGREDIENTS

Makes 450 g/1 lb/1 lb
- *450 g/1 lb/1½ cups apricot jam*
- *45 ml/3 tbsp/3 tbsp water*

1 *Place jam and water into a saucepan, heat gently, stirring occasionally until melted. Boil rapidly for 1 minute, then strain through a sieve (strainer).*

2 *Rub through as much fruit as possible, using a wooden spoon. Discard the skins left in the sieve (strainer).*

STORING

Pour the glaze into a clean, hot jar, seal with a clean lid and cool. Refrigerate for up to 2 months.

1 *Unwrap the cake and remove the lining paper. Place the cake on a cakeboard and roll the top with a rolling pin to flatten slightly.*

2 *Brush the top and sides of the cake with apricot glaze (see above), and dust the surface lightly with sieved (sifted) icing (confectioners) sugar.*

3 *Knead the marzipan into a smooth ball. Roll out to a 5 mm/¼ in thickness, to match the shape of the cake, and large enough to cover the top and sides, about 5–7.5 cm/2–3 in larger. Make sure the marzipan moves freely, then roll the marzipan loosely around the rolling pin.*

4 Place the supported marzipan over the cake and carefully unroll so that the marzipan falls evenly over the cake. Working from the centre of the cake, carefully smooth the marzipan over the top and down the sides, lifting the edges slightly to allow the marzipan to fit at the base of the cake without stretching or tearing the top edge.

5 Using a sharp knife, trim the excess marzipan from the base of the cake, cutting down on to the board.

6 Using clean, dry hands, gently rub the top of the cake in circular movements to make a smooth glossy finish to the marzipan.

7 Leave in a warm, dry place for at least 2 hours before covering with sugarpaste (fondant).

ROYAL ICING

Royal icing is the classic choice for all wedding, christening and other formal iced cakes, and is highly durable once dried.

A royal-iced cake has always been the traditional way of producing an English wedding or celebration cake. It is instantly recognizable by the classical lines and smooth finish, which certainly gives it a regal appearance.

To produce a beautifully royal-iced cake, it is essential to make the icing light and glossy in texture and of the correct consistency. Then with patience and practice, a good result can be achieved.

Everything must be spotless when making royal icing, and as dust-free as possible. Small particles can get into the icing and will come to the surface on a flat coat, or even cause the piping tubes to block.

Fresh egg whites or dried egg albumen may be used to make the icing – both produce good results. A little lemon juice helps to strengthen the albumen in fresh egg whites, but care must be taken not to add too much. Too much will make the icing short, causing it to break during piping, and making it difficult to obtain a smooth flat finish. Do not add glycerine to egg albumen as it does not set as hard as fresh egg-white icing.

Adding the icing (confectioners) sugar must be a gradual process, requiring plenty of mixing rather than beating during each addition of sugar, until the required consistency is reached. The icing should be light in texture and glossy in appearance.

Royal icing with too much icing (confectioners) sugar added too quickly will give a dull, heavy result and be grainy in appearance. It will be difficult to work with and, as it sets, will appear chalky and dull instead of sparkling white. It will also be difficult to pipe, soon becoming short and breaking off easily.

The prepared icing must be covered to exclude all air and prevent the surface from drying. Use damp cling film (plastic wrap) to seal the surface, or fill an airtight container to the top with icing. Covering with a damp cloth is fine for short periods but if left overnight the icing will absorb all the moisture, causing the consistency to be diluted.

If the icing is too stiff, add egg white or reconstituted egg albumen to make it softer. If the icing is too soft, gradually stir in more icing (confectioners) sugar for the required consistency.

Work from a small quantity of icing in a separate bowl from the main batch, covering it with damp muslin (cheesecloth) during use and keeping it well scraped down. If this small amount does become dry and cracked, at least it will not affect the whole batch of royal icing.

Royal Icing 1

This icing made with fresh egg whites is traditionally used to cover celebration cakes. Depending upon its consistency, it may be used for flat icing, peaked icing or piping designs on to cakes.

Makes 450 g/1 lb/1½ cups
- *2 egg whites*
- *1.5 ml/¼ tsp/¼ tsp lemon juice*
- *450 g/1 lb/3 cups icing (confectioners) sugar, sieved (sifted)*
- *5 ml/1 tsp/1 tsp glycerine*

Peaked royal icing has been used to coat little fruit cakes for a witty and attractive festive gift.

Royal Icing Consistencies

The consistency of royal icing varies for different uses. Stiff icing is necessary for piping, slightly softer for flat icing or peaked icing, and slacker for run-outs.

PIPING CONSISTENCY
When a wooden spoon is drawn out of the icing, it should form a fine, sharp point, termed as 'sharp peak'. This consistency flows easily for piping but retains a definite shape produced by the nozzle.

FLAT OR PEAKED ICING CONSISTENCY
When the spoon is drawn out of the icing it should form a fine point which curves over at the end, termed as 'soft peak'. This consistency spreads smoothly and creates a flat finish, but also pulls up into sharp or soft peaks.

RUN-OUTS
Use soft peak consistency to pipe the outlines, and thick cream consistency to fill in the shapes. This consistency flows to fill in the run-outs, but holds a rounded shape within the piped lines.

1 *Place the egg whites and lemon juice in a clean bowl. Using a clean wooden spoon, stir to break up the egg whites. Add sufficient icing (confectioners) sugar and mix well to form the consistency of unwhipped cream.*

2 *Continue mixing and adding small quantities of sugar every few minutes, until the desired consistency has been reached. Mix well after each addition of sugar.*

3 *Stir in the glycerine until the icing is well blended.*

Royal Icing 2

Dried powdered egg white is known as egg albumen and may be used in place of fresh egg whites for royal icing. Simply blend the egg albumen with water to reconstitute it as directed on the packet, then add the icing (confectioners) sugar. The dried egg white is more convenient to use as there are no egg yolks to dispose of and it produces a good, light, glossy icing which is easy to handle. Used as flat icing for tiered cakes, it sets hard enough to support the weight of the cakes, but still cuts easily without being brittle. This icing is suitable for flat or peaked icing, piping and run-outs.

Note Use double-strength dried egg albumen for run-outs so that the run-out pieces set hard enough to remove from the paper.

INGREDIENTS

Makes 450 g/1 lb/1½ cups
- *15 g/½ oz/1 tbsp dried egg albumen*
- *90 ml/6 tbsp/6 tbsp tepid water*
- *450 g/1 lb/3 cups icing (confectioners) sugar, sieved (sifted)*

1 *Put the egg albumen into a clean bowl. Using a clean spoon, gradually stir in the water and blend well together until the liquid is smooth and free from lumps.*

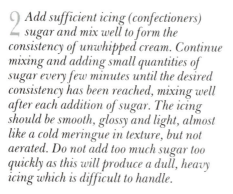

2 *Add sufficient icing (confectioners) sugar and mix well to form the consistency of unwhipped cream. Continue mixing and adding small quantities of sugar every few minutes until the desired consistency has been reached, mixing well after each addition of sugar. The icing should be smooth, glossy and light, almost like a cold meringue in texture, but not aerated. Do not add too much sugar too quickly as this will produce a dull, heavy icing which is difficult to handle.*

3 *Allow the icing to settle before using it; cover the surface with a piece of damp cling film (plastic wrap) and seal well, excluding all the air.*

4 *Stir the icing thoroughly before use as this will disperse the air bubbles, then adjust the consistency if necessary by adding more sieved (sifted) icing (confectioners) sugar or reconstituted egg albumen.*

To Royal-ice a Round Cake

1 *The method for royal icing a round cake is the same as for icing a square cake, but easier as there are only two surfaces to ice – the top and side. Following the instructions for royal icing a square cake, spread the top of the cake evenly with icing.*

2 *Draw a straight edge across the top; repeat if unsatisfactory. Neaten the top edge and leave the icing to dry for at least two hours in a warm, dry place.*

To Royal-ice a Round Cakeboard

3 *Spread the side of the cake evenly with icing and leave the cake on the turntable. Neaten the top edge with a metal palette knife (spatula).*

4 *Hold the side scraper firmly on to the side of the cake, resting on the cakeboard. Hold the cakeboard and turntable with one hand and the scraper with the other; turn the cake and turntable continuously in one revolution in one direction and at the same time hold the side scraper against the icing, pulling it towards you in the opposite direction to smooth the icing. Draw the side scraper gradually off the cake.*

1 When the icing is completely dry, place the cake on to the turntable, and ensure the cakeboard is free from dry icing. Spread a thin layer of icing onto the cakeboard, neaten the edge of the board with a palette knife (spatula).

2 Place the side scraper onto the board and turn the cake and turntable in one revolution, drawing the side edge towards you to smooth the icing. Neaten the edge and leave to dry. Repeat with a second layer of icing.

5 *Neaten the top edge and the cakeboard edge. Leave the cake to dry before repeating the procedure to cover the cake with three or four thin layers of icing. Use a slightly softer consistency of icing for the final layer.*

To Royal-ice a Square Cake

ROYAL ICING CHART

QUANTITY OF ROYAL ICING	CAKE SIZE
450 g/1 lb/1½ cups	12 cm/5 in square 15 cm/6 in round
675 g/1½ lb/2¼ cups	15 cm/6 in square 18 cm/7 in round
900 g/2 lb/3 cups	18 cm/7 in square 20 cm/8 in round
1.1 kg/2½ lb/3¾ cups	20 cm/8 in square 23 cm/9 in round
1.4 kg/3 lb/4½ cups	23 cm/9 in square 25 cm/10 in round
1.6 kg/3½ lb/5¼ cups	25 cm/10 in square 28 cm/11 in round
1.8 kg/4 lb/6 cups	28 cm/11 in square 30 cm/12 in round
2 kg/4½ lb/6¾ cups	30 cm/12 in square 33 cm/13 in round

Royal Icing Quantity Guide

It is always difficult to estimate how much royal icing will be needed to cover a cake. The quantity varies according to how the icing is applied and to the thickness of layers. The design also has to be taken into consideration – depending upon whether it is just piping, or run-outs and sugar pieces.

Do not attempt to make up large quantities of royal icing in one go. The best method is to make up and use the royal icing in 450 g/1 lb/1½ cup batches (see recipes pages 41 and 42). Each batch of icing will then be fresh and free from any impurities which may occur when larger quantities are made for one cake.

The chart (left) is just a guide to the quantities needed for covering various cakes with two or three thin layers of flat royal icing.

1 Make a quantity of royal icing to soft peak consistency. Cover with clean, damp muslin (cheesecloth). Place the marzipanned cake on a turntable.

2 Using a small palette knife (spatula), spread the icing back and forth over the top of the cake to eliminate any air bubbles before spreading smoothly. Remove the excess icing from the top edges of the cake with the metal palette knife (spatula). Take the cake off the turntable and place on a rigid surface.

3 With the cake directly in front, hold the straight edge comfortably and place it on the top edge at the far side of the cake. Steadily pull the straight edge across the top of the cake in one continuous movement to smooth the icing. If the top is not smooth enough, repeat the movement until it is smooth, or re-spread the top of the cake with icing, neaten the edge and start again. Do not worry about this first layer being perfect.

4 Trim away the excess icing from the top edges of the cake with the clean metal palette knife (spatula) to neaten. Then leave the icing to dry for about two hours or overnight in a warm, dry place.

5 Replace the cake on the turntable and using the small palette knife (spatula), smoothly spread one side of the cake with icing to cover evenly. Remove the excess icing from the dry icing on the top edge of the cake and at both corners.

6 Place the cake on a rigid surface and, positioning a side scraper at the far corner of the cake so that it rests on the cakeboard, pull the scraper across the side of the cake in one movement to smooth the icing. If the surface is not satisfactory, repeat the process.

7 Trim away the excess icing from the top edge and the corners of the cake to neaten. Ice the opposite side of the cake in the same way. Neaten the edges and along the cakeboard and leave to dry for at least two hours. Repeat the process to ice the remaining two opposite sides of the cake. Leave to dry overnight before continuing to add further layers of icing.

8 Ice the cake with another two or three thin coats of icing, repeating the method above, until the surface is smooth and flat. For the final coat of icing, to obtain a really smooth finish, use a slightly softer consistency of icing.

To Royal-ice a Square Cakeboard

1 Ensure the icing is completely dry and the cakeboard is free from dry icing. Ice the two opposite sides at a time, smoothing with a side scraper and neaten the edges of the board.
2 Leave to dry. Then repeat to ice the remaining sides and leave to dry. Repeat with a second layer of icing.

Peaked Royal Icing

Royal icing is very versatile and can be smoothed onto a cake to achieve a perfectly flat finish for decorating, or peaked and swirled to give a texture.

To make beautifully even peaks, the icing must be of soft peak consistency.

1 Spread the top and sides of a marzipanned cake evenly with royal icing. Smooth the top of the cake with a straight edge and the side with a side scraper so the icing is fairly even and completely covers the cake.

2 Using a small, clean palette knife (spatula) dip one side of the blade into the bowl of icing. Starting at the base and working to the top edge of the cake, press the palette knife (spatula) with icing onto the iced cake, pulling sharply away to form a peak. Repeat to form about three or four peaks, then re-dip the palette knife (spatula) into the bowl of icing and repeat to make more peaks down the side of the cake, in between the first line, about 10 mm/$\frac{1}{2}$ in apart. Continue until the side is complete.

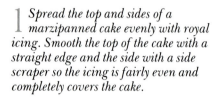

3 Repeat to peak the top, leaving a smooth area for decorations if desired.

4 If the top is to be flat, follow the guide for flat icing the top of a cake and then, when completely dry, spread the sides with soft-peak royal icing and peak as above.

SUGARPASTE (FONDANT)

Pink-coloured sugarpaste or fondant has been used over a sponge base to create this appealing present-shaped cake for a special birthday.

Sugarpaste (fondant) has become increasingly popular during the last few years. Now celebration cakes are often presented as softly rounded, smooth cakes instead of the sharp, crisp, classical lines of a traditionally iced cake.

There are so many advantages when using this type of icing, the most obvious being that it is quick and easy to make and a treat to use. Being soft and pliable, the icing may be rolled out to any shape and used to cover freshly marzipanned cakes, producing an instant result. Even the least experienced cake decorator can achieve a smooth, glossy, professional finish and – with the minimum amount of decoration – finish the cake.

Although a recipe for a sugarpaste (fondant) is included, there are certainly times when ready-made icing is better or more convenient to use. There are several types of sugarpaste (fondant) or ready-to-roll icing on the market. All have more or less the same ingredients, but are packaged under many different names. Textures may vary and some are certainly better to handle than others. It is a good idea to try a small quantity first to see if it is suitable for the cake you wish to ice.

Sugarpaste (fondant) can be purchased in 225 g/8 oz/½ lb packs from supermarkets and shops, or up to 5 kg/11 lb boxes from cake-icing specialists. Sugarpaste (fondant) is available in white, champagne, pink and many other colours. This is worth considering if you need a large quantity for a wedding cake, as it ensures the colour is even throughout. Kneading food colouring into large quantities of sugarpaste (fondant) is hard work and time-consuming.

Sugarpaste (fondant icing) may be tinted at home in any shade by kneading in a few drops of food colouring until the whole quantity is evenly coloured. It can be used very successfully for covering all types of cakes – for modelling, making sugar flowers, leaves and cut-out sugar decorations.

Sugarpaste (Fondant Icing)

INGREDIENTS

Makes 575 g/1¼ lb/1¼ lb
- *1 egg white*
- *30 ml/2 tbsp/2 tbsp liquid glucose*
- *10 ml/2 tsp/2 tsp rosewater*
- *450 g/1 lb/1½ cups icing (confectioners) sugar, sieved (sifted)*
- *icing (confectioners) sugar to dust*

1 *Place the egg white, liquid glucose and rosewater into a clean bowl. Mix together to break up the egg white. Add the icing (confectioners) sugar and combine with a wooden spoon until the icing begins to bind together.*

2 *Knead together with the fingers until the mixture forms into a ball.*

3 *Place on a surface lightly dusted with icing (confectioners) sugar and knead until smooth and free from cracks.*

4 *If the icing is too soft to handle and is sticky, knead in some more sieved (sifted) icing (confectioners) sugar until firm and pliable. If the sugarpaste should dry out and become hard, knead in a little boiled water until the icing is soft and pliable.*

STORING

Wrap the icing completely in cling film (plastic wrap), or store in a polythene (polyethylene) bag with all the air excluded.

SUGARPASTE CHART

Cake Tin Sizes	12 cm/5 in Square	15 cm/6 in Square	18 cm/7 in Square	20 cm/8 in Square	23 cm/9 in Square	25 cm/10 in Square	28 cm/11 in Square	30 cm/12 in Square
	15 cm/6 in Round	18 cm/7 in Round	20 cm/8 in Round	23 cm/9 in Round	25 cm/10 in Round	28 cm/11 in Round	30 cm/12 in Round	33 cm/13 in Round
QUANTITIES								
Sugarpaste (fondant)	450 g/ 1 lb	675 g/ 1½ lb	800 g/ 1¾ lb	900 g/ 2 lb	1.1 kg/ 2½ lb	1.5 kg/ 3¼ lb	1.8 kg/ 4 lb	1.9 kg/ 4¼ lb

1 Place the marzipanned cake, on the cakeboard, onto a turntable and brush the surface evenly with a little sherry or cooled boiled water. Dust a work surface with sieved (sifted) icing (confectioners) sugar to prevent the sugarpaste from sticking. Roll out the sugarpaste (fondant) to 5 mm/¼ in thickness, using more sieved (sifted) icing (confectioners) sugar if necessary, to the chosen shape of the cake.

2 Trim the sugarpaste (fondant) to 6.5 cm/2½ in larger than the top of the cake, making sure the icing moves freely. Lift the sugarpaste carefully over the top of the cake, supported by a rolling pin. Brush off any excess icing (confectioners) sugar. Unroll the sugarpaste over the cake to cover evenly.

3 Dust your hands with cornflour (cornstarch), and smooth the icing over the top and then down the sides of the cake. Ease the excess icing toward the base, excluding any air bubbles between the surfaces. Trim off excess icing at base of cake using a small knife.

4 Dust your hands with more cornflour (cornstarch), and gently rub the surface of the sugarpaste in circular movements to make it smooth and glossy. Place the cake in a cake box and leave in a warm, dry place to dry the sugarpaste.

5 Knead the trimmings together and seal in cling film (plastic wrap) or a polythene (polyethylene) bag and use to cover the cakeboard, or for decorations.

To Cover Any Shaped Cakeboard with Sugarpaste (Fondant)

Complete the effect of a novelty or classic cake by continuing the coloured fondant or sugarpaste covering onto the cakeboard.

1 *Lightly dust a surface with icing (confectioners) sugar. Tint the sugarpaste (fondant) to the required colour to match the cake. Brush the cakeboard with a little apricot glaze.*

2 *Roll out the sugarpaste (fondant) to 5 mm/¼ in thickness to the shape of the cakeboard. Ensure the sugarpaste moves freely and lift over the cakeboard. Dust your hands with cornflour (cornstarch), and smooth the surface, trimming off excess icing using a small palette knife (spatula). Keep the blade level with the edge of the board and take care to keep the edge of the sugarpaste (fondant) straight.*

3 *Leave the iced board in a warm place overnight to dry. Then place the iced cake carefully in position.*

PETAL PASTE

Petal paste is used only for making cake decorations. It is exceptionally strong and can be moulded into very fine flowers or cut into individual sugar pieces which dry very quickly. Liquid glucose and gum tragacanth are available from chemists or cake-icing specialists. Petal paste can also be purchased commercially in a powdered form ready to mix, which is very convenient for small quantities but is rather expensive if using large amounts.

INGREDIENTS

Makes 575 g/1¼ lb/1¼ lb
- *10 ml/2 tsp/2 tsp (powdered) gelatine*
- *25 ml/5 tsp/5 tsp cold water*
- *10 ml/2 tsp/2 tsp liquid glucose*
- *10 ml/2 tsp/2 tsp white vegetable fat*
- *450 g/1 lb/3½ cups icing (confectioners) sugar, sieved (sifted)*
- *5 ml/1 tsp/1 tsp gum tragacanth*
- *1 egg white*

Petal paste can be used to make tiny little flowers for a special celebratory or formal birthday cake.

1 *Place the gelatine, water, liquid glucose and white fat in a heatproof bowl over a saucepan of hot water until melted, stirring occasionally. Remove the bowl from the heat.*

2 *Sift the icing (confectioners) sugar and gum tragacanth into a bowl. Make a 'well' in the centre and add the egg white and gelatine mixture. Mix together with a wooden spoon to form a soft paste.*

3 *Knead on a surface dusted with icing (confectioners) sugar until smooth, white and free from cracks.*

4 *Place in a polythene (polyethylene) bag or wrap in cling film (plastic wrap) and seal well to exclude all the air. Leave for two hours before use, then re-knead and use small pieces at a time, leaving the remaining petal paste well sealed.*

FOOD COLOURINGS AND TINTS

Food colourings and tints have changed dramatically over the last few years. At one time food colourings were only available in bottles in a range of primary colours. These liquid colours are still available from most supermarkets and shops and are adequate for tinting icings, frosting, butter icing, marzipan and sugarpaste. With careful blending many other colours and shades can be achieved. Since the colourings are fairly diluted, it is impossible to achieve a richer colour without diluting the consistency of the icing. So for stronger colours, concentrated food colouring pastes produce better results.

PASTE, POWDER AND LIQUID COLOURS

In specialist cake-icing and decorating shops, food colourings are available in a far greater range. Good quality colours appear as pastes, powders and liquids. They are very concentrated and need to be added drop by drop, using a cocktail stick to stir and carefully tint the icing to a delicate shade. An exceptional variety of colours are available so there is no need to blend the colours to obtain the shade of icing you want. Since they are so concentrated, the consistency of the icing is not affected. The colours are also permanent and do not fade.

Remember that food colourings, when added to icings or kneaded into marzipan or sugarpaste, change on standing and dry a deeper or a lighter colour than when first mixed. Colour sample amounts of icing in the daylight and leave them for at least 15 minutes to assess if you have achieved the desired colour. If you are matching icing with fabrics or flowers, allow coloured samples to dry thoroughly before deciding. If several batches of coloured icing are to be made, keep some icing in reserve so the colour can be matched. Always remember that a cake should look edible, so keep the colours to pastel shades – a hint of colour is better than too much.

Celebration cakes may require more subtle shading and tinting. Moulded and cut-out flowers, sugar pieces and cakes' surfaces can now be coloured with 'blossom tints', or painted with 'lustre colours' when the flowers, sugar pieces or icings

are dry. This also gives you an opportunity to add colour at the last minute, and prevents the risk of colours running into the icing when the atmosphere is damp. These products also hold their colour without fading. Such specialist food colours are available only from cake-decorating shops.

FOOD-COLOURING PENS

These pens look like fibre-tip pens but are filled with edible food colourings. They come in a range of primary colours as well as black, brown and purple. Their uses are endless, especially for quickly decorating, writing or applying details to models or sugar pieces.

Use them like a pen to write or draw a design onto dry royal icing run-outs, small sugar plaques or even to mark a design directly onto an iced cake. But these pens are indelible – so make no mistakes!

Marzipan or sugarpaste (fondant) is easily tinted with food colouring; break off small pieces and work in gradually until evenly blended.

USING CHOCOLATE TO DECORATE CAKES

A traditional festive log on a chocolate theme, coated with a deliciously rich chocolate ganache topping and decorated with chocolate flakes.

Chocolate is a very versatile ingredient to work with. Since it is an expensive product, however, it should be used with great care to obtain the best results. Chocolate is sold in many forms – milk, plain and white; in bars, dots, as thick, richly-flavoured spreads, and as powdered cocoa and drinking chocolate.

Choosing Chocolate

There are basically four grades of chocolate for cooking – *couverture*, cooking chocolate, eating or dessert chocolate and chocolate-flavoured cake covering.

COUVERTURE is the finest, most expensive chocolate used for confectionery and special chocolate work. It contains the highest proportion of cocoa butter, which gives the chocolate its fine flavour and texture. When using, it must be tempered to obtain the high gloss and hard texture.

COOKING CHOCOLATE is available in different grades; the quality of the chocolate depends on how much cocoa butter it contains. This affects the flavour, colour and texture. Cooking chocolate is a good all-rounder, is less expensive to buy and ideal for all recipes using cooked chocolate.

EATING OR DESSERT CHOCOLATE has slightly less cocoa butter but a wonderful flavour and refined texture. It is versatile for cooking, but is rather expensive. It is better to select this type of chocolate for special desserts, gateaux or homemade chocolates. When it is melted, it remains quite thick, so it is not suitable for smoothly coated cakes.

CHOCOLATE-FLAVOURED CAKE COVERING actually contains so little cocoa butter that it can no longer be called "chocolate". It has a poorer flavour than the other alternatives and the texture is soft and rather greasy. Points in its favour are that it is easier to use and is less expensive to buy. It is a good all-round cooking product and may be used for all chocolate recipes.

All these grades of chocolate are obtainable as plain (semisweet), milk or white chocolate. The plainer the chocolate, the harder the texture and the stronger the flavour. Milk chocolate is milder and sweeter. White chocolate, containing only cocoa butter and no dark cocoa solids, has no distinctive flavour.

To Melt Chocolate

Break the chocolate into small pieces and place in a large, dry, clean bowl over a saucepan of *hand-hot* water. Ensure that the base of the bowl does not touch the water. Do not beat, but stir it occasionally until it has completely melted; this you cannot hurry and the chocolate temperature should not exceed 38–43°C/100–110°F. Otherwise, when it eventually sets, the surface will be covered with a white fat bloom. Never allow moisture, steam or condensation to come into contact with chocolate or it will become thick and unstable. Leave the bowl over water during use, unless you require the chocolate to become thicker. Any left-over chocolate can always be re-used so there is no waste.

Chocolate can be melted in a microwave set at the lowest setting if time is short, but only if the chocolate is being used to add to other ingredients. For coating and spreading, the chocolate becomes too warm and the surface dries with a streaked appearance.

Coating

1 Stand cakes, candies or biscuits (cookies) on a wire cooling rack, spaced a little apart. Make sure all items to be coated are at room temperature. Place a large piece of greaseproof (wax) paper underneath to catch the excess chocolate. Depending on the size of the piece being coated, use a ladle full of chocolate that will coat the whole item at one coating.

2 Pour the chocolate quickly over, allowing the excess to fall onto the paper below. Tap the cooling rack against the counter surface to level the chocolate. Repeat with another layer after the first one has set, if liked. Return the fallen chocolate from the greaseproof (wax) paper back into the bowl.

Dipping Fruit

1 Have everything ready before starting. All items to be dipped should be at room temperature, otherwise the chocolate will set before smoothly coating. Use confectioners' dipping forks or a large dinner fork and have several sheets of baking parchment ready to take the dipped items.

2 Place the items individually into the chocolate, turn once with the dipping fork to coat evenly. Lift out with the fork, tap gently on the side of the bowl and allow the excess chocolate to fall. Place on the paper, mark or decorate the top, and leave to set.

Chocolate Leaves

Choose real leaves from flowers, herbs and plants which are small, firm and have well-defined veins.

1 *Melt 125 g/4 oz/4 squares white, plain or milk chocolate. Pick as many fresh leaves as possible, wash them and then dry thoroughly on kitchen paper.*

2 *Using a medium-sized paintbrush, thickly coat the underside of each leaf with melted chocolate, taking care not to paint over the edge of the leaves or the leaf will not peel away from the chocolate.*

3 *Place the leaves to set on baking parchment – chocolate side uppermost – in a cool place. Just before using, peel the real leaves away from their chocolate impressions. The chocolate leaves make exquisite decorations.*

A chocolate cake is always irresistible; not only is the sponge of this cake chocolate, but there is a rich chocolate icing and decorations of chocolate-dipped cherries and chocolate leaves.

Chocolate Curls

1 Melt 125 g/4 oz/4 squares plain, milk or white chocolate. Pour melted chocolate onto a rigid surface such as marble, wood or plastic laminate. Spread evenly backwards and forwards with a palette knife until smooth.

2 When the chocolate has just set, but has not become hard, hold a sharp knife at a 45° angle to the chocolate. Draw the knife across the surface to shave off thin curls from the chocolate.

3 To make larger curls or *caraque*, draw the knife down the whole length or width of the chocolate to form long curls.

4 Make chocolate shavings in the same way, but let the chocolate set a little harder before beginning. Then draw the knife only halfway across the surface to shave off fine flakes.

5 To make tiny curls, use a potato peeler to shave curls off the side of a block of chocolate. This must be at room temperature, unless you are using chocolate-flavoured cake covering, which is just the right texture for curling. Alternatively grate chocolate on a coarse grater.

Chocolate Cut-outs

1 Melt 125 g/4 oz/4 squares milk, plain or white chocolate. Pour the melted chocolate onto baking parchment. Spread as evenly as possible with a palette knife (spatula).
2 Pick up the corners of the paper and drop a few times to level and remove air bubbles from the chocolate.
3 When the chocolate can be touched without sticking to the fingers, place another piece of paper on the top. Turn the whole sheet of chocolate over, then peel off the backing paper. Turn the chocolate sheet over.
4 To cut out shapes: use any shaped cocktail, biscuit (cookie), plain or fluted cutters. Press onto the chocolate, cut out and remove the shapes.
5 To cut out squares or triangles: carefully measure and mark the size of the squares required. Using a fine sharp knife or scalpel and the straight edge of a ruler, cut along the marked lines and remove the shapes. Cut diagonally in half for triangles.
6 Leave in a cool place to set hard before using.

Piped Chocolate

There are easy ways of piping chocolate; one is by using chocolate and hazelnut spread which is the ideal consistency. Place in a greaseproof (wax) paper piping bag fitted with a small star nozzle. With this you can pipe a border of shells, stars or whirls.

Melted chocolate is more difficult to pipe through a metal nozzle, as the coldness of the metal sets the chocolate before you start. Add a few drops of glycerine to the chocolate to thicken it, rather than allowing the chocolate to cool and thicken naturally. Then pipe the chocolate through a nozzle as quickly as possible.

For piping threads or lines of chocolate, use a greaseproof (wax) paper piping bag, snip off the point to the size of the hole required and pipe thin threads of chocolate in straight or zig-zag lines.
To Colour White Chocolate – white chocolate is very versatile and can be coloured. Use oil-based or powdered food colourings, as liquids added to chocolate will cause it to thicken and become unusable.

Piped Chocolate Pieces

1 Melt 25 g/1 oz/1 square white, plain or milk chocolate. Draw the chosen designs onto a piece of paper. Place greaseproof (wax) paper over the top and secure the corners with tape.
2 Fill a greaseproof (wax) paper piping bag with chocolate. Fold down the top and snip off the end.

3 Pipe fine threads of chocolate following the designs, or pipe free-hand designs. Leave to set, then carefully slide a thin palette knife (spatula) under each piece to release. Use for decorating cakes and gateaux.

Chocolate Run-outs

Choose any simple biscuit- (cookie-) cutter, in shapes such as animals, birds, hearts, flowers, bells, horseshoes, numerals or letters.

1 *Draw or trace the chosen shape several times on a piece of paper to allow for breakages. Place a piece of baking parchment over the top and stick down the edges. Using two greaseproof (wax) paper piping bags, fill each with melted chocolate and fold down the tops. Snip off the point from one piping bag and pipe a thread of chocolate around the edge of the design.*

2 *Cut the end off the remaining piping bag and fill in the run-out with melted chocolate so that it looks rounded. Leave to set.*

3 *Pipe on any details, if necessary, then allow to set hard. Carefully peel off the paper and use as desired.*

MARZIPAN DECORATING IDEAS

Marzipan is smooth, soft and easy to work with – an ideal base for royal icing and sugarpaste (fondant). It may be tinted in various shades with food colourings, or cut into shapes, or moulded into flowers, animals and figures.

Used as a cake covering on its own, it offers colour, texture and flavour without the sweetness of icing or sugarpaste (fondant). Once the cake has been covered in marzipan, it may be decorated very simply by crimping the edges and applying marzipan cut-outs, or moulded leaves, flowers, animals or fruit.

Crimper Designs

These easy and effective designs are obtained by using crimping tools, which are available from most kitchen shops or cake-decorating specialists. They come with a variety of shaped end-pieces – curved lines, scallops, ovals, 'V', hearts, diamonds and zig-zags. To obtain an even crimped design, first practise on a spare piece of freshly-made marzipan. Crimping must always be worked on fresh marzipan.

Cover the cake with marzipan, but do not allow it to dry. Before beginning, dust the crimper with cornflour (cornstarch) to prevent sticking. Place the crimper on the edge of the cake and squeeze firmly to mark the marzipan. Gently release and lift the crimper, taking care it does not spring apart or it will tear the marzipan. Place the crimper end next to the marked section and continue the pattern all around the top of the cake. If desired, use on the base and sides of cakes as well, or make a design across the top.

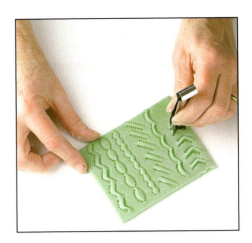

Cut-out Decorations

Cut-outs present a simple way of decorating a cake with coloured marzipan.
● Tint several pieces of marzipan with different food colouring, kneading each piece lightly until evenly coloured. Roll out each piece evenly on a surface lightly dusted with sieved (sifted) icing (confectioners) sugar, until about 3 mm/⅛ in thick.
● Using small aspic, cocktail or biscuit (cookie) cutters, cut out a selection of shapes. Arrange them in an attractive design on the cake – either as a border or as a central design – and secure with a coating of apricot glaze.

● Small flower and leaf cutters may be used to make a flower design; an arrangement of stems and other leaves can be cut out from thin strips of coloured marzipan. Mark the veins with a knife and bend the leaves over a piece of dowel until dry.
● Individual cut-out decorations look bright and cheerful on a marzipanned or iced cake. Suggestions for designs include a candle and flame. Cut out a template as a guide for making the coloured marzipan pieces and assemble them on the cake. Other possibilities include book or nursery rhyme characters or scenes from birthday or Christmas cards. Build the shapes by cutting out each piece from different-coloured marzipan.

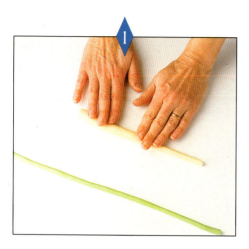

Rope or Plait

These attractive decorations, made from marzipan, are a quick and simple way to finish the top and base of a cake.

1 To make a rope, simply use two coloured pieces of marzipan rolled into pencil-thin lengths.

2 Join the two ends together and twist to form a rope.

1 To make a plait, use three coloured pieces of marzipan or *just one colour* and roll them into pencil-thin lengths.

2 Join the ends together and plait the pieces neatly.

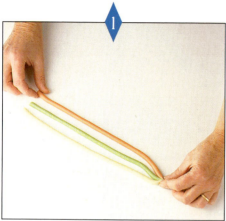

Basket Weave

This is fun to do, but takes a little more time and patience. When finished, however, it looks impressive.

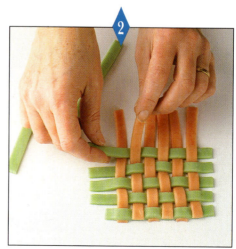

1 Work with one or two colours of marzipan. Roll out one piece at a time to 5 mm/¼ in thickness and cut into 5 mm/¼ in wide strips.

2 Arrange several strips in parallel lines a little apart, then weave strips of marzipan in and out to form a basket weave.

Easy Modelling

Marzipan can be moulded like plasticine into many different shapes by copying simple pictures. The decorator can create a still-life of fruits or flowers, or model animals or people. Tint the marzipan to the required shade and mould each piece individually. Assemble the scenes or characters by pressing the pieces together and allow them to dry in a warm place. Use food colouring pens to mark in details.

Simple Flowers

These are also quick and easy to make. Flower cutters can be obtained from icing specialists. Colour the marzipan as required and roll it out thinly. Dip the cutters into cornflour (cornstarch) and cut out the flowers. Bend the petals to give some shape, and mould different-coloured centres or stamens to fit in the centre. Once the blossoms are completely dry, store them in a box until required.

DECORATING WITH SUGARPASTE (FONDANT)

A cake covered in sugarpaste (fondant) looks so different from a royal iced cake – so soft and delicate that it hardly needs decorating; the soft lines and silky finish only demand a dainty finish.

Marbling

Sugarpaste (fondant) lends itself to tinting in all shades, and a very effective way of colouring is to marble the paste. Use it to cover a cake and the cakeboard completely and use the trimmings for cut-out or moulded decorations.

1 *Add a few drops of food colouring in drops over the icing.*

2 *Do not knead the food colouring fully into the icing.*

3 *When it is rolled out, the colour is dispersed in such a way that it gives a marbled appearance to the sugarpaste (fondant).*

Marbling is a wonderful effect easily achieved with sugarpaste or fondant and edible food colourings, as shown with this blue and orange candle-shaped novelty cake.

Frills and Flounces

Frills and flounces are a delicate way of finishing cakes covered smoothly with sugarpaste (fondant). They can be made from ordinary sugarpaste (fondant) but, being soft when worked, the frill has a tendency to drop. To counter this, it is advisable to knead a half teaspoon of gum tragacanth into 225 g/8 oz/½ lb sugarpaste (fondant) 24 hours before use. Alternatively knead one-third petal paste into two-thirds sugarpaste (fondant) until evenly blended. Tint the paste evenly to the colour required.

TO MAKE A FRILL

Frills made from a blend of sugarpaste (fondant) and petal paste are used to stunning decorative effect on this formal wedding cake.

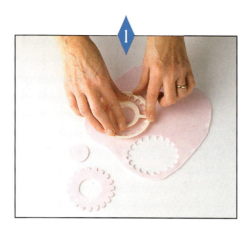

1 *On a surface lightly dusted with cornflour (cornstarch), roll out thinly a small piece of sugarpaste (fondant). Cut out a 7.5 cm/3 in round, using a plain or fluted cutter. Cut out the centre of the round using a 4 cm/1½ in plain cutter. Alternatively, use a special frill cutter, as here.*

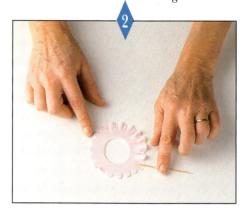

2 *Using the end of a cocktail stick or toothpick sprinkled with cornflour (cornstarch), place on the outer edge of the circle. Roll the cocktail stick along the edge with the fingers until the edge of the icing begins to frill. Move round the edge of the icing until the edge is completely frilled.*

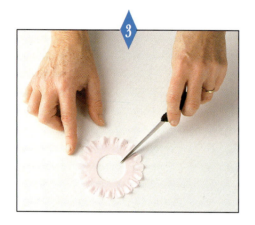

3 *Cut the ring open with a sharp knife.*

4 *Gently ease the frill open and attach it to the cake, securing with a line of royal icing or egg white.*

TO MAKE A FRILLED PLAQUE

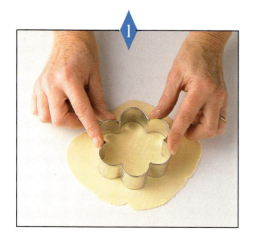

1 *Colour the sugarpaste (fondant) and roll out thinly. Cut out the shape and size of the plaque required, using an oval or round plain or fluted cutter.*

2 *Frill the edge following the instructions above.*

3 *When the plaque is dry, pipe with royal icing to decorate, or use food colouring pens to write on the plaque.*

Embossing

This wonderful technique provides an instant way of decorating a cake covered with sugarpaste (fondant). It is similar to crimping in that the cake has to be freshly covered with the icing to work the design.

There are embossing tools in a large range of patterns and designs available from cake-icing specialists. Many other tools may be used to impress a pattern into the sugarpaste (fondant) – spoon handles, tops of icing nozzles, anything small with a defined pattern on it.

Colour may be added by dipping the embossing tool into petal dust before embossing the icing, or by painting part or all the design with food colouring and a fine brush, or with petal dust or food colouring pens, when the sugarpaste (fondant) is dry.

TO EMBOSS A PATTERN

Choose the design you wish to emboss onto the cake. Practise on a small piece of sugarpaste (fondant) to create the design before embarking on the cake.

Ensure the cake is freshly covered in sugarpaste (fondant) and dust the embossing tool with cornflour (cornstarch) or petal dust. Take care to press the embossing tool to the same depth and angle each time to make an even design. Re-dust with petal dust to colour the design or with cornflour (cornstarch) to prevent sticking.

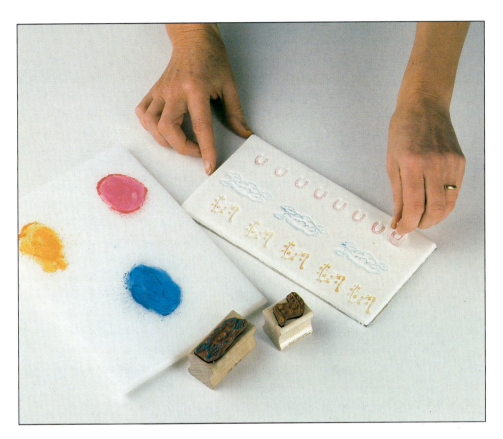

Embossers are a simple way to create a beautiful edging to a formal cake; a horseshoe-shaped embosser is used here for good luck.

Crimping

These quick, easy and effective designs are obtained by the use of crimping tools which are available from most kitchen shops or cake-decorating specialists. They come in different-shaped end pieces, curved lines, scallops, ovals, 'V', hearts, diamonds and zig-zags. To obtain an even crimped design, first practise on a spare piece of sugarpaste (fondant) and always crimp in fresh sugarpaste.

1 *Cover the cake with sugarpaste (fondant), but do not allow it to dry. Dust the crimper with cornflour (cornstarch) to prevent sticking. Place the crimper on the edge of the cake and squeeze firmly to mark the sugarpaste (fondant). Gently release and lift the crimper – taking care it does not spring apart or it will tear the sugarpaste (fondant). Place the crimper end next to the patterned paste, squeeze, lift and repeat all around the top of the cake.*

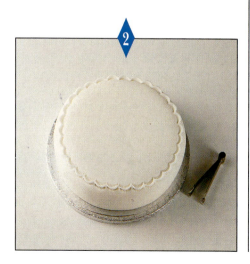

2 *Use on the base and sides of cakes as well, if desired, or make a design across the top. Always crimp a cake which has been freshly covered.*

Cut-out Decorations

Cut-outs make an instant decoration for an iced cake.

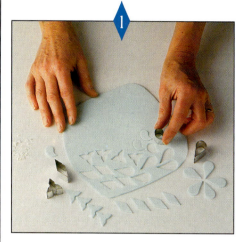 

1 *Simply colour the sugarpaste (fondant) in the chosen colours, roll out thinly on a surface lightly dusted with icing (confectioners) sugar and cut out small shapes using aspic or cocktail cutters.*

2 *Lightly press these shapes onto the top and sides of the cake to make a border design and to decorate the sides, securing them with egg white, if necessary. Alternatively, allow the cut-out pieces to dry and store in a box in a warm dry place until required for finishing the cake.*

Cut-out sugar pieces in a variety of different shapes have been created to decorate this special birthday cake.

Sugar Pieces and Extensions

Delicate pieces cut out from petal paste need to be fine and strong as generally they are attached to the edges of the cake, extending the design. There are many wonderful shapes to create from petal paste, so work out the design first. Tint the paste a pale shade, or leave it white and dust the pieces with petal dust when they are dry.

Roll out the petal paste in small quantities as it dries quickly. Roll it so thinly that you can almost see through it. Using cutters of varying shapes or a template, cut out the pieces you require. Allow them to dry, then attach them to the cake using royal icing.

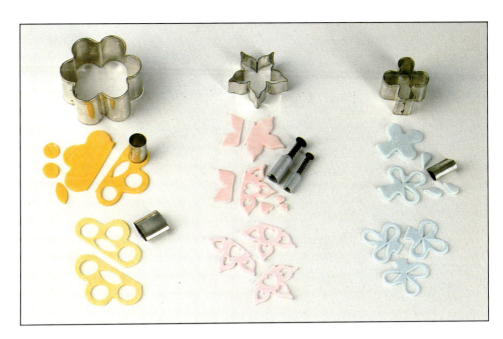

Ribbon Insertion

This technique creates the illusion that a single piece of ribbon has been threaded through the sugarpaste (fondant) icing. The design can be straight, diagonal or curved and combined with crimper work or dainty piping. The sugarpaste should feel firm on the surface, but soft underneath. Finish off the ribbon insertion with tiny bows, fine piping or crimping.

Plan the design on paper first, make a template and mark the design accurately onto the cake. Choose the colour and the width of the ribbon required and cut as many pieces as necessary to complete the design. The ribbon pieces should be slightly larger than the spaces, leaving enough room to tuck the ends in.

The technique of ribbon insertion takes a little time to master, but is stunningly effective on special celebratory cakes.

1 *Using a very fine blade or scalpel, cut the slits accurately in the icing following the marked lines.*

2 *Insert one end of the ribbon into the first slit using a pin or fine blade, and tuck the other end of the ribbon into the second slit.*

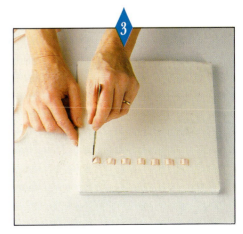

3 *Leave a space and repeat, until all the slits are filled.*

Cut-out Sugarpaste Flowers

Using flower cutters to make sugarpaste (fondant) flowers must be the simplest way to make a large quantity of flowers quickly. Flower cutters are available from cake-icing specialists and are available in a variety of flower shapes – daisy, rose, simple blossoms, fuchsia and orchids, to name but a few. The most popular shape is the plunger blossom cutter. This comes in three sizes with a plunger which ejects the blossom in the perfect shape.

Plunger Blossom Flowers

Sugarpaste (fondant) or petal paste may be used for these flowers. If you need to wire them onto stems to make sprays, the petal paste is stronger.

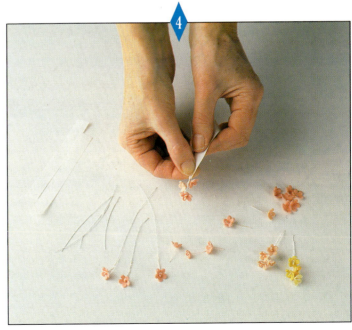

1 Tint the sugar- or petal paste to the shade you require. Roll out the sugar- or petal paste very thinly on a lightly cornfloured (cornstarched) surface. Cut out the flower shape with a plunger cutter and place on a piece of foam sponge.

2 Eject the flower by pressing the plunger into the sponge to bend the paste to shape the flower. Repeat to make small, medium and large blossoms.

3 If the flowers are to have a stamen in the centre, make a pin hole in each blossom as it is made. When dry, pipe a bead of royal icing on to the back of the stamen and thread through the sugar blossom to secure.

4 When dry, wire these together using fine florist's wire to make sprays.

PIPING TECHNIQUES

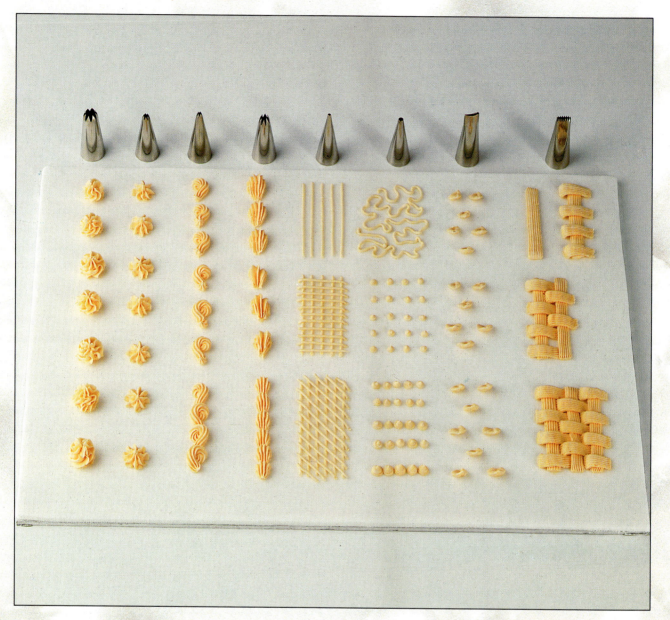

Simple Piping

From left to right: swirls, stars, scrolls, shells, building up a trellis design, filigree work and beads or dots, building up a basket weave design.

Piping is a skill worth mastering. All that is needed is a good-quality piping bag or a greaseproof (wax) paper piping bag fitted with a straight-sided metal nozzle. This can turn cream, butter icing or royal icing into stars, shells, scrolls or lines to create a simple decoration on a cake.

Although it appears complicated and difficult to do, with practice and following a few guide lines, it is amazing how quickly you will become confident using a piping bag and nozzle. Take every opportunity to pipe instead of spreading or swirling creams, meringue and icing, and you will soon become adept.

To Make a Greaseproof (Wax) Paper Piping Bag

1 Cut out a 38 × 25 cm/15 × 10 in rectangle of greaseproof (wax) paper or baking parchment. Fold diagonally in half to form two triangular shapes, each with a blunt end. Cut along the fold line.

Fold the blunt end of the triangle over into a sharp cone into the centre and hold in position.

2 Then fold the sharp end of the triangle over the cone shape. Hold all the points together at the back of the cone, ensuring the point of the cone is sharp.

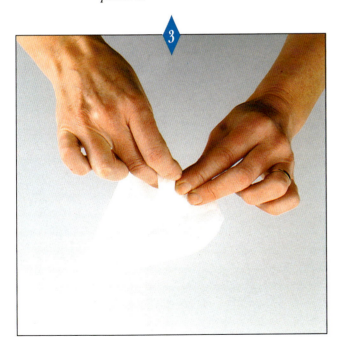

3 Turn the points inside the top edge of the cone and crease firmly.

4 Secure with sticky tape or staple if desired.

Piping Equipment and Tips

COMMERCIALLY-MADE PIPING BAGS
These are available ready-made in washable fabric from most cake specialists or kitchen shops. They are especially good to use if you are a beginner as they are easy to handle. Sizes vary from small to large and are ideal for piping cream, buttercream and meringue icing.

PAPER PIPING BAGS
The great advantage of the greaseproof (wax) paper piping bag is that they can be made in advance in various sizes and may be used with or without an icing nozzle. If they are used without a nozzle, simply fill the bag with icing, fold down the top and snip off the end straight to pipe lines, or into a 'V' shape to pipe leaves. After use they can be thrown away. If the icing runs out while using a bag, simply fill a new bag, transferring the icing nozzle first, if necessary. Choose good quality greaseproof (wax) paper or baking parchment for making the bags and follow the instructions on the previous page.

ICING NOZZLES
These are available in a wide variety of shapes and sizes, so it can be quite daunting to know which type to choose. As a beginner, it is advisable to start with a small selection of straight-sided metal piping nozzles as they give a clean, sharp icing result. Begin with two writing nozzles and small, medium and large star nozzles. After mastering the use of these, build up your collection as you try new piping designs. Kept clean and stored carefully in a box or rigid container, the nozzles will never need replacing and are worth the extra expense. Always clean icing nozzles with a nozzle cleaning brush so that the ends do not become bent or damaged.

ICING
Before using any piping equipment, it is essential to have the buttercream or icing at the correct consistency. When a wooden spoon is drawn out of the icing, it should form a fine but sharp point. If the icing is too stiff it will be very difficult to squeeze out of the bag; if too soft, the icing will be difficult to control and the piped shapes will lose their definition.

BASIC PIPING
When piping a celebration cake with royal icing, it is a good idea to practise piping on a board or work surface before starting on the cake. Always ensure the icing is the correct colour and consistency before beginning.

Use a greaseproof (wax) paper piping bag fitted with a straight-sided metal nozzle as this gives a clean, sharp icing pattern. Half-fill the bag with icing – do not be tempted to fill it to the top, as the fuller the icing bag is, the harder it is to squeeze the icing out of the nozzle. This results in aching wrists and hands and poor piping. A good guide is: the smaller the icing nozzle, the less icing you require.

Hold the piping bag comfortably with the nozzle through the first two fingers and thumb, like holding a pencil. Apply the pressure at the top of the bag. The wrists and arms should be relaxed, ready to guide the nozzle.

Simple Piping

Piping is the obvious choice when decorating a cake, but it is easy to be discouraged by attempting too complicated a design. Choose a simple star icing tube and fit it into a greaseproof (wax) paper piping bag to pipe swirls, scrolls and shells.

TO PIPE A SWIRL
Fit the greaseproof (wax) paper piping bag with a star nozzle, half-fill with icing, fold down the top, and squeeze the icing to the end of the nozzle. Place the tip of the icing nozzle just onto the surface of the cake. Press out the icing and pipe a swirl in a circular movement. Stop pressing the bag and pull up sharply to break off the icing. Repeat, piping swirls around the top edge and base of the cake, as desired.

TO PIPE A STAR
Pipe a star shape also from the same nozzle. Hold the bag straight above, at right angles to the surface of the cake. Press the icing out forming a star on the edge of the cake, then pull off sharply to break the icing. Repeat to make a neat border.

TO PIPE SCROLLS
Use the star nozzle and hold the piping bag at an angle so that the nozzle is almost on its side in front of you. Press out the icing onto the top edge of the cake to secure the scroll. Pipe outwards in a circular movement and return the piping nozzle to the edge of the cake. Stop pressing the bag and break off the icing. Repeat again but pipe the icing away from the cake in a circular movement, then return the piping nozzle just to the edge. This is called reverse scrolls, piping scrolls inwards and outwards. For a straight scroll design, pipe the scrolls in one direction only.

TO PIPE SHELLS
Using the star nozzle, hold the piping bag at an angle to the cake so that the nozzle is almost on its side in front of you. Press out some icing and secure to the surface of the cake, pressing gently. Move the nozzle forward, then slowly up, over and down, almost like a rocking movement. Stop pressing and break off the icing by pulling the nozzle towards you. Repeat by piping the icing onto the end of the first shell and continue to make a shell edging.

TO PIPE LINES
Fit a greaseproof (wax) paper bag with a plain writing nozzle; the smaller the hole the finer the lines will be. Fill the bag with icing and pipe a thread of icing, securing the end to the surface of the cake. Continue to pipe the icing just above the surface of the cake, allowing the thread to fall in a straight or curved line. Stop pressing and break off the icing by pulling the nozzle towards you.

To pipe a trellis design, pipe parallel lines of icing in one direction, then over-pipe the lines in the opposite direction. A third series of lines may be piped horizontally across the lattice work to give a better finish.

BASKET WEAVE
Fit a greaseproof (wax) paper piping bag with a ribbon nozzle. Pipe a vertical line from the top of the cake to the bottom. Follow by piping 2 cm/¾ in lines horizontally across the vertical line at 1 cm/½ in intervals. Pipe another vertical line of icing on the edge of the horizontal lines, then pipe short lines of icing in between the spaces across the vertical line to form a basket weave. Repeat all around the cake.

TO PIPE LEAVES

Half-fill a greaseproof (wax) paper piping bag with icing and press the icing to the end of the bag. Cut the end of the piping bag into an inverted 'V'. Place the tip on the surface of the cake. Press out the icing to form a leaf shape, then sharply break off the icing. Repeat to make a pretty border, to add to stems or flowers, or to make a design.

FILIGREE OR CORNELLI WORK

Half-fill a greaseproof (wax) paper piping bag, fitted with a plain writing nozzle, with icing. Hold the icing bag like a pen between the thumb and forefinger. Pipe a continuous thread of icing into 'W' and 'M' shapes, keeping the flow of icing constant; work in all directions, not in lines.

You will need larger nozzles to pipe butter icing and fresh cream. They are, however, available in a wide range of designs for piping swirls, stars, shells and scrolls as described here.

TO PIPE BEADS OR DOTS

To pipe beads of icing is relatively simple, but the icing must be of a softer consistency than usual. This prevents the bead from ending in a sharp point.

Fit a greaseproof (wax) paper piping bag with a No. 3 plain nozzle. Half-fill with icing and fold down the top. Press the icing out just above the surface of the cake to form a rounded bulb. Pull upwards sharply to break off the icing. Repeat to make a border of nicely rounded beads.

Piped Sugar Pieces

Piped sugar pieces are really very useful decorations to make. They can be piped in advance and, when dry, stored in boxes between layers of tissue paper. Any simple shape may be copied by piping royal icing, made with double-strength egg albumen without the addition of glycerine. Use a No. 0 or 1 fine plain writing nozzle.

1 *Draw the chosen design several times on a piece of paper. Cover with a piece of run-out silk or baking parchment and secure at each corner with tape. Fit a greaseproof (waxed) paper piping bag with a No. 1 plain writing nozzle and quarter-fill with royal icing. Fold down the top. Pipe a continuous thread of icing to follow the design showing through the overlay.*

2 *Repeat, moving the base paper underneath the run-out silk or baking parchment to pipe more designs.*

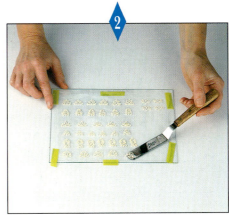

Icing Run-outs

Icing run-outs are one of the most ex-acting forms of cake decoration. They can be made in any shape or form by simply tracing over a chosen design or pattern. Small run-outs can be made in advance and kept between layers of greaseproof (wax) paper in a box stored in a dry place. Larger run-outs and col-lars are more difficult to store as they may warp during storage. They are bet-ter made when needed, dried complete-ly, and applied directly to the cake.

Since run-outs are made from royal icing, they are very fragile. It is wise to choose a small solid shape at first, and make more than required to allow for breakages. When you are confident in making the smaller solid shapes, practise making finer pieces, figures and scenes.

ROYAL ICING

This is a demanding medium. The con-sistency and texture of the icing must be just right, or the run-outs will be difficult to handle. Use double-strength dried egg albumen, or egg whites with no additives such as glycerine or lemon juice. When the spoon is lifted, a soft peak should form which will bend at the tip. This is the consistency required for piping the outline of the run-outs.

Icing to fill in the run-out must be soft enough to flow with the help of a paint-brush, but hold its shape until tapped, when it becomes smooth. Dilute the royal icing with reconstituted double-strength egg albumen and test a little on a flat surface to determine the consistency. Leave the icing to stand overnight if possible, covered with damp muslin (cheesecloth), allowing any air bubbles to come to the surface. Stir until the air bubbles have dispersed before using.

To Make an Icing Run-out

Draw or trace the chosen design several times on a piece of paper, spaced well apart. Cover the design with a piece of perspex or glass and cover with a sheet of run-out silk or fine waxed paper. Secure the paper to a flat surface with sticky tape or beads of icing.

Fit a greaseproof (wax) paper piping bag with a No. 1 writing nozzle. Half-fill with icing of a slightly stiffer consistency to pipe the outline. Fill a second piping bag with soft icing.

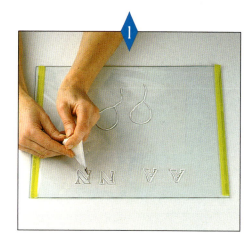

1 *With the first bag, fitted with the writing nozzle, pipe carefully over the outline of the design. Use a continuous thread of icing or one with as few breaks as possible. Begin by squeezing out a little icing at the least focal point of the run-out to secure the icing thread to the paper. Lift the thread of icing just above the surface and squeeze the bag, gently following the outline of the tracing, and allow the thread to fall on the marked line around the shape of the run-out. Stop squeezing to prevent the icing thread from running on, and join the icing at the point where it started.*

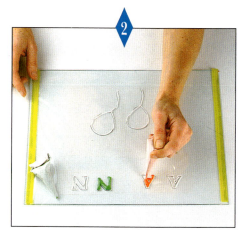

2 *Snip the pointed end off the bag half-filled with soft icing and fill in the run-out. Start by piping around the inside edge to keep the outline soft, with less chance of breaking. Work towards the centre, filling the shape so that the icing looks rounded and over-filled and not flat, as the icing shrinks as it sets.*

Use a fine paintbrush or cocktail stick to brush over the run-out, ensuring the area is completely filled, and that the icing is smooth and rounded. Gently tap the perspex so that any air bubbles rise to the surface; burst any with a pin. Lift the perspex or glass off the design, move and repeat the design.

3 *If the run-out is large, leave it in position to dry. For smaller run-outs, carefully release from the run-out silk or fine waxed paper and transfer to a flat board and leave to dry. Cover the drawing design with more run-out silk or waxed paper and repeat to make as many run-outs as required.*

Leave the run-outs under a spotlight, if possible, to dry the surface quickly. Otherwise place in a warm, dry place

overnight until they have set hard. The more quickly they dry, the glossier the run-outs will be. Pipe any detail onto the run-out at this stage and allow to dry. Carefully peel off the paper from the run-out and store the icing decoration in a box between layers of greaseproof (wax) paper until required. Arrange the run-outs on top of the cake and secure with small beads or a line of royal icing.

Simple Flowers Piped With a Petal Nozzle

Many simple flowers can be piped with the aid of a petal nozzle. The size of the nozzles are small, medium and large, and right- and left-handed. Fit the nozzle in a greaseproof (wax) paper piping bag and half-fill with royal icing; fold down the top. Practise several times to get the feel of the nozzle, and it is easier to use an icing nail or piping turntable.

ROSE
Secure a piece of greaseproof (wax) paper to the piping turntable with a bead of icing. Using a petal nozzle, pipe the cone-shaped centre on to the paper and, turning the turntable at the same time, keep the nozzle upright with the thick end of the nozzle at the base.

Pipe a petal two-thirds of the way round the centre cone, turning the turntable at the same time as piping the petal. Repeat to pipe another three petals, at the same time keeping the top of the petal curled outwards.

To pipe the final petals, hold the piping bag at an angle instead of upright. These last petals should be almost flat, to make the rose look in full bloom.

TO PIPE A ROSEBUD
Pipe the centre cone and three petals close together.

DAISY
Use the icing turntable and a square of greaseproof (wax) paper secured with a bead of icing. Hold the petal nozzle on the side so it is flat. Pipe a tiny petal shape in a flat loop, at the same time turning the turntable. Continue to pipe about 12 tiny petals in a circle. Using yellow icing, pipe several small beads to fill the centre.

PANSY
Pipe the pansy petals like the daisy, using white, yellow or purple icing. Holding the petal nozzle flat, pipe the petal shape in a large rounded loop while turning the turntable. Pipe another two petals, one on each side, broad side to the centre. Pipe the fourth petal to join up the circle. Pipe the last petal the opposite way round. Pipe yellow threads of icing in the centre. Using food colouring pens, colour in the markings of the pansy.

FORGET-ME-NOTS
Half-fill the piping bag with white royal icing on the broad side of the nozzle, and pale blue royal icing on the narrow side. Fold down the top and press the icing to the end of the nozzle.

Hold the petal nozzle almost flat to the turntable, with the broad side of the nozzle towards the centre. Pipe a rounded petal, at the same time revolving the turntable. Pipe another four petals, each overlapping the first, to form a circle. Pipe a bead of yellow icing in the centre of the bi-coloured petals.

APPLE BLOSSOM
Pipe these as for forget-me-nots but substitute pale pink for half the icing and white for the remaining icing. Finish with piped green dots in the centre.

A selection of piped flowers in a variety of types, sizes and shades, showing the versatility of this decorative technique.

NARCISSUS
Pipe the white narcissus petals in the same manner as the forget-me-nots, but move the nozzle out and in again to form a long shaped petal. Pipe the first three petals apart, then pipe the remaining three petals in between. Pipe a coil of yellow icing from a No. 1 plain writing nozzle to form the centre. Paint the top with orange food colouring if you wish a bolder variety.

Flowers Piped from a Greaseproof (Wax) Paper Piping Bag without a Nozzle

There are many simple flower forms which can be piped from a greaseproof (wax) paper piping bag by snipping an inverted 'V' from the end of the bag. The piped icing forms into tiny leaf or petal shapes and when grouped into circles or clusters, they form simple flower shapes. Colour the icing to suit the cake design, and give the blossoms contrasting centres.

TO PIPE FLOWER FORMS
Tint the icing to the colour you require. Half-fill a greaseproof (wax) piping bag, fold down the top and press the icing to the point. Flatten the point with your fingers and cut an inverted 'V' with a pair of sharp scissors.

Secure a square of greaseproof (wax) paper to the piping turntable with an icing bead. Pipe a circle of petals. Add a double row of petals if desired. Using yellow or white icing, pipe beads or coils of icing into the centre of each flower.

SIMPLE DECORATIONS

Everyday ingredients, used with imagination and flair, are very useful for decorating cakes. Most require very little time. It is particularly rewarding to add the finishing touches to simple cakes, turning them into something a little more special. The ingredients and ideas that follow may inspire you to create your own designs.

A selection of simple and edible cake decorations: glacé and crystallized fruits, citrus fruits, nuts, sweets (candies) and ready purchased decorations.

Icing (Confectioners) Sugar

This is an ingredient which, when used carefully, can transform the appearance of a cake. Simply dusting the surface with the sugar makes a sponge cake more appealing.

Try placing a patterned doiley on top of a cake, or arranging 1 cm/½ in strips of paper in lines or a lattice pattern on top of the cake; then dredge thickly with the icing (confectioners) sugar. Carefully remove the doiley or paper strips, revealing the pattern in sugar. It looks most effective when used on a chocolate or coffee cake where there is a strong colour contrast.

Cocoa and Coffee

These may be used in a similar way to obtain a strong contrast on a light-coloured cake, such as white icing or cream-finished gateaux. Mix cocoa or coffee with a little icing (confectioners) sugar and use to dredge thickly to transfer the doiley or paper-lattice design.

A skewer, cocktail stick or toothpick dipped into cocoa or coffee, then pressed onto the surface of an iced cake will also produce a decorative design.

Citrus Fruits

These fruits are very versatile and offer effective edible decorations from both the fruit and the rind.

Cut oranges, lemons or limes into wedges, segments or round slices, with or without the rind, and use to decorate cakes or gateaux.

The rind, when cut into thin strips using a zester or *canelle* cutter, can transform the appearance of a simply-iced cake. Use to make a fine shred border, or arrange on top of cream whirls. To make decorative stars, crescents or diamonds, cut thin strips of lemon, orange or lime rind from the fruit, taking care not to include the white pith. Using tiny aspic or cocktail cutters, cut out the desired shapes. Arrange them on glacé- or butter-iced cakes as a continuous border design, perhaps using the same shape but different-coloured rinds, or cut the rind to form flowers, stems and leaves.

Glacé or Crystallized Fruits

Preserved fruits are always a good standby and can give a charming finish to a cake. Angelica can be cut into stems, leaves and diamond shapes. Glacé cherries in green, red or yellow can be used whole, cut into halves or thin wedges and arranged as petal shapes to make flowers, or cut into slices and used in a border design. Crystallized fruit, although expensive, makes a colourful finish to a rich or plain cake. Slice the fruit thinly and arrange the colourful slices in abstract designs over the top of the cake. Brush with apricot glaze to give a glossy finish.

Nuts

These are also versatile as a quick decoration. Whole assorted nuts arranged over the top of a cake and glazed with honey or sugar syrup look particularly tempting. Nuts dipped in caramel are also attractive, and chopped nuts are invaluable for coating the sides of iced cakes or creamy gateaux.

Commercially-made Decorations

Always have a selection of these to use as standby decorations. Applied with care, they make a very pretty finish to a simple cake. Sugar flowers, jelly diamonds, crystallized flower petals, and marzipan fruits all make eye-catching toppings on swirls of icing, or pressed on to make a border pattern. Coloured almonds, dragées, yellow mimosa balls, hundreds and thousands (multicoloured titbits), chocolate chips and coloured sugar strands make quick and colourful instant coatings, toppings and designs.

Sweets (Candies)

Always a favourite for children's cakes, these decorations come in all shapes, colours and sizes. White or dark chocolate buttons are classic options, while yogurt-coated nuts and raisins offer a healthy alternative. Jelly beans, chocolate beans and liquorice sweets can all be used for simple finishes and decorations on party, novelty or simple cakes.

Flowers

Tiny fresh flowers positioned at the last minute look delectable. Even better are sugar-frosted flowers preserved by the egg white and sugar; they will last for several weeks once they are completely dry. Teamed with fine ribbons tied into tiny bows, they impart a romantic, feminine appeal.

A more practical alternative is offered by silk or artificial flowers which are available from cake-icing specialists or from department stores. Chosen carefully for colour and size, they make instant, re-usable decorations on many cakes.

Use ribbons to decorate cakeboard edges, or make loops and bows for cake tops and flower sprays. Fresh flowers can be used as they are or sugar-frosted or choose silk or paper flowers.

Ribbons

Invaluable for decorating cakes, it is the one non-edible decoration which simply transforms the plainest cake into something quite special. There are over 100 colours available, ranging in width from 1 mm–5 cm/¹⁄₁₆–2 in with plain and fancy edges. Choose double-faced polyester satin ribbons and use to make loops, bows for cakes and flower sprays, and circle around the sides of cakes. Band the cakeboards with ribbons to match the cake design and colour. The best selection of ribbons are from cake-icing and decorating suppliers, who also make matching ribbon bows.

Sugar-frosted Flowers and Leaves

Choose fresh, simple, small flowers with fairly flat petals such as violets, primroses, tiny daffodils, freesias, fuchsias. If possible, pick or buy the flowers just before you need to frost them and ensure they are young blooms. You will need 1 egg white, lightly beaten and caster (superfine) sugar.

1 *Dry the flowers with kitchen paper and leave a small stem intact, if possible. Using a fine paintbrush, paint both sides of the flower petals and stem with egg white.*

2 *Spoon the sugar over the flower petals to coat evenly on both sides, and carefully shake to remove excess sugar.*

3 *Place in a warm place on a wire rack covered with kitchen paper until dry. To help keep their shape, some flowers are better dried with the stems upwards and the petals flat on the paper. Sugar-frost the leaves in the same way, choosing firm leaves with distinctive shapes.*

4 *When completely dry, store the flowers in a box between layers of kitchen paper, taking care not to damage them. Use to decorate all types of cakes.*

Sugar-frosted Fruits

Choose small, fresh fruits in peak condition such as grapes, cherries, strawberries, lychees, Cape gooseberries and kumquats. You will need 1 egg white, lightly beaten and caster (superfine) sugar.

1 Wipe the fruit with kitchen paper so that the surface is completely dry.
2 Brush each piece of fruit evenly with egg white. Spoon the sugar over the fruit to cover evenly. Leave to dry on kitchen paper.
3 Arrange in a fruit bowl, place in separate paper cases to serve as petit fours, or keep to decorate cakes.

Making Basic Caramel

Care must be taken when making caramel. The sugar syrup is boiled at a very high temperature, turning the syrup a golden amber colour. It has endless uses – for dipping fruits and nuts, crushing for cake coating, or drizzling into shapes for decorating. You will need 150 ml/¼ pt/⅔ cup water and 175 g/6 oz/¾ cup caster (superfine) sugar.

1 Place the water in a saucepan. Bring to the boil, remove the saucepan from the heat and stir in the sugar. Heat gently until the sugar has completely dissolved. Remove the spoon.
2 Bring the syrup to the boil, boil rapidly for several minutes until the bubbles begin to subside and the syrup begins to turn a pale golden brown. Watch carefully at this stage, as the syrup continues to darken when it is taken off the heat.
3 The caramel is ideal for using when it has become a rich golden brown. Allow the bubbles to subside, then use as required.

Caramel Coating

Pour hot caramel thinly over a baking sheet lined with a piece of lightly-oiled foil. Leave until cold, then crush the hardened candy with a rolling pin. Use to coat the sides of an iced cake or gateau.

Making praline and abstract shapes in caramel.

Abstract Caramel Designs

Using a teaspoon, drizzle threads of caramel onto a piece of lightly-oiled foil to make small abstract shapes. If the caramel in the pan begins to set, warm the saucepan over a gentle heat until it begins to melt. When the shapes are set on the foil, lift them off carefully and use for decorations.

To Make Praline

1 Scatter 75 g/3 oz/¾ cup of almonds or hazelnuts over a baking tray and toast at 200°C/400°F/Gas mark 6 until golden brown.
2 Line a board with foil and brush lightly with oil. Make the caramel according to the recipe above. When the bubbles subside, add the warm toasted nuts to the pan. Carefully shake the pan to mix well, then pour the mixture thinly over the oiled foil. Leave to cool.
3 Peel off the foil and crush the caramel and nuts finely with a rolling pin to make a coarse praline. Alternatively place in a food processor and process until finely ground.

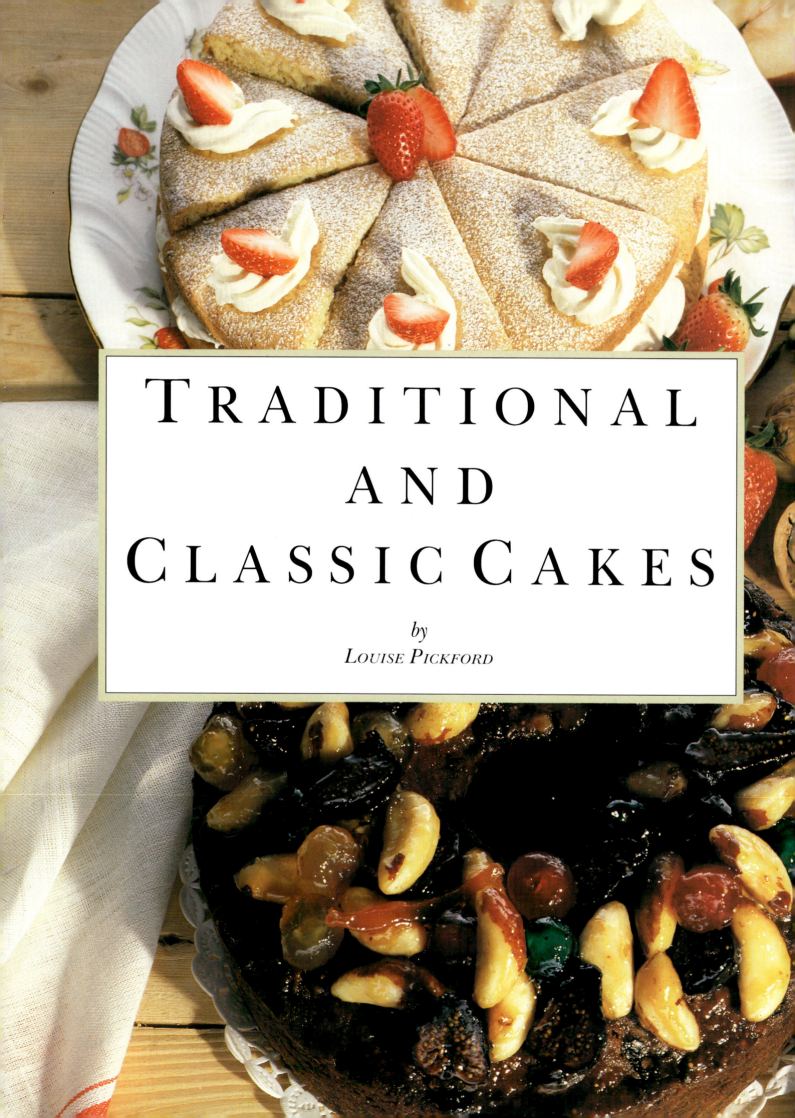

TRADITIONAL
AND
CLASSIC CAKES

by

LOUISE PICKFORD

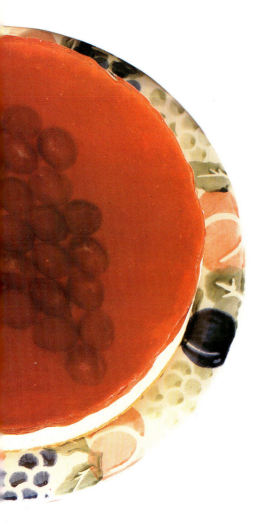

INTRODUCTION

*T*RADITIONAL AND CLASSIC CAKES *provides a collection of classic recipes, many of which are long-standing family favourites. There are 25 mouthwatering recipes, ranging from the quick and easy, to those that can be prepared in advance and stored, to the more elaborate dessert cakes or gateaux. Examples of all the various methods of cake making — creaming, whisking, rubbed-in, melted, all-in-one and yeasted — can be found in this chapter. Traditional cakes are decorated in a variety of exciting and innovative ways.*

So that you can choose exactly the right cake for a given occasion, the recipes have been divided into five relevant sections.

• QUICK AND EASY: *four delicious cakes, ideal for the arrival of that unexpected guest. These recipes require as little preparation and baking time as possible. Included is a classic* Victoria Sandwich, *with six different ideas for decoration. It is the perfect sponge cake.*

• TEATIME TREATS: *six very different cakes, all adaptations of classic family cakes from around the world. These include a Middle Eastern-style nut and syrup*

sponge, Spiced Honey Nut Cake, *the American classic* Angel Food Cake, *and the French yeast cake,* Savarin with Fresh Berries.

● CAKES TO KEEP: *four very familiar cakes, traditionally baked to be stored and used as desired. All are moist cakes which mature with age. Included are such favourites as* Dundee Cake *and* Caramel Frosted Gingerbread.

● FESTIVE CAKES: *what better opportunity could there be for baking one of these wonderful cakes than for a festive occasion such as Easter or Christmas. Five luxurious recipes for traditional cakes include a rich fruit* Glazed Christmas Ring, *an international classic;* Italian Panforte, *a speciality of Siena; and the French yule log* Bûche de Noël.

● GATEAUX: *this final section numbers a wide selection of cakes with the most elaborate decorations in the chapter. From the exotic frozen* Iced Paradise Cake, *to the sumptuous spiced* Chocolate and Fresh Cherry Cake, *these recipes would grace the table at any social gathering.*

These classic cakes, with their imaginative decorations, are the basis of traditional cake baking at its most rewarding.

Quick and Easy

MAPLE–PECAN BROWNIES

An adaptation of the classic American chocolate brownies, using pecan nuts and maple syrup, to give a delicious alternative.

INGREDIENTS

Makes 12

- *125 g/4 oz/¹⁄₂ cup butter, melted*
- *75 g/3 oz/good ¹⁄₃ cup light soft brown sugar*
- *90 ml/6 tbsp/6 tbsp maple syrup*
- *2 eggs*
- *125 g/4 oz/1 cup self-raising flour*
- *75 g/3 oz/¹⁄₂ cup pecan nuts, chopped*
- *125 g/4 oz/³⁄₄ cup plain (semisweet) chocolate chips*
- *50 g/2 oz/¹⁄₄ cup unsalted butter*

DECORATION

- *12 pecan nuts*

STORING

Transfer to an airtight container as soon as brownies are cold. Best eaten the day of making.

MATERIALS AND EQUIPMENT

- *greaseproof (wax) paper*
- *25 × 18 cm/10 × 7 in rectangular cake tin (pan)*

FREEZING

Recommended before the decoration stage. Open-freeze until very firm, and then wrap. Defrost at room temperature.

1 *Preheat oven to 180°C/350°F/Gas 4. Grease and line the cake tin (pan) with the greaseproof (wax) paper.*

2 *Place the melted butter, sugar, 60 ml/4 tbsp/4 tbsp maple syrup, eggs and flour in a bowl and beat for 1 minute until smooth.*

3 *Stir in the nuts and transfer to the prepared tin (pan). Smooth the surface and bake for 30 minutes, until risen and firm to the touch. Remove from the oven, cool in the tin (pan) for 10 minutes and transfer to a wire rack to cool.*

4 *Melt the chocolate chips, butter and remaining syrup in a small pan over a low heat. Cool slightly.*

5 *Spread over the cooled cake with a palette knife (spatula). Leave for 5 minutes to set.*

6 *Mark out 12 rectangles with a knife and place a whole pecan nut in the centre of each one. Leave until set and cut into rectangles along the marked lines.*

ALMOND AND RASPBERRY SWISS ROLL

A light and airy whisked sponge cake is rolled up with a fresh cream and raspberry filling, making a classic Swiss (jelly) roll.

INGREDIENTS

Serves 8
- 3-egg quantity whisked sponge cake mixture replacing 25 g/1 oz/ 2 tbsp plain (all-purpose) flour with 25 g/1 oz/2 tbsp ground almonds
- a little caster (superfine) sugar
- 225 ml/8 fl oz/1 cup double (heavy) cream
- 225 g/8 oz/½ lb fresh raspberries

DECORATION

- caster (superfine) sugar
- reserved raspberries
- 16 flaked almonds, toasted

MATERIALS AND EQUIPMENT

- 33 × 23 cm/13 × 9 in Swiss (jelly) roll tin (pan)
- baking parchment
- greaseproof (wax) paper

STORING

Best eaten the day of making.

FREEZING

Recommended at the end of step 3. Wrap and freeze the sponge flat, and defrost at room temperature.

1 Preheat oven to 200°C/400°F/Gas 6. Grease and line the tin (pan) with baking parchment.

2 Make the whisked sponge mixture, transfer to the prepared tin (pan) and bake for 10–12 minutes, until risen and springy to the touch.

3 Place a sheet of greaseproof (wax) paper over the tea-towel (dishtowel) and sprinkle with caster (superfine) sugar. Turn out the cake onto the sheet, and leave to cool with the tin (pan) in place. Remove the tin and peel away lining paper.

4 Reserve a little cream for decoration, and whip the rest until it holds its shape. Fold in all but eight raspberries and spread the mixture over the cooled cake, leaving a narrow border around the edge.

5 Carefully roll the cake up from a narrow end to form a Swiss (jelly) roll. Sprinkle liberally with caster (superfine) sugar.

6 Whip the remaining cream until it just holds its shape, and spoon the cream along the centre of the cake. Decorate with the reserved raspberries and toasted flaked almonds.

VICTORIA SPONGE WITH SIX IDEAS FOR DECORATION

This classic creamed sponge cake is presented with six different ideas for decorating for any given occasion.

INGREDIENTS

Serves 6
- 125 g/4 oz/½ cup butter, softened
- 125 g/4 oz/½ cup caster (superfine) sugar
- 2 eggs, lightly beaten
- 125 g/4 oz/1 cup self-raising flour
- 2.5 ml/½ tsp/½ tsp baking powder
- 2.5 ml/½ tsp/½ tsp vanilla essence (extract)

MATERIALS AND EQUIPMENT

- greaseproof (wax) paper
- 2 × 18 cm/7 in sandwich tins (shallow cake pans)
- piping bag fitted with a large star nozzle
- pastry brush
- small star nozzle

STORING

Best eaten on day of making.

FREEZING

Freeze before decorating stage, for up to three months. Defrost at room temperature.

1 Preheat oven to 180°C/350°F/Gas 4. Grease and base-line the tins (pans) with greaseproof (wax) paper.

2 Cream the butter and sugar together until pale and light. Gradually beat in the eggs, a little at a time, until combined.

3 Sift the flour and baking powder together and fold into the creamed mixture with the vanilla essence (extract). Transfer to the prepared tins (pans), smooth the surface of each and bake for 20–25 minutes, until risen and firm to the touch.

4 Remove from the oven, cool in the tins (pans) for 10 minutes and transfer to a wire rack to cool.

Decoration 1

- 60 ml/4 tbsp/4 tbsp raspberry jam
- 90 ml/6 tbsp/6 tbsp double (heavy) cream, whipped
- icing (confectioners) sugar to dust

1 Spread the jam and cream over one sponge cake and top with the second sponge cake.

2 Cut the greaseproof (wax) paper into seven strips, 1 cm/½ in wide. Lay the strips at equal distances over the top of the cake and sprinkle over a liberal dusting of icing (confectioners) sugar.

3 Carefully lift off the strips of paper, being careful not to let any icing (confectioners) sugar fall off or smudge.

Decoration 2

- 2 drops almond essence (extract)
- 125 g/4 oz/¼ lb fresh raspberries
- 90 ml/6 tbsp/6 tbsp double (heavy) cream, whipped
- caster (superfine) sugar

1 Make the sponge cakes as above, substituting the vanilla essence (extract) with 2 drops almond essence (extract).

2 Reserve eight raspberries and a little cream and fold the remaining raspberries into the rest of the cream. Use to sandwich the two cakes together.

3 Sprinkle the cake with a little caster (superfine) sugar.

4 Transfer the remaining cream to the piping bag, fitted with the large star nozzle, and pipe eight swirls onto the top of the cake. Decorate each swirl of cream with a reserved raspberry.

Decoration 3

- 60 ml/4 tbsp/4 tbsp strawberry jam
- 225 g/8 oz/½ lb strawberries
- 90 ml/6 tbsp/6 tbsp double (heavy) cream
- 45 ml/3 tbsp/3 tbsp strawberry jam

1 Make the sponge cakes as above.

2 Spread the jam over one sponge cake. Hull and thinly slice the strawberries.

3 Fold the outside slices of the strawberries into the whipped cream, spread over the jam and sandwich the two sponge cakes together.

4 To make the glaze, boil the strawberry jam in a pan, then strain through a sieve (strainer). Brush a little glaze over the top of the cake and arrange the strawberry slices, in circles, attractively over the top.

5 Brush the remaining glaze over the top.

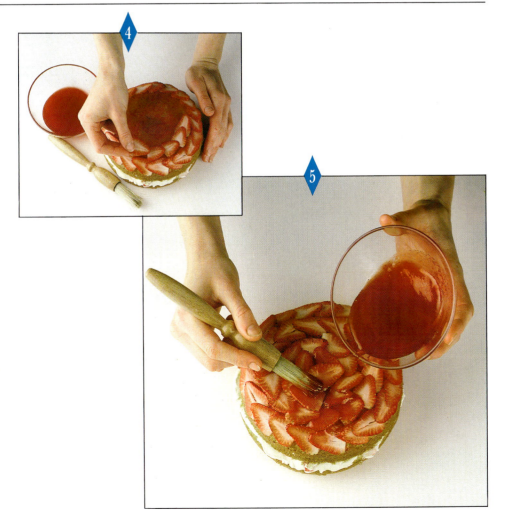

Decoration 4

- 25 g/1 oz/¼ cup cocoa powder
- 125 g/4 oz/¾ cup plain (semisweet) chocolate chips
- 50 g/2 oz/¼ cup unsalted butter
- 1 egg, lightly beaten
- 175 g/6 oz/1½ cups icing (confectioners) sugar, sifted
- 90 ml/6 tbsp/6 tbsp double (heavy) cream, whipped
- a few reserved chocolate chips

1 Make the cake as above, substituting 25 g/1 oz/2 tbsp plain (all-purpose) flour with the cocoa powder.

2 Melt the chocolate chips and butter together in a bowl over a pan of gently simmering water. Remove from the heat, cool slightly and beat in the egg and icing (confectioners) sugar. Continue beating until thick and glossy and leave to cool.

3 Sandwich the two sponge cakes together with one quarter of the icing and use the rest to completely cover the top and sides of the cake. Swirl a pattern over the top with a palette knife (spatula).

4 Transfer the whipped cream to the piping bag fitted with the small star nozzle, and pipe small stars around the top of the cake.

5 Decorate the stars with a few chocolate chips, spacing them evenly around the cake.

Decoration 5

- 40 ml/2½ tbsp/2½ tbsp coffee essence (extract)
- 125 g/4 oz/½ cup unsalted butter
- 225 g/8 oz/2 cups icing (confectioners) sugar, sifted
- 50 g/2 oz/⅓ cup walnuts, chopped
- eight walnut halves

1 Make the sponge cake as above, substituting the vanilla essence (extract) with 7.5 ml/½ tbsp/½ tbsp coffee essence (extract).

2 Cream the butter and sugar together with the remaining coffee essence (extract), until smooth and glossy. Sandwich the two sponge cakes together with half the icing.

3 Spread one-third of the remaining icing around the sides of the cake. Place the chopped walnuts on a tray or a sheet of greaseproof (wax) paper, and roll the sides of the cake over the nuts to coat.

4 Spread remaining icing over the top of the cake. Swirl over a pattern and decorate with the walnut halves.

Decoration 6

- 45 ml/3 tbsp/3 tbsp orange juice
- grated rind of 1 orange
- 25 g/1 oz/2 tbsp unsalted butter
- 275 g/10 oz/2½ cups icing (confectioners) sugar, sifted
- 15 ml/1 tbsp/1 tbsp warm water
- crystallized orange slices

1 Make the cake as above, substituting 15 ml/1 tbsp/1 tbsp orange juice for the vanilla essence (extract). Add the grated orange rind.

2 Cream the butter and 25 g/1 oz/2 tbsp of sugar together with 15 ml/1 tbsp/1 tbsp orange juice, until pale and light. Use to sandwich the two sponge cakes together.

3 Beat the remaining icing (confectioners) sugar, orange juice and warm water together to form a thick, glossy, glacé icing. Pour over the cake in one motion to coat the top and sides. Decorate with the crystallized orange slices.

STRAWBERRY SHORTCAKE

This is a cross between a shortbread and a cake, resulting in a light biscuit-textured sponge. It is quick and easy to prepare, and the strawberry, cream and port filling makes it that little bit special. Serve on a summer's day for a perfect lunchtime dessert.

INGREDIENTS

Serves 8
- 225 g/8 oz/½ lb fresh strawberries, hulled
- 30 ml/2 tbsp/ 2 tbsp ruby port
- 225 g/8 oz/2 cups self-raising flour
- 10 ml/2 tsp/2 tsp baking powder
- 75 g/3 oz/6 tbsp unsalted butter, diced
- 40 g/1½ oz/3 tbsp caster (superfine) sugar
- 1 egg, lightly beaten
- 15–30 ml/1–2 tbsp/1–2 tbsp milk
- a little melted butter
- 225 ml/8 fl oz/1 cup double (heavy) cream

DECORATION
- icing (confectioners) sugar
- 5 reserved strawberries

MATERIALS AND EQUIPMENT
- baking parchment
- 2 × 20 cm/8 in loose-bottom round cake tins (pans)
- piping bag fitted with a large star nozzle

STORING

Best eaten the day of making.

FREEZING

Recommended at the end of step 4. Wrap and freeze, defrost at room temperature.

1 Preheat oven to 220°C/425°F/Gas 7. Grease and base-line the cake tins (pans).

2 Reserve five strawberries for decoration, cut the rest into slices and marinate in the port for 1–2 hours. Strain and reserve both the strawberries and port.

3 Sift the flour and baking powder into a bowl. Rub in the butter until the mixture resembles fine breadcrumbs and stir in the sugar. Work in the egg and 15 ml/1 tbsp/1 tbsp of milk to form a soft dough, adding a further 15 ml/1 tbsp/1 tbsp if the dough is too firm.

4 Knead the dough on a lightly-floured surface and divide in two. Roll out each half, mark one half into eight wedges, and transfer to the prepared tins (pans). Brush each with a little melted butter and bake for 15 minutes until risen and golden. Remove from the oven, cool in the tins (pans) for 10 minutes and transfer to a wire rack to cool.

5 Cut the marked cake into wedges. Reserving a little cream for decoration, whip the rest until it holds its shape, and fold in the reserved port and strawberry slices. Spread over the whole cake.

6 Whip the remaining cream and transfer to the piping bag. Dust each wedge with icing (confectioners) sugar and pipe a swirl onto each one.

7 Arrange the wedges, overlapping slightly, on top of the filling. Cut four of the reserved strawberries in half, and use to decorate each swirl. Place the final strawberry in the centre of the cake.

Teatime Treats

PEAR AND CARDAMOM SPICE CAKE

Fresh pear and cardamom – a classic combination of flavours – are used together in this moist fruit and nut cake to provide a delicious, mouth-watering teatime treat.

INGREDIENTS

Serves 8–12
- 125 g/4 oz/½ cup butter
- 125 g/4 oz/½ cup caster (confectioners) sugar
- 2 eggs, lightly beaten
- 225 g/8 oz/2 cups plain (all-purpose) flour
- 15 ml/1 tbsp/1 tbsp baking powder
- 30 ml/2 tbsp/2 tbsp milk
- crushed seeds from 2 cardamom pods
- 50 g/2 oz/⅓ cup walnuts, chopped
- 15 ml/1 tbsp/1 tbsp poppy seeds
- 575 g/1¼ lb/1¼ lb dessert pears, peeled, cored and thinly sliced

DECORATION

- 3 walnut halves
- reserved pear slices
- 45 ml/3 tbsp/3 tbsp clear honey

STORING

Keeps in an airtight container for several days.

MATERIALS AND EQUIPMENT

- greaseproof (wax) paper
- 20 cm/8 in loose-bottom round cake tin (pan)

FREEZING

Recommended. Wrap and freeze, defrost at room temperature.

1 Preheat oven to 180°C/350°F/Gas 4. Grease and base-line the tin (pan) with the greaseproof (wax) paper.

2 Cream the butter and sugar together until pale and light. Gradually beat in the eggs, a little at a time, until incorporated. Sift the flour and baking powder together, and fold in with the milk.

3 Stir in the cardamom, chopped nuts and poppy seeds. Reserve one-third of the pear slices, and chop the rest. Fold the chopped pears into the creamed mixture.

4 Transfer to the prepared tin. Smooth the surface, making a small dip in the centre.

5 Place the three walnut halves in the centre of the cake mixture, and fan the reserved pear slices around the walnuts, covering the cake mixture. Bake for 1¼– 1½ hours, or until a skewer, inserted in the centre, comes out clean.

6 Remove the cake from the oven and brush with the clear honey. Cool in the tin (pan) for 20 minutes, and transfer to a wire rack to cool completely.

ANGEL FOOD CAKE

This is a true American classic. Although this is similar to a whisked sponge cake, it differs, in that it contains no egg yolks. This results in a delicate snowy white texture. The cream of tartar helps to stiffen the egg whites, and the addition of the sugar forms a light meringue mixture. The cake is baked in a non-stick tube tin (tubular cake pan) which is not greased. This enables the mixture to cling to the sides of the tin (pan) as it rises. The traditional whipped frosting is a basic Italian meringue mixture, which has a hot sugar syrup whisked into it.

INGREDIENTS

Serves 20
- 60 g/2½ oz/5 tbsp plain (all-purpose) flour
- 15 ml/1 tbsp/1 tbsp cornflour (cornstarch)
- 340 g/11½ oz/scant 1½ cups caster (superfine) sugar
- 12 egg whites
- 5 ml/1 tsp/1 tsp cream of tartar
- 7.5 ml/1½ tsp/1½ tsp vanilla essence (extract)
- 60 ml/4 tbsp/4 tbsp water
- 10 ml/2 tsp/2 tsp golden syrup (light corn syrup)

DECORATION

- 15 g/½ oz/2 tbsp each desiccated coconut, chopped pistachio nuts, chopped candied orange peel
- gold and silver dragées

MATERIALS AND EQUIPMENT

- 25 cm/10 in non-stick tube tin (tubular cake pan)
- sugar thermometer
- turntable
- palette knife (spatula)

STORING

Best stored before frosted, in an airtight container, for 2–3 days.

FREEZING

Recommended, again before icing, for up to 2 months. Wrap and freeze, defrost at room temperature and frost the cake as above.

1 Preheat oven to 180°C/350°F/Gas 4. Sift the flour, cornflour (cornstarch) and 50 g/2 oz/¼ cup of the sugar together three times.

2 Whisk 10 of the egg whites with the cream of tartar until stiff, and gradually whisk in 175 g/6 oz/¾ cup of the remaining sugar, a tablespoon at a time, until thick and glossy.

3 Fold in the sifted flours and sugar and 5 ml/1 tsp/1 tsp vanilla essence (extract) until combined, and transfer to the tin (pan). Bake for 35–40 minutes until risen and golden. Remove from the oven, invert the cake in its tin (pan), and leave to cool.

4 Make the frosting. Heat the remaining sugar and water in a small pan until the sugar dissolves. Increase the heat and boil until the temperature reaches 115°C/220°F on the sugar thermometer (or until it reaches the thread stage).

5 Meanwhile, as soon as the mixture boils, whisk the remaining egg whites until very stiff and dry. Pour the syrup, in a steady stream, into the centre of the egg whites, whisking continually, until thick and glossy. Beat in the golden syrup (light corn syrup) and remaining vanilla essence (extract) and continue beating for 5 minutes until the frosting is cooled.

6 *Carefully remove the cooled cake from its tin (pan), place on the turntable and coat with the frosting, using a palette (spatula) knife to make a swirling pattern and peak effect.*

7 *Sprinkle over the coconut, pistachios and orange peel, and decorate with gold and silver dragées.*

HAZELNUT PRALINE AND APRICOT GENOESE

Genoese is the name associated with the most classic of all whisked sponge cakes. Here it is layered with an apricot- and maple-flavoured buttercream, and topped with apricots and whole praline-coated hazelnuts. Delicious and elegant, this is an ideal cake for any occasion.

INGREDIENTS

Serves 12
- 4-egg quantity Genoese sponge cake mixture substituting 25 g/1 oz/2 tbsp plain (all-purpose) flour with 25 g/1 oz/2 tbsp toasted ground hazelnuts
- 75 g/3 oz/6 tbsp granulated sugar
- 75 g/3 oz/3/4 cup unblanched hazelnuts
- 6 egg yolks
- 175 g/6 oz/3/4 cup caster (superfine) sugar
- 150 ml/5 fl oz/2/3 cup milk
- 350 g/12 oz/1 1/2 cups unsalted butter, diced
- 30 ml/2 tbsp/2 tbsp maple or golden syrup (light corn syrup)
- 15 ml/1 tbsp/1 tbsp apricot brandy or apricot juice from canned apricots
- 400 g/14 oz can apricot halves in natural juice, drained

DECORATION

- 12 praline-coated hazelnuts
- 4 reserved apricot halves

STORING

Place in an airtight container and keep in a cool place for up to two days.

MATERIALS AND EQUIPMENT

- greaseproof (wax) paper
- 23 cm/9 in spring-release round tin (pan)
- baking tray (sheet)
- blender or food processor
- turntable
- piping bag fitted with a medium star nozzle

FREEZING

Recommended before the decorations are added. Open-freeze until very firm and wrap. Defrost at room temperature and decorate.

1 Preheat oven to 180°C/350°F/Gas 4. Grease, line and flour the tin (pan) and lightly oil the baking tray (sheet).

2 Prepare the Genoese sponge cake mixture and transfer to the prepared tin (pan). Bake for 35 minutes until risen and springy to the touch. Remove from the oven, cool in the tin (pan) for 10 minutes and transfer to a wire rack to cool completely.

3 To make the praline, heat the granulated sugar and nuts together in a small heavy-based pan, until the sugar melts. Increase the heat, and stir with a wooden spoon until the sugar turns golden. Be careful not to allow the sugar to burn. Remove immediately from the heat.

4 Carefully scoop out 12 coated nuts with a metal spoon and place on the oiled tray (sheet). Pour the remaining mixture onto the tray (sheet) and set aside until completely cold and set hard. Break this into pieces and grind in a blender or food processor to form a rough paste. Cover and set aside.

5 To make the icing, beat egg yolks and caster (superfine) sugar together until pale and thick. Heat the milk until it just boils and pour over the creamed mixture, still beating. Return to the pan and stir over a low heat, until the mixture coats the back of the spoon. Do not let the mixture become too hot or it will curdle. Remove from the heat and strain through a fine sieve (strainer) into a large bowl.

6 Beat the mixture for a minute or two, until tepid. Gradually beat in the butter, a little at a time, until the mixture thickens and becomes glossy. Beat in the maple syrup and apricot brandy or fruit juice. (Just before the mixture thickens it will appear to be curdling. Continue beating and the correct consistency will be achieved.)

7 Cut the cold cake into 3 equal layers. Reserve 4 apricot halves and chop the rest. Dry well and fold the chopped fruit into one-third of the icing along with 45 ml/3 tbsp/3 tbsp of praline paste.

8 Place one layer of sponge cake on the turntable, spread with half the filling, top with the next layer of sponge cake and repeat.

9 Reserve a little of the remaining icing for decoration. Use the rest to cover the top and sides of the cake. Coat the sides with a further 45 ml/3 tbsp/3 tbsp praline paste and swirl a pattern over the top with a palette knife (spatula).

10 Transfer the remaining icing to the piping bag and pipe 24 rosettes around the top of the cake. Cut the reserved apricot halves into thin slices and decorate alternate rosettes. Top the other rosettes with the whole praline coated nuts. Fan the remaining apricot slices in the centre of the cake.

SPICED HONEY NUT CAKE

A combination of ground pistachio nuts and breadcrumbs replaces the flour in this recipe, resulting in a light, moist sponge cake. Soaking the cooled cake is typical of many Middle Eastern cakes, and the combination of pistachio, lemon and cinnamon is mouth-watering.

INGREDIENTS

Serves 8
- 125 g/4 oz/1/2 cup caster (superfine) sugar
- 4 eggs, separated
- grated rind and juice of 1 lemon
- 125 g/41/2 oz/11/4 cups ground pistachio nuts
- 50 g/2 oz/1/2 cup dried breadcrumbs
- 1 lemon
- 90 ml/6 tbsp/6 tbsp clear honey
- 1 cinnamon stick
- 15 ml/1 tbsp/1 tbsp brandy

DECORATION

- shredded lemon rind
- cinnamon stick
- chopped pistachio nuts

STORING

Place in an airtight container for up to two days.

MATERIALS AND EQUIPMENT

- greaseproof (wax) paper
- 20 cm/8 in square cake tin (pan)
- skewer

FREEZING

Recommended at the end of step 3. Wrap and freeze. Defrost at room temperature and continue.

1 Preheat oven to 180°C/350°F/Gas 4. Grease and base-line the tin (pan).

2 Beat the sugar, egg yolks, lemon rind and juice together until pale and creamy. Fold in 110 g/4 oz/1 cup of the ground pistachio nuts and all the breadcrumbs.

3 Whisk the egg whites until stiff and fold into the creamed mixture. Transfer to the prepared tin (pan) and bake for 45 minutes, until risen and springy to the touch. Remove from the oven, cool in the tin (pan) for 10 minutes and transfer to a wire rack to cool completely.

4 Meanwhile to make the syrup, peel the lemon and cut the rind into very thin strips. Squeeze the juice into a small pan and add the honey and cinnamon stick. Bring to the boil, add shredded rind, and simmer fast for 1 minute. Cool slightly and stir in the brandy.

5 Place the cold cake onto a serving plate, prick all over with a skewer and pour over the cooled syrup, lemon shreds and cinnamon stick.

6 Sprinkle over the reserved pistachio nuts.

ST CLEMENTS MARBLED CROWN

A tangy orange-and-lemon marbled cake is transformed into a spectacular centrepiece by the pretty arrangement of fresh flowers in the centre of the ring. The icing is decorated with crystallized fruits, dragées and sugared almonds, creating a dramatic jewelled effect.

INGREDIENTS

Serves 8
- 175 g/6 oz/³/4 cup butter
- 75 g/3 oz/good ¹/3 cup light soft brown sugar
- 3 eggs, separated
- grated rind and juice 1 orange
- 160 g/5¹/2 oz/1¹/3 cups self-raising flour
- 75 g/3 oz/6 tbsp caster (superfine) sugar
- grated rind and juice of 1 lemon
- 15 g/¹/2 oz/2 tbsp ground almonds
- 350 ml/³/4 pt/1 US pt double (heavy) cream
- 15 ml/1 tbsp/1 tbsp Grand Marnier

DECORATION
- 16 crystallized orange and lemon slices
- silver dragées
- 8 gold sugared almonds
- fresh flowers

STORING

Best eaten the day of making.

MATERIALS AND EQUIPMENT
- 850 ml/1¹/2 pt/3³/4 cups capacity ring mould
- skewer

FREEZING

Recommended at the end of step 5. Wrap and freeze. Defrost at room temperature and ice and decorate.

1 Preheat oven to 180°C/350°F/Gas 4. Grease and flour the mould.

2 Make orange cake mixture. Cream half the butter and the soft brown sugar together until pale and light. Gradually beat in the egg yolks, orange rind and juice until incorporated, and fold in 75 g/3 oz/³/4 cup of the flour.

3 Make lemon cake mixture. Cream the remaining butter and caster (superfine) sugar together, stir in the lemon rind and juice and fold in the remaining flour and ground almonds. Whisk the egg whites until stiff, and fold in.

4 Spoon the two mixtures alternately into the prepared tin (pan).

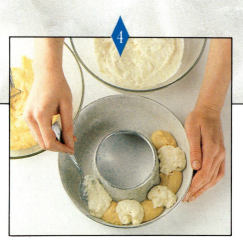

5 Using a skewer or small spoon, swirl through the mixture, to create a marble effect. Bake for 45–50 minutes, until risen and a skewer, inserted into the cake, comes out clean. Cool in the tin (pan) for 10 minutes and transfer to a wire rack to cool completely.

6 Whip the cream and Grand Marnier together until lightly thickened. Spread over the cooled cake and swirl a pattern over the icing.

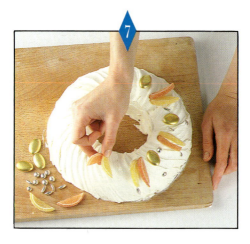

7 Decorate the ring with the crystallized fruits, dragées and almonds to resemble a jewelled crown. Arrange a few pretty, fresh flowers in the centre.

SAVARIN WITH FRESH BERRIES

A classic French yeast cake soaked with a rum syrup and glazed, is served with fresh cream and a mixture of fresh berries – choose your favourite fruits.

INGREDIENTS

Serves 8
- 15 ml/1 tbsp/1 tbsp dried yeast
- 40 ml/2½ tbsp/2½ tbsp caster (superfine) sugar
- 90 ml/6 tbsp/6 tbsp tepid milk
- 225 g/8 oz/2 cups strong plain (all-purpose) flour
- pinch salt
- 4 eggs, beaten
- 125 g/4 oz/½ cup unsalted butter, softened
- 120 ml/4 fl oz/½ cup clear honey
- 60 ml/4 tbsp/4 tbsp water
- 30 ml/2 tbsp/2 tbsp lemon juice
- 30 ml/2 tbsp/2 tbsp dark rum or Grand Marnier
- 45 ml/3 tbsp/3 tbsp apricot glaze

DECORATION

- 150 ml/¼ pt/⅔ cup double (heavy) cream
- 125 g/4 oz/¼ lb summer fruits
- lemon balm leaves

STORING

Best eaten on the day of making.

MATERIALS AND EQUIPMENT

- 1.5 l/2½ pt/6¼ cup capacity ring mould
- piping bag fitted with a large star nozzle

FREEZING

Recommended before the decorations are added. Open-freeze until very firm, wrap and re-freeze for up to two months.

1 Grease and flour the ring mould. Blend the yeast, 7.5 ml/½ tbsp/½ tbsp sugar, milk and 15 ml/1 tbsp/1 tbsp flour together. Cover and leave in a warm place for 15 minutes, until frothy.

2 Sift the remaining flour and salt into a bowl and stir in the remaining sugar. Make a well in the centre and beat in the frothed yeast mixture, eggs and butter, until smooth and glossy. Heat the oven to 200°C/400°F/Gas 6.

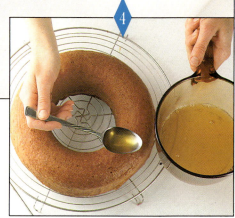

3 Transfer to the prepared tin (pan), cover and leave in a warm place for 30 minutes, or until the batter almost reaches the top of the tin (pan). Bake for 35 minutes until risen and golden. Remove from the oven, cool in the tin (pan) for 5 minutes and transfer to a wire rack. Prick the cake all over with a skewer.

4 To make the syrup, heat the honey, water and lemon juice together and boil for 3 minutes, until thick and syrupy. Remove from the heat. Stir in the rum and spoon over the cooling cake. Leave to cool completely.

5 Heat the apricot glaze until it just boils, remove from the heat and brush over the cooled cake.

6 Whip the cream until thick and transfer to the piping bag. Pipe swirls all around the top of the cake and decorate with the berries and lemon balm leaves.

Cakes to Keep

CARAMEL FROSTED GINGERBREAD

This is an unusual gingerbread, made with all golden syrup (light corn syrup) rather than a mixture of syrup and treacle (molasses). It gives a lighter mixture – and the addition of desiccated (shredded) coconut adds a wonderful flavour and texture.

INGREDIENTS

Makes 18–20
- 300 g/11 oz/1½ cups light soft brown sugar
- 225 g/8 oz/1 cup unsalted butter
- 275 ml/10 fl oz/1¼ cup golden syrup (light corn syrup)
- 90 ml/6 tbsp/6 tbsp stem (preserved) ginger syrup
- 350 g/12 oz/3 cups self-raising flour
- 125 g/4 oz/2 cups desiccated (shredded) coconut
- 25 g/1 oz/2 tbsp chopped stem (preserved) ginger
- 5 ml/1 tsp/1 tsp ground ginger
- 2.5 ml/½ tsp/½ tsp bicarbonate of soda (baking soda)
- 300 ml/½ pt/1¼ cups milk
- 1 egg, lightly beaten

DECORATION
- 50 g/2 oz/1 cup desiccated (shredded) coconut

MATERIALS AND EQUIPMENT
- greaseproof (wax) paper
- 25 × 20 cm/10 × 8 in rectangular deep cake tin (pan)

STORING

This moist gingerbread will keep well in an airtight container for up to two weeks without the icing, and up to one week with the icing.

FREEZING

Recommended at the end of step 3. Wrap and freeze. Defrost and continue.

1 Preheat oven to 180°C/350°F/Gas 4. Grease and line the tin (pan).

2 Heat 225 g/8 oz/¾ cup of the sugar, 175 g/6 oz/¾ cup butter, the golden syrup (light corn syrup), and 60 ml/4 tbsp/4 tbsp of stem ginger syrup together gently, until melted. Combine the flour, coconut, stem ginger, ground ginger and bicarbonate of soda (baking soda), in a large bowl. Gradually beat in the melted syrup mixture, milk and egg, and continue beating for 1 minute.

3 Transfer to the prepared tin (pan) and bake for 1½ hours, or until a skewer, inserted in the centre, comes out clean. Remove from the oven, cool in the tin (pan) for 10 minutes and transfer to a wire rack to cool completely.

4 Melt the remaining sugar, butter and stem ginger syrup together. Increase the heat and boil for 1 minute. Remove from the heat and allow the bubbling to stop. Pour over the cooled cake, in one smooth motion, letting a little drizzle over the edges.

5 Immediately sprinkle over the coconut, mark into 18–20 fingers with a sharp knife and leave in a cool place until the caramel icing has set. Cut along the marked lines into fingers.

DUNDEE CAKE

This is the perfect fruit cake for those who prefer a lighter-style cake. It has a wonderful fruit and nut flavour and a light, slightly crumbly texture.

INGREDIENTS

Serves 16–20
- 175 g/6 oz/¾ cup butter
- 175 g/6 oz/scant ¾ cup light soft brown sugar
- 3 eggs
- 225 g/8 oz/2 cups plain (all-purpose) flour
- 10 ml/2 tsp/2 tsp baking powder
- 5 ml/1 tsp/1 tsp ground cinnamon
- 2.5 ml/½ tsp/½ tsp ground cloves
- 1.5 ml/¼ tsp/¼ tsp ground nutmeg
- 225 g/8 oz/1⅓ cups sultanas (golden raisins)
- 175 g/6 oz/1 cup raisins
- 175 g/6 oz/1 cup glacé cherries, halved
- 125 g/4 oz/¾ cup chopped mixed (candied) peel
- 50 g/2 oz/⅓ cup blanched almonds, chopped
- grated rind 1 lemon
- 30 ml/2 tbsp/2 tbsp brandy

DECORATION
- 75–125 g/3–4 oz/⅔ cup whole blanched almonds

MATERIALS AND EQUIPMENT
- greaseproof (wax) paper
- 20 cm/8 in round deep cake tin (pan)

STORING
All fruit cakes improve in flavour if left in a cool place for up to three months. Wrap the cake in a double layer of foil.

FREEZING
Although suitable for freezing, it is unnecessary, as the cake keeps well.

1 Preheat oven to 170°C/325°F/Gas 3. Grease and line the tin (pan).

2 Cream the butter and sugar together until pale and light. Add the eggs, one at a time, beating well after each addition.

3 Sift the flour, baking powder and spices together and fold into the creamed mixture alternately with the remaining ingredients, until evenly incorporated.

4 Transfer to the prepared tin (pan), smooth the surface, making a small dip in the centre.

5 Decorate the top of the cake mixture by pressing the almonds in decreasing circles over the entire surface. Bake for 2–2¼ hours until a skewer, inserted in the centre, comes out clean.

6 Remove from the oven, cool in the tin (pan) for 30 minutes, and transfer to a wire rack to cool completely.

FIG, BANANA AND BRAZIL NUT TEABREAD

Mashed bananas are a classic ingredient in tea-breads. Combined here with dried figs and brazil nuts, they make an exceptionally moist and flavoursome cake.

INGREDIENTS

Serves 8–12
- 225 g/8 oz/2 cups plain (all-purpose) flour
- 10 ml/2 tsp/2 tsp baking powder
- 5 ml/1 tsp/1 tsp ground mixed spice
- 125 g/4 oz/½ cup butter, diced
- 125 g/4 oz/scant ½ cup light soft brown sugar
- 2 eggs, lightly beaten
- 30 ml/2 tbsp/2 tbsp milk
- 30 ml/2 tbsp/2 tbsp dark rum
- 2 medium bananas, peeled and mashed
- 125 g/4 oz/⅔ cup dried figs, chopped
- 50 g/2 oz/½ cup brazil nuts, chopped

DECORATION

- 8 whole brazil nuts
- 4 whole dried figs, halved
- 30 ml/2 tbsp/2 tbsp apricot jam
- 5 ml/1 tsp/1 tsp dark rum

MATERIALS AND EQUIPMENT

- greaseproof (wax) paper
- 900 g/2 lb/5 cup loaf tin (bread pan)
- pastry brush

STORING

The flavour of this cake will improve if kept in an airtight container, in a cool place, for three to four days.

FREEZING

Recommended *before* glazing. When cold, wrap the cake and freeze. Defrost and heat the glaze before brushing over the cake.

1 Preheat oven to 180°C/350°F/Gas 4. Grease and base-line the loaf tin (bread pan).

2 Sift the flour, baking powder and mixed spice into a bowl. Rub in the butter until the mixture resembles fine breadcrumbs. Stir in the sugar.

3 Make a well in the centre and work in the eggs, milk and rum until combined. Stir in the remaining ingredients and transfer to the prepared tin (pan).

4 Press the whole brazil nuts and halved figs gently into the mixture, to form an attractive pattern. Bake for 1¼ hours, or until a skewer, inserted in the centre, comes out clean. Remove from the oven, cool in the tin (pan) for 10 minutes and transfer to a wire rack.

5 Heat the jam and rum together in a small saucepan. Increase the heat and boil for 1 minute. Remove from the heat and pass through a fine sieve (strainer). Cool the glaze slightly and brush over the cake while still warm. Leave to cool completely and serve cut into slices.

CARROT CAKE

So easy to make, this is a wonderfully moist and tasty cake, enriched with grated carrots and vegetable oil – a classic 'all in one' cake. The chopped nuts impart an even fuller flavour.

Although often served with a simple dusting of icing (confectioners) sugar, the cream cheese icing and marzipan carrots make the cake a little more special.

INGREDIENTS

Serves 8
- 225 g/8 oz/1 cup caster (superfine) sugar
- 3 eggs
- 200 ml/7 fl oz/scant 1 cup vegetable oil
- grated rind and juice of 1 orange
- 225 g/8 oz/2 cups self-raising wholemeal (wholegrain) flour
- 5 ml/1 tsp/1 tsp ground cinnamon
- 2.5 ml/½ tsp/½ tsp. ground nutmeg
- 2.5 ml/½ tsp/½ tsp salt
- 350 g/12 oz/¾ lb grated carrot, squeezed dry
- 125 g/4 oz/good 1 cup walnuts, ground
- 225 g/8 oz/½ lb cream cheese
- 30 ml/2 tbsp/2 tbsp clear honey
- 15 ml/1 tbsp/1 tbsp orange juice

DECORATION
- 50 g/2 oz/¼ cup ready-made marzipan
- orange food colouring
- angelica
- 2 walnut halves (optional)

STORING

This cake keeps for up to one week in an airtight container.

MATERIALS AND EQUIPMENT
- greaseproof (wax) paper
- 20 cm/8 in round cake tin (pan)

FREEZING

Recommended before adding the carrots. Open-freeze until very firm before wrapping.

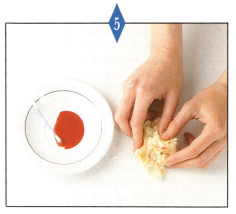
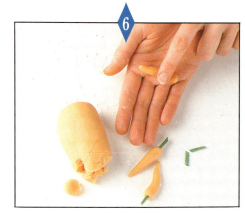

1 Preheat oven to 180°C/350°F/Gas 4. Grease and base-line the cake tin (pan).

2 Beat the sugar, eggs, oil, orange rind and juice together until light and frothy. Sift in the flour, spices and salt and beat for a further minute. Stir in the carrots and nuts and transfer to the prepared tin (pan).

3 Bake for 1½–1¾ hours until risen. Test with a skewer and remove from the oven, if done. Cool in the tin (pan) for 10 minutes and transfer to a wire rack to cool completely.

4 To make the icing, beat the cheese, honey and 15 ml/1 tbsp/1 tbsp orange juice together until smooth. Chill for 30 minutes to firm up.

5 Tint the marzipan with the food colouring to resemble the colour of carrots.

6 Break off small pieces and roll between your palms to form carrot shapes.

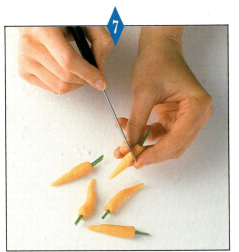

7 Using a small knife, press marks around the sides and stick a small piece of angelica in the top of each one to resemble the stalk.

8 Remove the icing from the refrigerator and spread over the top of the cooled cake. Arrange the carrots, in a bunch, in the centre of the cake and decorate with the walnut halves, if using.

Festive Cakes

GLAZED CHRISTMAS RING

A good, rich fruit cake is a must at Christmas. This one is particularly festive with its vibrant, glazed fruit and nut topping. Made here in a tube tin (pan), it gives the cake an unusual shape, but it is as equally successfully made in a 25 cm/10 in round cake tin (pan). If using the latter, cook for an extra 15–30 minutes, checking the centre with a skewer.

INGREDIENTS

Serves 16–20

- 225 g/8 oz/1⅓ cups sultanas (golden raisins)
- 175 g/6 oz/1 cup raisins
- 175 g/6 oz/1 cup currants
- 175 g/6 oz/1 cup dried figs, chopped
- 90 ml/6 tbsp/6 tbsp whiskey
- 45 ml/3 tbsp/3 tbsp orange juice
- 225 g/8 oz/1 cup butter
- 225 g/8 oz/scant 1 cup dark soft brown sugar
- 5 eggs
- 250 g/9 oz/2¼ cups plain (all-purpose) flour
- 15 ml/1 tbsp/1 tbsp baking powder
- 15 ml/1 tbsp/1 tbsp ground mixed spice
- 125 g/4 oz/⅔ cup glacé cherries, chopped
- 125 g/4 oz/1 cup brazil nuts, chopped
- 50 g/2 oz/⅓ cup chopped mixed (candied) peel
- 50 g/2 oz/⅓ cup ground almonds
- grated rind and juice 1 orange
- 30 ml/2 tbsp/2 tbsp thick-cut orange marmalade

DECORATION

- 150 g/5 fl oz/1 cup thick-cut orange marmalade
- 15 ml/1 tbsp/1 tbsp orange juice
- 175 g/6 oz/1 cup mixed colour glacé cherries
- 75 g/3 oz/¾ cup whole brazil nuts
- 125 g/4 oz/⅔ cup dried figs, halved

MATERIALS AND EQUIPMENT

- greaseproof (wax) paper
- 25 cm/10 in tube tin (tubular cake pan)

STORING

Ideal for storing for up to three months. Wrap in a double layer of foil, and keep in a cool dry place.

FREEZING

Suitable, but unnecessary, as the cake keeps well.

1 Place the sultanas, raisins, currants and figs into a large bowl. Pour over 60 ml/4 tbsp/4 tbsp of the whiskey and the orange juice and leave to marinate overnight.

2 Preheat oven to 170°C/325°F/Gas 3. Grease and double-line the tin (pan).

3 Cream the butter and sugar together until pale and light. Beat in the eggs one at a time, beating well after each addition, until incorporated. Add a little flour if the mixture starts to curdle.

4 Sift remaining flour, baking powder and mixed spice together. Fold into the creamed mixture, alternating with the remaining ingredients, except for the whiskey. Transfer the mixture to the prepared tin (pan), smooth the surface, making a small dip in the centre. Bake for 1 hour, reduce the oven temperature to 150°C/300°F/Gas 2 and bake for a further 1¾–2 hours. Test with a skewer, to ensure the cake is cooked.

5 Remove from the oven, prick the cake all over with a skewer and pour over the reserved whiskey. Leave to cool in the tin (pan) for 30 minutes and transfer to a wire rack to cool completely.

6 To decorate, heat the marmalade and orange juice together and boil gently for 3 minutes. Stir in the cherries, nuts and figs. Remove from the heat and cool slightly.

7 Spoon the glazed fruits and nuts over the cake in an attractive pattern and leave to set.

PANFORTE

This rich, spicy nougat-type cake is a speciality of Siena in Italy, where it is traditionally baked at Christmas. It is a combination of chopped candied peel and nuts, which are mixed with a sugar syrup before baking.

INGREDIENTS

Serves 8
- 275 g/10 oz/2 cups mixed candied exotic peel, to include: papaya, pineapple, orange, lemon and citron
- 125 g/4 oz/²⁄₃ cup unblanched almonds
- 50 g/2 oz/¹⁄₂ cup walnut halves
- 50 g/2 oz/¹⁄₂ cup plain (all-purpose) flour
- 5 ml/1 tsp/1 tsp ground cinnamon
- 1.5 ml/¹⁄₄ tsp/¹⁄₄ tsp each nutmeg, cloves and coriander
- 175 g/6 oz/³⁄₄ cup caster (superfine) sugar
- 60 ml/4 tbsp/4 tbsp water

DECORATION
- icing (confectioners) sugar

STORING

This cake will keep well for several weeks in an airtight container.

MATERIALS AND EQUIPMENT
- 20 cm/8 in loose-bottom round cake tin (pan)
- rice paper
- sugar thermometer

FREEZING

Unsuitable and unnecessary as it stores well.

1 Preheat oven to 180°C/350°F/Gas 4. Grease and base-line the tin (pan) with a sheet of rice paper.

2 Combine the mixed candied peel and nuts in a bowl. Sift in the flour and spices and mix well.

3 Heat the sugar and water in a small pan, until the sugar dissolves. Increase the heat and boil until the mixture reaches 115°C/220°F on a sugar thermometer, or until it reaches the thread stage.

4 Remove from the heat and pour onto the fruit mixture, stirring with a wooden spoon until well coated. Transfer to the prepared tin (pan), pressing into the sides with a metal spoon.

5 Bake for 25–30 minutes, until the mixture is bubbling all over. Remove from the oven and cool in the tin (pan) for 5 minutes.

6 With a lightly-oiled palette knife (spatula) work around the edges of the cake, to loosen and remove from the tin (pan) leaving the base in place. Leave to go cold.

7 Remove from the base and decorate with a generous dusting of icing (confectioners) sugar.

CASSATA SICILIANA

This is a chilled cake from Sicily, where it is traditional to cover the cake with a layer of almond paste and to decorate the top with an exotic selection of glacé fruits.

INGREDIENTS

Serves 12
- 4-egg quantity whisked sponge cake mixture made into a 23 cm/9 in round sponge cake
- 100 ml/3½ fl oz/scant ½ cup Marsala
- 350 g/12 oz/1¾ cups ricotta cheese
- 30 ml/2 tbsp/2 tbsp clear honey
- 1.5 ml/¼ tsp/¼ tsp vanilla essence (extract)
- grated rind and juice ½ lemon
- 125 g/4 oz/¾ cup mixed candied peel, finely chopped
- 75 g/3 oz/½ cup plain (semisweet) chocolate chips
- 175 g/6 oz/1½ cups ground almonds
- 75 g/3 oz/6 tbsp caster (superfine) sugar
- 75 g/3 oz/¼ cup icing (confectioners) sugar, sifted
- 1 egg white, lightly whisked
- 5 ml/1 tsp/1 tsp lemon juice
- 2 drops almond essence (extract)
- green food colouring
- 45 ml/3 tbsp/3 tbsp apricot glaze

DECORATION

- 225 g/8 oz/½ lb mixed glacé fruits

MATERIALS AND EQUIPMENT

- 20 cm/8 in round spring form tin (pan)
- cling film (plastic wrap)
- small rolling pin
- cakeboard

STORING

This cake will keep in an airtight container in a cool place for two days, before adding the fruit decoration.

FREEZING

Recommended at the end of step 4. Can be frozen in its tin (pan). Defrost at room temperature and continue.

1 Line the tin (pan) with cling film (plastic wrap).

2 Cut the whisked sponge cake into 3 equal layers. Trim one to fit into the base of the prepared tin (pan). Cut the second into strips to line the sides of the tin. Brush with a little of the Marsala. Reserve the trimmings and the final sponge layer.

3 To make the filling, beat the ricotta, honey, 15 ml/1 tbsp/1 tbsp Marsala, vanilla essence (extract), lemon rind and juice together until very smooth. Chop the sponge trimmings and stir into the cheese mixture, with the peel and chocolate chips. Spoon into the sponge cake case, pressing into the sides.

4 Smooth the surface and trim the reserved layer of sponge cake to fit tightly over the filling. Pour over the remaining Marsala and cover with cling film (plastic wrap). Place a weight on top of the cake and chill for several hours, until firm.

5 Meanwhile, make the icing. Combine the almonds, caster (superfine) sugar and icing (confectioners) sugar together. Make a well in the centre and work in the egg white, lemon juice and almond essence (extract) to form a soft pliable paste. Add a few drops of food colouring and knead on a clean surface, dusted with a little icing (confectioners) sugar, until smooth and evenly coloured. Wrap and keep cool until required.

6 *Remove the cake from the refrigerator and turn out of the tin (pan). Remove the cling film (plastic wrap) and brush with warmed apricot glaze. Roll out the almond paste to a circle a little larger than the cake, and use to cover, pressing gently to the top and sides. Smooth over the icing with a palette knife (spatula) or small rolling pin. Transfer to a cakeboard.*

7 *Make an attractive arrangement of mixed glacéd fruits in the centre of the cake.*

BUCHE DE NOEL

This is the traditional French Christmas cake, filled with a purée of chestnuts, flavoured with honey and brandy, and coated with a classic chocolate ganache. The meringue mushrooms add a whimsical touch to the decoration of this festive cake.

INGREDIENTS

Serves 8
- 3-egg quantity whisked sponge cake mixture substituting 25 g/1oz/2 tbsp plain (all-purpose) flour with 25 g/1 oz/2 tbsp cocoa powder
- 1 egg white
- 50 g/2 oz/¼ cup caster (superfine) sugar, plus extra for sprinkling
- 225 g/8 oz/½ lb unsweetened chestnut purée
- 30 ml/2 tbsp/2 tbsp clear honey
- 30 ml/2 tbsp/2 tbsp brandy
- 300 ml/½ pt/1¼ cups double (heavy) cream
- 150 g/5 oz/scant 1 cup plain (semisweet) chocolate chips

DECORATION

- meringue mushrooms
- icing (confectioners) sugar
- holly leaves
- 4 chocolate flakes, crumbled

MATERIALS AND EQUIPMENT

- baking tray (sheet)
- greaseproof (wax) paper
- 33 × 23 cm/13 × 9 in Swiss (jelly) roll tin (pan)
- food processor
- piping bag fitted with a 5 mm/¼ in plain nozzle
- baking parchment
- star nozzle
- square cakeboard

STORING

The chocolate log will keep for up to two days in the refrigerator, in an airtight container. Do not assemble mushrooms until just before serving, as they will soften.

FREEZING

Recommended before decoration, although the meringue mushrooms can be frozen separately before assembly. Open-freeze the log until solid and wrap.

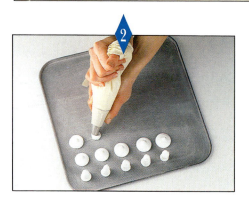

3 Make the whisked sponge cake mixture and transfer to the prepared Swiss (jelly) roll tin (pan). Bake for 10–12 minutes until risen and springy to the touch.

4 Lay a sheet of baking parchment onto a lightly dampened tea-towel (dishtowel) and sprinkle liberally with caster (superfine) sugar. Turn the cake over onto the paper and leave to cool completely with the tin (pan) in place.

5 To make the filling, blend the chestnut purée with the honey and brandy in a food processor until smooth, and gradually blend in half the cream until thick. Chill until required.

6 To make the icing, heat the chocolate and remaining cream in a small pan over a low heat, until melted. Transfer to a bowl, cool and chill for 1 hour. Remove from the refrigerator and beat until thick.

1 Preheat oven to 110°C/220°F/Gas ¼. Grease and flour a baking tray (sheet). Grease and line the tin (pan).

2 To make the meringue mushrooms, whisk the egg white until stiff and gradually beat in the sugar a little at a time, until thick and glossy. Transfer to the piping bag, fitted with the plain nozzle. Pipe 8 tall 'stalks' and 8 shorter 'caps' onto the prepared baking tray. Bake for 2½–3 hours, until crisp and dried out. Remove from the oven and leave to cool completely. Increase the temperature to 200°C/400°F/Gas 6.

7 Remove the Swiss (jelly) roll tin (pan) and peel away the lining paper from the sponge. Spread with all but 30 ml/2 tbsp/2 tbsp chestnut filling, leaving a border around the edges. Roll up from one narrow end, to form a roll. Transfer to a cakeboard.

8 Coat the top and sides of the roll with the icing, leaving the ends plain. Swirl a pattern over the icing with a palette knife (spatula), to resemble tree bark. Sprinkle the crumbled flakes over the rest of the board.

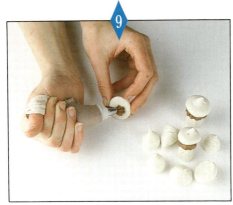

9 Remove the meringue 'stalks' and 'caps' from the baking tray. Transfer the reserved chestnut filling to the piping bag, fitted with the star nozzle. Pipe a swirl onto the underside of each mushroom 'cap'. Press gently onto the 'stalks' to form the mushroom decorations.

10 Place a small cluster of mushrooms on top of the chocolate log, arranging the rest around the board. Sprinkle over a little icing (confectioners) sugar and add a few festive holly leaves if wished.

121

KULICH

This Russian yeasted cake – Kulich – is known under other names in many Eastern European countries. Traditionally made at Easter time in Slavic countries, this delicious spiced cake was baked in special moulds. For convenience the recipe has been converted for use in either clay flower pots, or coffee tins (cans). Capacity and sizes have been given for both.

INGREDIENTS

Makes 2 cakes
- 15 ml/1 tbsp/1 tbsp dried yeast
- 90 ml/6 tbsp/6 tbsp tepid milk
- 75 g/3 oz/6 tbsp caster (superfine) sugar
- 500 g/1 lb 2 oz/4½ cups plain (all-purpose) flour
- pinch saffron strands
- 30 ml/2 tbsp/2 tbsp dark rum
- 2.5 ml/½ tsp/½ tsp ground cardamom
- 2.5 ml/½ tsp/½ tsp ground cumin
- 50 g/2 oz/¼ cup unsalted butter
- 2 eggs plus 2 egg yolks
- ½ vanilla pod, finely chopped
- 25 g/1 oz/2 tbsp each: chopped mixed candied peel, chopped crystallized ginger, chopped almonds and currants

DECORATION

- 75 g/3 oz/¼ cup icing (confectioners) sugar, sifted
- 7.5–10 ml/1½–2 tsp/1½–2 tsp warm water
- a drop almond essence (extract)
- 2 candles
- blanched almonds
- mixed candied peel

MATERIALS AND EQUIPMENT

- greaseproof (wax) paper
- 2 × 15 cm/6 in clay flower pots or 2 × 500 g/1 lb 2 oz/1⅛ lb coffee tins (cans)

FREEZING

Recommended before the cakes are iced. Wrap and freeze. Defrost and continue.

STORING

Best eaten the day of making.

1 Blend the yeast, milk, 25 g/1 oz/2 tbsp sugar and 50 g/2 oz/½ cup flour together, until smooth. Leave in a warm place for 15 minutes, until frothy. Soak the saffron in the rum for 15 minutes.

2 Sift the remaining flour and spices into a bowl and rub in the butter. Stir in the remaining sugar, make a well in the centre and work in the frothed yeast mixture, the saffron liquid and remaining ingredients to form a fine dough.

3 Knead on a lightly floured surface for 5 minutes until smooth and pliable. Place in an oiled bowl, cover and leave to rise in a warm place for 1–1½ hours, until doubled in size.

4 Preheat oven to 190°C/375°F/Gas 5. Grease, base-line and flour the pots or tins (cans).

5 Knock back (punch down) the dough. Divide in two and form each lump into rounds. Press into the prepared pots, cover and leave in a warm place for a further 30 minutes, until the dough comes two-thirds of the way up the sides.

6 Bake for 35 minutes if using the coffee tins (cans) or 50 minutes if using the clay pots. Test with a skewer and remove from the oven. Transfer to a wire rack and leave to cool.

7 Blend the icing (confectioners) sugar, water and almond essence (extract) together until smooth, to form a thick glacé icing. Pour over the top of each cake, allowing it to drizzle down the sides, and decorate with the candles, nuts and peel.

Gateaux

ICED PARADISE CAKE

A whisked sponge cake mixture is piped into fingers. These are then used to line a loaf tin (bread pan).

This is a luxurious frozen gateaux, finished off with a coating of melted chocolate, butter and cream.

INGREDIENTS

Serves 12
- 3-egg quantity whisked sponge cake mixture substituting 15 g/$^{1}/_2$ oz/1 tbsp plain (all-purpose) flour with 15 g/$^{1}/_2$ oz/1 tbsp cornflour (cornstarch)
- 90 ml/6 tbsp/6 tbsp dark rum
- 250 g/9 oz/1$^{2}/_3$ cups plain (semisweet) chocolate chips
- 30 ml/2 tbsp/2 tbsp golden syrup (light corn syrup)
- 30 ml/2 tbsp/2 tbsp water
- 400 ml/14 fl oz/1$^{3}/_4$ cups double (heavy) cream
- 125 g/4 oz/2 cups desiccated (shredded) coconut, toasted
- 25 g/1 oz/2 tbsp unsalted butter
- 30 ml/2 tbsp/2 tbsp single cream (half-and-half)

DECORATION

- 25–50 g/1–2 oz/$^{1}/_3$ cup white chocolate chips
- a little desiccated (shredded) coconut or coconut curls
- a little cocoa powder

MATERIALS AND EQUIPMENT

- 2 large baking trays (sheets)
- 900 g/2 lb/5 cup loaf tin (bread pan)
- cling film (plastic wrap)
- piping bag fitted with a 1 cm/$^{1}/_2$ in plain nozzle
- greaseproof (wax) paper piping bag

STORING

This cake can be kept in the freezer for up to three months.

FREEZING

Recommended. Defrost in the refrigerator for 45 minutes, until soft enough to slice.

1 Preheat oven to 200°C/400°F/Gas 6. Grease and flour the baking trays (sheets). Line the loaf tin (bread pan) with a layer of cling film (plastic wrap).

2 Make the whisked sponge cake mixture and transfer to the piping bag. Pipe 28–30, 7 cm/3 in fingers onto the prepared trays (sheets) and bake for 8–10 minutes until risen and springy to the touch. Remove from the oven, cool slightly and transfer to a wire rack to cool completely.

3 Line the base and sides of the prepared loaf tin (pan) with sponge fingers, trimming them as necessary to fit the tin (pan). Brush with a little rum.

4 Melt 75 g/3 oz/$^{1}/_2$ cup of the chocolate chips, the syrup, water and 30 ml/2 tbsp/2 tbsp of rum in a bowl, over a pan of gently simmering water. Cool slightly.

5 Whip the double (heavy) cream until it holds its shape and stir in the chocolate mixture and toasted coconut. Pour into the tin (pan), tap the bottom gently to clear any air bubbles, and place the remaining sponge fingers over the top. Brush over the remaining rum. Cover with cling film (plastic wrap) and freeze for several hours, until firm.

6 Melt the remaining chocolate, butter and cream in a bowl, over a pan of gently simmering water. Remove from the heat and cool slightly.

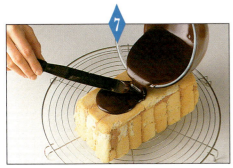

7 Remove cake from the freezer and unmould onto a wire rack. Pour over the icing in one smooth motion, to coat the top and sides of the cake. Use a palette knife (spatula) to smooth the sides, if necessary. Refrigerate for 10–15 minutes, until chocolate icing is set. (Alternatively, the cake can be returned to the freezer at this time.)

8 To make the decorations, melt the white chocolate chips and transfer to the greaseproof (wax) paper piping bag. Snip the end off the bag and drizzle a zig-zag pattern over the chocolate icing. Allow the cake to soften in the refrigerator for a further 20–30 minutes, or until a knife will cut through easily.

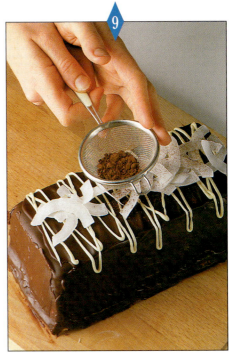

9 Just before serving, decorate the top with a little desiccated (shredded) coconut or coconut curls, and dust lightly with cocoa powder.

MOCHA BRAZIL LAYER TORTE

This wonderfully rich gateau is a layered cake or torte, consisting of both sponge cake and meringue discs. The combination of mocha and brazil nuts is particularly successful and the simple decorations give an elegant finish to this classic European cake.

INGREDIENTS

Serves 12
- 3 egg whites
- 225 g/8 oz/1 cup caster (superfine) sugar
- 45 ml/3 tbsp/3 tbsp coffee essence (extract)
- 75 g/3 oz/¾ cup brazil nuts, toasted and finely ground
- 275 g/10 oz/1¾ cups plain (semisweet) chocolate chips
- 4 eggs
- 125 g/4 oz/1 cup plain (all-purpose) flour
- 5 ml/1 tsp/1 tsp baking powder
- 30 ml/2 tbsp/2 tbsp water
- 575 ml/1 pt/2½ cups double (heavy) cream

DECORATION

- 50 g/2 oz/⅓ cup plain (semisweet) chocolate chips
- 12 chocolate-coated coffee beans

MATERIALS AND EQUIPMENT

- baking parchment
- 1 large baking tray (sheet)
- 20 cm/8 in round springform tin (pan)
- piping bag fitted with a 1 cm/½ in plain nozzle
- turntable
- large star nozzle

STORING

Best eaten the day of making. The chocolate triangles can be made in advance and stored in an airtight container, in a cool place, for up to one week.

FREEZING

Recommended at the end of step 9. Open-freeze until very firm, wrap and re-freeze. Defrost at room temperature, and continue.

1 Preheat the oven to 150°C/300°F/Gas 2. Draw 2 × 20 cm/8 in circles onto a large sheet of baking parchment. Place on a baking tray. Grease, base-line and flour the springform tin (pan).

2 Whisk the egg whites until stiff and gradually whisk in half the sugar, 15 g/½ oz/1 tbsp at a time, until thick and glossy. Fold in 15 ml/½ fl oz/1 tbsp coffee essence (extract) and nuts until evenly incorporated and transfer to the piping bag fitted with the plain nozzle. Starting in the centre, pipe circles of mixture onto the prepared paper.

3 Bake for 1¾–2 hours, until crisp and golden. Remove from the oven and transfer to a wire rack to cool completely. Peel away the baking parchment. Increase the oven temperature to 180°C/350°F/Gas 4.

4 To prepare the chocolate decorations, melt the 50 g/2 oz/⅓ cup plain (semisweet) chocolate chips and pour over a piece of baking parchment, spreading out to a very thin layer with a palette knife (spatula) and leave to set.

5 Melt 125 g/4 oz/¾ cup of the chocolate chips and cool slightly. Whisk the eggs and remaining sugar together in a bowl over a pan of gently simmering water, until very pale and thick and the whisk leaves a trail through the mixure. Remove from the heat, continue beating until cool and carefully stir in the melted chocolate. Sift the flour and baking powder together and fold into the whisked mixture, until incorporated. Transfer to the prepared tin (pan) and bake for 40–45 minutes, until risen and springy to the touch.

6 Remove from the oven, cool in the tin for 10 minutes and transfer to a wire rack to cool completely.

7 To make the icing, melt the remaining chocolate chips, coffee essence (extract) and the water together in a bowl over a pan of gently simmering water, and remove from the heat. Whip the cream until it holds its shape and stir into the mocha mixture, until combined.

8 Place the cooled cake onto the turntable and cut into 3 equal layers. Trim the meringue discs to the same size and assemble the gateau with a layer of sponge, a little of the icing and a meringue disc, finishing with a layer of sponge.

9 Reserve a little of the remaining icing for decoration; use the rest to completely coat the cake, forming a swirling pattern over the top.

10 Carefully peel away the paper from the set chocolate and cut out 12 triangles, 10 cm/4 in long and 2.5 cm/1 in wide at the top.

11 Transfer the reserved icing to a piping bag fitted with the star nozzle, and pipe 24 small rosettes around the top edge of the cake. Top alternately with the coffee beans and chocolate triangles.

BAKED CHEESE-CAKE WITH FRESH FRUITS

A rich, creamy, American-style cheesecake, baked on a sweet biscuit (graham cracker) base. It is topped with a selection of exotic fresh fruit; vary the decoration to suit the season.

INGREDIENTS

Serves 12
- 175 g/6 oz/1⅓ cups digestive biscuits or graham crackers, crushed
- 50 g/2 oz/¼ cup unsalted butter, melted
- 450 g/1 lb/1 lb curd cheese (farmer's-style cottage cheese)
- 150 ml/¼ pt/⅔ cup sour cream
- 125 g/4 oz/½ cup caster (superfine) sugar
- 3 eggs, separated
- grated rind 1 lemon
- 30 ml/2 tbsp/2 tbsp Marsala
- 2.5 ml/½ tsp/½ tsp almond essence (extract)
- 50 g/2 oz/½ cup ground almonds
- 50 g/2 oz/⅓ cup sultanas (golden raisins)

DECORATION

- 450 g/1 lb/1 lb prepared mixed fruits (figs, cherries, peaches, strawberries, hulled, halved and stoned, as necessary)

MATERIALS AND EQUIPMENT

- baking parchment
- 25 cm/10 in round springform tin (pan)

STORING

Refrigerate in an airtight container for up to three days.

FREEZING

Recommended. Open-freeze until very firm, before wrapping.

1 Preheat oven to 180°C/350°F/Gas 4. Grease and line the sides of the tin (pan).

2 Combine the biscuits (graham crackers) with the butter until well combined and press into the base of the prepared tin (pan). Smooth the surface with a metal spoon and chill for 20 minutes.

3 Meanwhile prepare the cake mixture. Beat the cheese, cream, sugar, egg yolks, lemon rind, Marsala and almond essence (extract) together until smooth and creamy.

4 Whisk the egg whites until stiff and fold into the creamed mixture with the remaining ingredients until evenly combined. Pour over the chilled biscuit (or cracker) base and bake for 45 minutes, until risen and just set in the centre.

5 Remove from the oven and leave in the tin (pan) in a warm, draught-free place, until completely cold. Carefully remove the tin (pan) and peel away the lining paper.

6 Chill the cheesecake for at least an hour before decorating with the prepared fruits, just before serving.

CHILLED GRAPE CHEESECAKE

An attractive and unusual topping decorates this classic chilled cheesecake. Use green grapes and white-grape juice if wished, for an equally attractive cheesecake.

INGREDIENTS

Serves 12
- 175 g/6 oz/1⅓ cups gingernuts (ginger cookies), crushed
- 50 g/2 oz/¼ cup unsalted butter, melted
- 350 g/12 oz/¾ lb cream cheese
- 200 g/7 oz/1 scant cup fromage frais
- 90 ml/6 tbsp/6 tbsp clear honey
- 2 eggs, separated
- 5 ml/1 tsp/1 tsp grated lemon rind
- 15 ml/1 tbsp/1 tbsp lemon juice
- 60 ml/4 tbsp/4 tbsp Muscat de Beaume de Venise (or other sweet white dessert wine)
- 15 ml/1 tbsp/1 tbsp powdered gelatine

- 125 g/4 oz/¼ lb red or green seedless grapes, halved
- small piece angelica
- 30 ml/2 tbsp/2 tbsp Muscat de Beaume de Venise (or other sweet white dessert wine)
- 7.5 g/1½ tsp/1½ tsp powdered gelatine
- 300 ml/½ pt/1¼ cups red or white grape juice

MATERIALS AND EQUIPMENT

- baking parchment
- 23 cm/9 in round springform tin (pan)
- fine paintbrush

STORING

Place in an airtight container and refrigerate for up to three days.

FREEZING

Recommended. Open-freeze until solid before wrapping.

1 Grease and line the sides of the tin (pan).

2 Combine the gingernuts (ginger cookies) with the butter until well combined. Press into the base of the prepared tin (pan). Smooth the surface with a metal spoon and chill for 20 minutes.

3 To prepare the cake mixture, beat the cheese, fromage frais, honey, egg yolks, lemon rind and juice, until smooth and creamy.

4 Heat the first quantity of wine and gelatine together in a small pan, over a low heat, until gelatine dissolves. Remove from the heat, stir in a little of the creamed mixture, and pour back into the remaining creamed mixture until combined.

5 Whisk the egg whites until stiff and fold into the creamed mixture, until evenly incorporated. Pour over the chilled biscuit (cookie) base and return to the refrigerator.

6 When the cheesecake is just setting, remove from the refrigerator and arrange the grapes over the top, in the shape of a bunch of grapes, and make a stalk from the angelica. Chill until completely set.

7 Heat the second quantity of wine and gelatine together as before, until dissolved. Pour in the grape juice and leave to go cold.

8 Using a small paintbrush, carefully dampen the edges of the lined tin (pan), directly above the set cheesecake.

9 Carefully pour over the cooled grape juice to cover the grapes and return to the refrigerator, until set.

10 Just before serving, remove the cheesecake from the refrigerator, remove the tin (pan) and carefully peel away the lining paper using a palette knife (spatula) to help.

131

COFFEE, PEACH AND ALMOND DAQUOISE

This is a traditional meringue gateau. The meringue mixture is piped into rounds, baked, and layered with a classic buttercream and peach filling. The French name for this classic style of gateau, 'succes', is then piped over the top of the finished cake.

INGREDIENTS

Serves 12
- 5 eggs, separated
- 425 g/15 oz/scant 2 cups caster (superfine) sugar
- 15 g/¹/₂ oz/1 tbsp cornflour (cornstarch)
- 175 g/6 oz/1¹/₂ cups ground almonds, toasted
- 125 ml/4¹/₂ fl oz/good ¹/₂ cup milk
- 275 g/10 oz/1¹/₄ cups unsalted butter, diced (room temperature)
- 45–60 ml/3–4 tbsp/3–4 tbsp coffee essence (extract)
- 2 × 400 g/14 oz cans peach halves in juice, drained

DECORATION

- 60 g/2¹/₂ oz/1¹/₂ cups flaked almonds, toasted
- icing (confectioners) sugar
- 3 reserved peach halves
- a few mint leaves (optional)

STORING

This cake will keep well in an airtight container, in a cool place, for several days.

MATERIALS AND EQUIPMENT

- baking parchment
- 3 baking trays (sheets)
- piping bag fitted with a 1 cm/¹/₂ in plain nozzle
- turntable
- small star nozzle

FREEZING

Recommended. Open-freeze at the end of step 6.

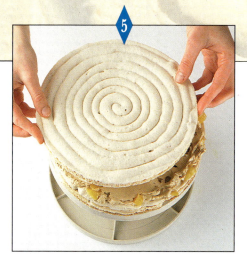

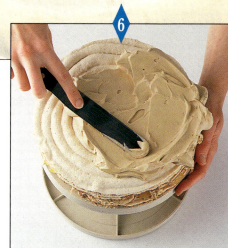

1 Preheat the oven to 150°C/300°F/Gas 2. Draw 3 × 23 cm/9 in circles onto 3 sheets baking parchment. Place on separate baking trays (sheets).

2 Whisk the egg whites until stiff and gradually whisk in 275 g/10 oz/1¹/₄ cups of the sugar, a little at a time, until thick and glossy. Fold in the cornflour (cornstarch) and almonds until evenly incorporated. Transfer the mixture to the piping bag fitted with the plain nozzle.

3 Starting in the centre of the prepared circles, pipe the mixture in a continuous tight coil, finishing just within the lines. Bake for 1³/₄–2 hours until lightly golden and dried out. Remove from the oven and transfer to a wire rack to cool completely. Peel away the baking parchment.

4 Using the 5 egg yolks, the remaining 150 g/5 oz/²/₃ cup caster (superfine) sugar, the milk and butter, make the crème au beurre icing. See Hazelnut Praline and Apricot Genoese steps 5 and 6 for the method. Substitute the coffee essence (extract) for the syrup and brandy.

5 Trim the meringue discs to 23 cm/9 in circles, and crush the trimmings. Reserve 3 peach halves, chop the rest and fold into half the icing with the crushed meringue. Use this to sandwich together the three meringue discs.

6 Reserve a little icing for decoration. Place the cake onto the turntable and use the remaining icing to coat the top and sides of the cake. Smooth over the sides with a palette knife (spatula).

7 Cover the top of the cake with the toasted almond flakes and dust liberally with icing (confectioners) sugar.

8 *Cut the reserved peaches into thin slices and use to decorate the outer edges of the cake, and garnish with a mint leaf. Place the reserved icing in a piping bag fitted with the star nozzle and use to pipe the word 'succes' in the centre of the cake.*

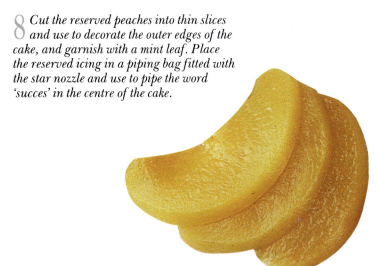

CHOCOLATE AND FRESH CHERRY GATEAU

The addition of spices to this attractive gateau adds an exotic kick. A compote of fresh cherries fills the hollowed-out centre, and the cake is coated with a rich chocolate icing. With the dipped cherries and chocolate-coated leaves, this is a cake for a special occasion.

INGREDIENTS

Serves 8
- 125 g/4 oz/½ cup butter
- 150 g/5 oz/⅔ cup caster (superfine) sugar
- 3 eggs, lightly beaten
- 175 g/6 oz/1 cup plain (semisweet) chocolate chips, melted
- 60 ml/4 tbsp/4 tbsp Kirsch
- 150 g/5 oz/1¼ cups self-raising flour
- 5 ml/1 tsp/1 tsp ground cinnamon
- 2.5 ml/½ tsp/½ tsp ground cloves
- 350 g/12 oz/¾ lb fresh cherries, stoned and halved
- 45 ml/3 tbsp/3 tbsp Morello cherry jam
- 5 ml/1 tsp/1 tsp lemon juice

FROSTING

- 125 g/4 oz/¾ cup plain (semisweet) chocolate chips
- 50 g/2 oz/¼ cup unsalted butter
- 60 ml/4 tbsp/4 tbsp double (heavy) cream

DECORATION

- 75 g/3 oz/½ cup white chocolate chips
- 14–18 fresh cherries
- a few rose leaves, washed and dried

MATERIALS AND EQUIPMENT

- greaseproof (wax) paper
- 20 cm/8 in springform tin (pan)
- 15 cm/6 in saucer
- baking parchment
- fine paintbrush

STORING

Place in an airtight container and consume within two days of making.

FREEZING

Recommended at the end of stage 8. Open-freeze until very firm before wrapping. Defrost at room temperature, and decorate.

1 Preheat oven to 170°C/325°F/Gas 3. Grease, base-line and flour the tin (pan)

2 Cream the butter and 125 g/4 oz/½ cup of sugar together, until pale and light. Gradually beat in the eggs, a little at a time, until incorporated. Stir in the melted chocolate and 30 ml/2 tbsp/2 tbsp of the Kirsch.

3 Sift the flour and spices together and fold into the creamed mixture. Transfer to the prepared tin (pan), smooth the surface and bake for 55–60 minutes or until a skewer, inserted in the centre, comes out clean. Remove from the oven, cool in the tin (pan) for 10 minutes, and transfer to a wire rack to cool.

4 Meanwhile, prepare the filling. Place the halved cherries, remaining Kirsch and sugar in a small pan. Heat gently to dissolve sugar, bring to the boil, cover and simmer for 10 minutes. Remove the lid and simmer for a further 10 minutes, until mixture is thick and syrupy. Leave to cool.

5 Cut the cake in half. Using the saucer as a template, cut out a circle, about 1 cm/½ in deep, from the centre of the bottom half. Crumble into the cherry syrup mixture, stirring well, to form a thick paste.

6 Use to fill the hollowed section of cake, smoothing over the surface. Cover with the top half of cake.

7 Heat the jam and lemon juice and boil for 1 minute. Strain through a fine sieve (strainer) and brush all over the cake.

8 To make the frosting, heat the chocolate, butter and cream in a small pan, until melted. Cool slightly, until the mixture starts to thicken. In one fluid motion, pour over the glazed cake, to completely cover the top and sides. Smooth over the sides with a palette knife (spatula), if necessary. Leave to set in a cool place.

9 *Melt the white chocolate chips in a small bowl over a pan of gently simmering water. Dip each cherry halfway into the white chocolate, so that it is half-white and half-red, and leave to set on baking parchment. Using the paintbrush, coat the underside of the rose leaves with a thick layer of the remaining chocolate. Leave to set on baking parchment.*

10 *When set, carefully peel away the leaves from the chocolate coating. Decorate the top of the cake with an arrangement of cherries and leaves.*

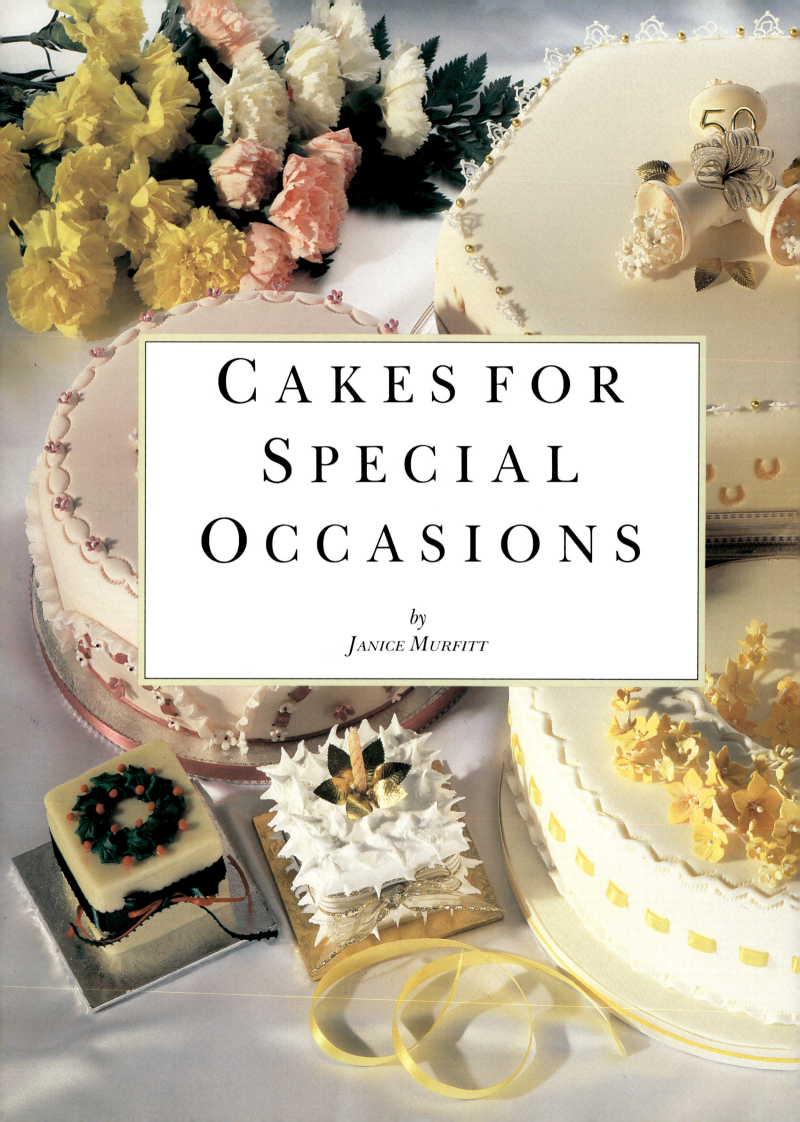

CAKES FOR
SPECIAL
OCCASIONS

by
JANICE MURFITT

INTRODUCTION

Cakes made for special occasions and special people warrant a lot of care and attention to detail. So take some time to plan. How many people are you hoping to serve? Is the cake for children or adults, a man or a woman? The answers to these questions will determine the choice of base (fruit or sponge), the cake size and shape, the choice of icing and the colour scheme.

Here you will find a wealth of ideas for cakes for all occasions, using many different decorating techniques, icings and colour schemes. There is a classic royal-iced

and an American-style butter-iced wedding cake, and a lovely fresh summer wedding cake made of tiered meringue rings, cream and soft fruits; there is a range of cakes for seasonal festivities, including fun miniature Christmas gift cakes and a traditional Easter simnel cake; and there are birthday, anniversary, christening and retirement cakes in all shapes and designs to suit everyone. Follow the step-by-step guides, but use your own ideas too and change the colours, decorations and ribbon trims, as wished, to create your own individual designs tailored to your particular special occasions.

CHOCOLATE LEAF WEDDING CAKE

Lovers of chocolate – this cake has been designed for you: a moist chocolate Madeira cake is covered with marzipan and chocolate-flavoured sugarpaste (fondant). The decorations consist of pretty coral-coloured sugar flowers and assorted chocolate leaves.

INGREDIENTS

Serves 130
- 30 × 25 cm/12 × 10 in oval, deep, chocolate-flavoured Madeira cake
- 25 × 20 cm/10 × 8 in oval, deep, chocolate-flavoured Madeira cake
- 120 ml/4 fl oz/½ cup apricot glaze
- 2.75 kg/6 lb/6 lb homemade or commercial white marzipan
- 3.25 kg/7 lb/7 lb sugarpaste (fondant)
- 450 g/1 lb/4 cups cocoa powder
- 350 g/12 oz/¾ lb petal paste
- yellow and pink food colouring
- 175 g/6 oz/1 cup plain chocolate chips, melted
- 125 g/4 oz/¾ cup white chocolate chips, melted
- 125 g/4 oz/¾ cup milk chocolate chips, melted
- 30 ml/2 tbsp/2 tbsp royal icing

DECORATION

- 3 m/3 yd × 2.5 cm/1 in wide peach ribbon
- 4 m/4 yd × 1 cm/½ in wide peach ribbon
- 5 m/5 yd × 5 mm/¼ in wide coral ribbon
- 1 m/1 yd × 5 mm/¼ in wide light coral ribbon

MATERIALS AND EQUIPMENT

- 35 × 30 cm/14 × 12 in oval silver cakeboard
- 25 × 20 cm/10 × 8 in thin oval silver cakeboard
- flower cutter
- blossom plunger cutter
- 30 peach pearl stamens
- flower tape and wire
- greaseproof (wax) paper piping bag
- No. 1 plain writing nozzle

TO MAKE THE CAKE

For a 30 × 25 cm/12 × 10 in and a 25 × 20 cm/10 × 8 oval cake, use quantities of cake mix suitable for a 30 cm/12 in and a 25 cm/10 in round cake. Bake the cakes one at a time and store for up to one week before icing.

1 To level the cakes, cut a slice off the top. Invert the cakes on to their cakeboards and brush with apricot glaze. Cover each cake with marzipan.

2 Divide the sugarpaste (fondant) into three pieces. Knead 125 g/4 oz/½ cup cocoa powder into each piece until the sugarpaste is evenly-coloured, then knead all the pieces together. Cover the larger cake using half the sugarpaste (fondant), so there is plenty of icing to manipulate, dusting the surface with plenty of cocoa powder and using cocoa powder on your hands to smooth the surface. Repeat to cover the smaller cake and the large cakeboard. Store in boxes in a warm, dry place for up to one week.

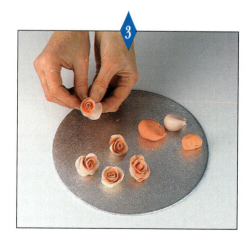

3 To make the sugar flowers, divide the petal paste into three pieces. Using the yellow and pink food colourings, tint one piece pale, one piece medium and one piece dark coral. Make five roses, starting with dark centres and working out to pale petals.

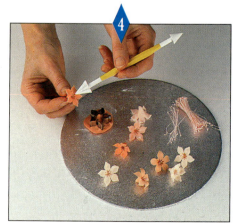

4 Make 25 cut-out flowers of varying shades of coral paste and add stamens.

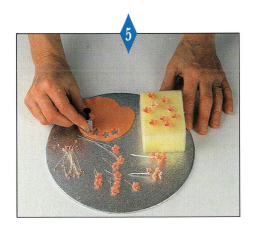

5 Make 40 plunger blossom flower sprays with the remaining stamens, wire and tape. Leave all the flowers to dry overnight and store in boxes in a warm, dry place. Using a piece of petal paste, press 30 blossom sprays in position to make an arrangement for the top.

6 To make the chocolate leaves, collect a variety of different-shaped leaves (rose, bay, camelia, fruit) and coat 30 with plain chocolate, 15 with white chocolate and 15 with milk chocolate. Store in a cool place until required, then peel off the leaves and keep the chocolate leaves separate on kitchen paper.

7 The day before the wedding, place the royal icing in a greaseproof (wax) paper piping bag fitted with a No. 1 plain writing nozzle. Measure and fit the wide peach ribbon around the larger cakeboard, securing it at the back with a pin. Fit the 1 cm/½ in wide peach ribbon around the base of the larger cake. Fix the fine coral ribbon over the top, and secure with a bead of royal icing. Arrange the cut-out flowers, roses and assorted chocolate leaves around the base of the cake, securing with royal icing.

8 Measure and fit the remaining 1 cm/½ in wide ribbon around the base of the small cake with the coral ribbons over the top, securing with royal icing. Carefully place the cake in position on top of the larger cake so that the backs of the cakes are level.

9 Arrange the sprays of blossom, cut-out flowers and chocolate leaves at intervals around the base of the small cake on the edge of the larger cake. Secure all decorations with royal icing. Carefully remove the top cake. Place the sugar flower arrangement onto the top of the cake and arrange the chocolate leaves so they come over the edge. Secure each leaf with royal icing. Using the remaining fine ribbon and fine wire, make some ribbon loops with tails. Press these into the arrangement. Re-box the cakes until the next day, then re-assemble just before the reception.

CLASSIC WEDDING CAKE

The sharp, classical lines of this royal-iced wedding cake give it a very regal appearance. This traditional all-white cake has just a hint of peach in the ribbon decoration.

INGREDIENTS	DECORATION	MATERIALS AND EQUIPMENT
Serves 100	• 4 m/4 yd × 2.5 cm/1 in wide white ribbon	• 35 cm/14 in square silver cakeboard
• 30 cm/12 in square rich fruit cake	• 2 m/2 yd × 2 cm/¾ in wide peach ribbon	• a sheet of perspex or glass
• 75 ml/5 tbsp/5 tbsp apricot glaze	• 1 m/1 yd × 5 mm/¼ in wide peach ribbon	• run-out silk or greaseproof (wax) paper
• 1.8 kg/4 lb/4 lb homemade or commercial white marzipan	• fresh 'paper white' flowers	• greaseproof (wax) paper piping bags
• 1.8 kg/4 lb/6 cups royal icing (for covering)		• No. 3 plain writing nozzle and medium star nozzle
• 900 g/2 lb/3 cups royal icing made with double-strength egg albumen (for run-outs)		• tiny vase

1 Brush the fruit cake with apricot glaze and cover with marzipan. Place the cake on the cakeboard.

2 Make the royal icing for covering the cake. Flat ice the top and sides of the cake with three or four smooth layers of royal icing. Leave the cake to dry overnight, then ice the cakeboard. Place in a cake box and store in a warm, dry place. Reserve the remaining royal icing for decoration.

3 Make up the royal icing for the run-outs, unless you have plenty left over from the flat icing, in which case add double-strength egg albumen to dilute it. Trace over the templates provided, cover with a piece of perspex or glass, and cover with run-out silk or greaseproof (wax) paper. Tape down to secure. As each run-out is piped and filled in, move the perspex or glass along to reveal the template, and repeat the procedure.

4 Make six corner pieces and six side pieces, allowing for breakage. Pipe in the details when the pieces are dry.

5 Measure and fit the white ribbon around the cakeboard and sides of the cake, securing with a bead of royal icing. Fit the wide peach ribbon over the top of each white band, securing with icing. Make some loops and bows from thin peach ribbon for the top arrangement.

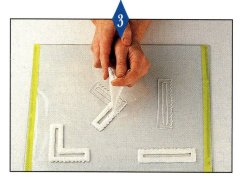

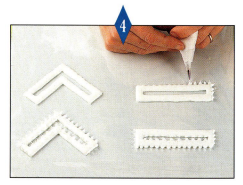

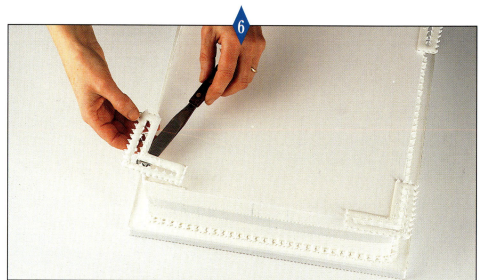

6 Carefully release the run-out pieces and half-fill a greaseproof (wax) paper piping bag fitted with a No. 3 plain writing nozzle with the reserved royal icing. Pipe a line of icing at one corner. Carefully place a corner run-out in position; press very gently to make sure the run-out is secure. Repeat to attach all the corner pieces and the side pieces.

7 Pipe a bead edging in between the run-outs on the top edge of the cake. Using a medium-sized star nozzle, pipe a star edging around the base of the cake. Make a pretty arrangement of fresh flowers in a tiny vase to go on top of the cake, and decorate with ribbons and bows.

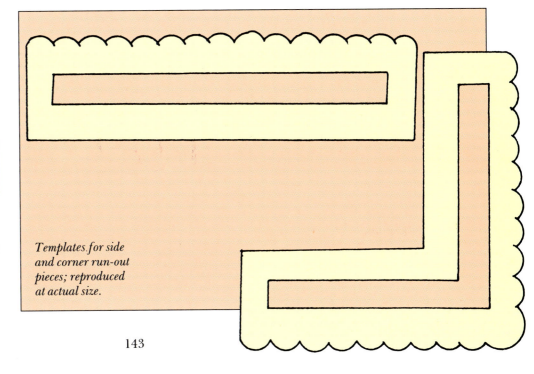

Templates for side and corner run-out pieces; reproduced at actual size.

MIDSUMMER WEDDING CAKE

This lovely meringue wedding cake is fresh and light, and is ideal for a summer wedding when all the soft fruits are in abundance.

INGREDIENTS

Serves 40
- *8 egg whites*
- *5 ml/1 tsp/1 tsp cream of tartar*
- *500 g/1 lb 2 oz/2¼ cups caster (superfine) sugar*
- *550 ml/1 pt/2½ cups double (heavy) cream*
- *300 ml/½ pt/1¼ cups whipping cream*
- *350 g/12 oz/2 cups redcurrants*
- *350 g/12 oz/2 cups white currants*
- *350 g/12 oz/2 cups raspberries*
- *350 g/12 oz/2 cups fraises des bois or tiny strawberries*
- *350 g/12 oz/2 cups blueberries*
- *30 ml/2 tbsp/2 tbsp Kirsch*

DECORATION

- *8 tiny pink rosebuds*
- *small fresh strawberry leaves*
- *1½ m/1½ yd × 2 cm/¾ in wide white ribbon*
- *1½ m/1½ yd × 1 cm/½ in wide dark pink ribbon*
- *1½ m/1½ yd × 5 mm/¼ in wide plain dark pink ribbon*
- *1½ m/1½ yd × 5 mm/¼ in wide plain light pink ribbon*

MATERIALS AND EQUIPMENT

- *30 cm/12 in round silver cakeboard*
- *4 large baking sheets*
- *baking parchment*
- *nylon piping bags*
- *1 cm/½ in plain and small star gateau nozzles*

1 *Preheat the oven to the lowest setting 110°C/220°F/Gas ¼. Line two large baking sheets with non-stick baking parchment. Draw a 25 cm/10 in circle on one sheet and 18 cm/7 in and 15 cm/6 in circles on the remaining sheet of paper. Invert the sheets of paper.*

2 *To make the meringue, whisk 4 egg whites and 2.5 ml/½ tsp/½ tsp cream of tartar in a large clean bowl until stiff. Very gradually whisk in 250 g/9 oz/1 good cup of caster (superfine) sugar, whisking really well between each addition, until the meringue stands up in stiff peaks. Place the meringue in a large nylon piping bag fitted with a 1 cm/½ in plain gateau nozzle.*

3 *Pipe a continuous circle of meringue following the marked lines on each circle. Then pipe a coil from the centre to the edge to fill in each round. Pipe leftover meringue into 5 small rounds in between the circles. Bake in the oven for 2–3 hours until the meringue is dry and the paper peels away easily from the base.*

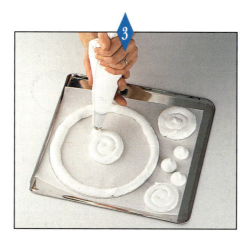

4 *Meanwhile line two more baking sheets with baking parchment and draw a 23 cm/9 in, a 10 cm/4 in and a 5 cm/2 in circle onto one sheet of paper and a 20 cm/8 in, a 13 cm/5 in and a 7.5 cm/3 in circle on the remaining sheet of paper. Invert the two papers.*

5 *Using the remaining egg whites, cream of tartar and sugar, make the meringue circles following the above instructions. When all the meringues are cold, cut around the paper to separate them. Store them in airtight containers on the paper in a warm, dry place until required.*

6 *Measure and fit the white and the wide pink ribbons around the edge of the cakeboard, securing with a pin.*

7 *Place the creams into a bowl and whip until just thick; reserve one-third for piping. Whisk the remaining cream until slightly thicker.*

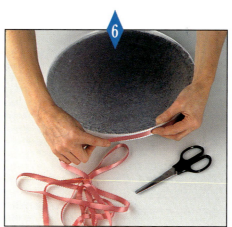

8 *Reserve several stems of red and white currants for decoration and remove the stems and hulls from the remaining fruits. Mix all the fruits together in a large bowl and sprinkle with Kirsch. Add the fruit to the cream and fold in until well blended. Place one-third of the reserved cream in a nylon piping bag fitted with a small star gateau nozzle.*

9 *Place the largest circle of meringue on the cakeboard and spread evenly with the cream and fruit mixture to give about a 2 cm/3/4 in deep layer. Top with the next size of meringue round and spread with more of the filling. Cover with the next meringue layer and repeat to use all the layers.*

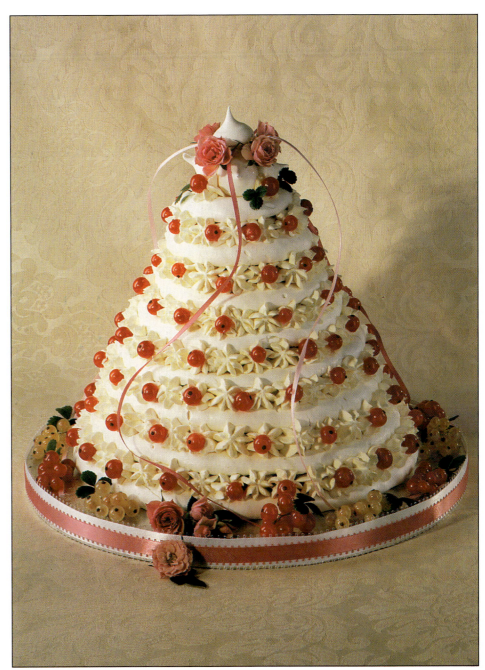

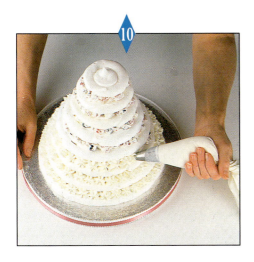

10 *Pipe small stars of cream in between the layers to seal in the filling and to decorate the joins. Pipe a swirl of cream on the top and arrange 4 tiny meringue rounds in a circle and one on the top.*

11 *Press individual redcurrants or other fruits if you prefer into alternate cream stars and 4 tiny rosebuds around the top. Measure and fit 3 dark and 3 light ribbon lengths from the top of the cake to the board. Decorate the board with the reserved currants, leaves and rosebuds. Keep in a cold place for up to 4 hours. Serve from the top, removing the rounds as required.*

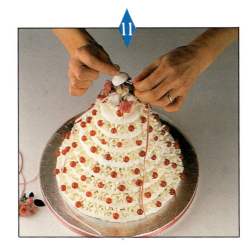

BASKET-WEAVE WEDDING CAKE

This wonderful wedding cake can be made in any flavour. The butter icing design is really very easy and looks so special.

INGREDIENTS

Serves 150
- 1 × 25 cm/10 in, 1 × 20 cm/8 in and 1 × 15 cm/6 in square Madeira cakes
- 2.75 kg/6 lb/6 lb butter icing

DECORATION

- 1½ m/1½ yd × 2.5 cm/1 in wide pale lilac ribbon
- 2½ m/2½ yd × 5 mm/¼ in wide deep lilac ribbon
- 30 fresh lilac-coloured freesias or simple flowers

MATERIALS AND EQUIPMENT

- 30 cm/12 in square silver cakeboard
- 20 cm/8 in thin silver cakeboard
- 15 cm/6 in thin silver cakeboard
- 12 greaseproof (wax) piping bags
- basket-weave and No. 4 plain writing nozzles

1 Make and bake the cakes one at a time, allow to cool, wrap in foil and store in a tin for up to one week before decorating.

2 If the cake tops have domed, cut a slice off to level the cakes, then invert the cakes onto their appropriate cakeboards. (It is quite a good idea to buy two larger thin cakeboards to sit the smaller cakes on while they are being decorated, to keep the edges neat. Allow an extra 2.5–5 cm/1–2 in.)

3 Make the butter icing in three batches. A food processor is worth using to obtain a very light texture and well mixed icing.

4 Spread each cake evenly with butter icing, dipping the palette knife (metal spatula) in hot water for easy spreading. Use a side scraper to smooth the sides and the palette knife to smooth the top. Leave in a cool place to set for at least one hour.

5 Make the remaining quantities of butter icing and make up at least 12 greaseproof (wax) paper piping bags. Fit a basket-weave nozzle in one bag and a No. 4 plain writing nozzle in a second greaseproof (wax) paper piping bag. Fill each with icing and fold down the tops.

6 Start piping the basket-weave design by piping a line of icing from the plain nozzle onto the corner of the large cake, from the base of the cake to the top. Using the basket-weave nozzle, pipe three horizontal lines across the vertical line, starting at the top of the cake and equally spacing the lines apart. Pipe another vertical line of icing on the edge of the

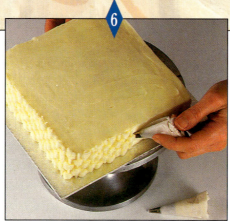

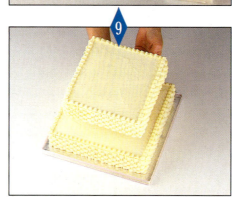

horizontal lines, then pipe three horizontal lines across this between the spaces formed by the previous horizontal lines to form a basket-weave. Pipe all around the side of the cake and neaten the top edge with a shell border, using the basket-weave nozzle. Repeat for the second cake.

7 To decorate the small cake with piping, pipe the top first by starting on the edge with one straight plain line, then pipe across with the basket-weave nozzle, spacing the lines equally apart, about the width of the nozzle. When the top is complete, carry on working the design around the sides, making sure the top and side designs meet. Leave all the cakes overnight in a cold place to set before assembling the cake.

8 Measure and fit the wide and narrow lilac ribbons around the board, securing with a pin. Use the remaining narrow ribbon to tie eight small bows with long tails. Select the flowers and trim off the stems.

9 To assemble the cake, carefully place the middle cake in position on the base cake, keeping it on the thin cakeboard the same size as the cake. Use a palette knife at the back of the cake to position it. Place the top cake on its board in position, using the palette knife at the back.

10 Position the bows on the top and base corners of the cakes. Place the flowers on each side of each cake at the corners of the board and a tiny arrangement on the top. This cake will keep all day in a cool place; if the weather is warm, position the flowers at the last minute to prevent wilting.

CHAMPAGNE WEDDING CAKE

An unusual combination of colours – champagne sugarpaste (fondant) and coffee-coloured ribbons and decorations – gives the cake an elegant, delicate appearance.

INGREDIENTS

Serves 120

- 1 × 25 cm/10 in, 1 × 20 cm/8 in and 1 × 15 cm/6 in round rich fruit cakes
- 120 ml/4 fl oz/½ cup apricot glaze
- 2.5 kg/5½ lb/5½ lb homemade or commercial white marzipan
- 3.25 kg/7 lb/7 lb champagne-coloured sugarpaste (fondant)
- 450 g/1 lb/1½ cups royal icing
- 575 g/1¼ lb/1¼ lb petal paste
- old gold and dark brown food colourings

DECORATION

- 5 m/5 yd × 2 cm/¾ in wide champagne ribbon
- 2 m/2 yd × 5 mm/¼ in wide champagne ribbon
- 4 m/4 yd × 1 cm/½ in wide coffee ribbon
- 2 m/2 yd × 5 mm/¼ in wide coffee ribbon
- 6 champagne-coloured cake pillars
- fresh cream or white flowers

MATERIALS AND EQUIPMENT

- 30 cm/12 in, 25 cm/10 in and 20 cm/8 in round silver cakeboards
- greaseproof (wax) paper piping bags
- No. 0 and 1 plain writing nozzles
- greaseproof (wax) paper
- crimping tool
- 5 acrylic cake skewers

1 Place each cake on its cakeboard and brush with apricot glaze. Cover each cake with marzipan.

2 Reserving 900 g/2 lb/2 lb of sugarpaste (fondant) for the cakeboards, use the remainder to smoothly cover each cake, starting with the largest cake. Leave in boxes overnight to dry in a warm, dry place. Knead all the sugarpaste (fondant) and trimmings together and cover the cakeboards. Replace the cakes on their boards and return to their boxes.

3 Make up the royal icing and the petal paste. Tint both icings with old gold food colouring to obtain the champagne colour of the sugarpaste (fondant) icing. Using a greaseproof (wax) paper piping bag fitted with a No. 1 plain writing nozzle, half-fill with royal icing. Measure and fit the wide champagne-coloured ribbon around each cakeboard, securing it with a pin.

4 To make the templates, measure and fit a band of greaseproof (wax) paper the same height around each cake. Fold the largest strip of paper into 6 equal sections, the next size into five sections and the small band into four sections. Place a plate on the edge of each template so that it comes halfway down the width. Draw around the shape and cut out.

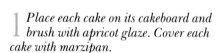

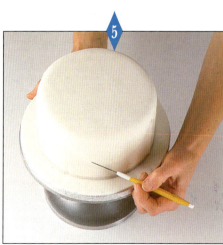

5 Fit the appropriate template around each cake and mark the scalloped shape with an icing marker or pin. Remove the template. Fit the wide coffee-coloured ribbon around the base of each cake and secure with a bead of royal icing.

6 Knead the remaining sugarpaste (fondant) into the petal paste and, using a small piece at a time, make the frills one at a time (see Making Frills, overleaf). On the large cake pipe a line of icing following the design and apply the frill, pressing gently onto the cake. Once the first 6 frills have been fitted, apply the second layer of frills. Use a crimping tool to neaten the join. Repeat on each cake.

7 Pipe the bead and scroll design following the top edge of the frills and in-between the frills at the base. Colour some of the royal icing dark brown and over-pipe the design using a No. 0 plain writing nozzle. Tie 15 coffee-coloured bows and 15 champagne-coloured bows made from the fine ribbons and attach above and below the frills, where they join. Leave the cakes in their boxes to dry.

8 Just before the wedding, place the cake pillars in position on the large and middle tier cakes. Press the skewers through the pillars into the cake. Mark the skewers level with the top of the pillars and carefully remove. Cut off the excess skewer above the pillars. Reassemble the cakes with the skewers and pillars, carefully placing each cake on top of the other. Decorate with a fresh flower arrangement on top of the cake and insert flowers in-between the pillars.

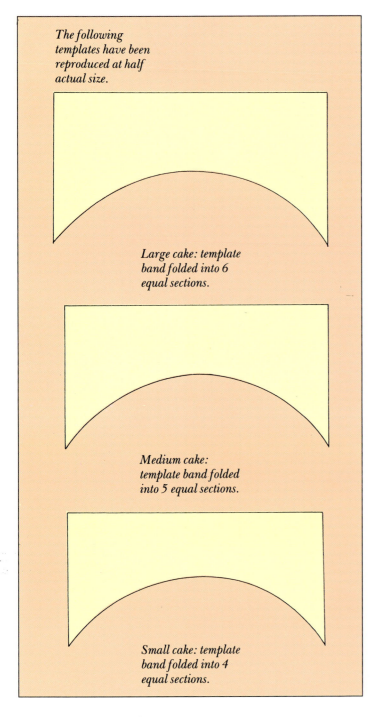

The following templates have been reproduced at half actual size.

Large cake: template band folded into 6 equal sections.

Medium cake: template band folded into 5 equal sections.

Small cake: template band folded into 4 equal sections.

MAKING FRILLS

1 *Make one frill at a time, as follows. Roll out the paste thinly and cut out a round using a 7.5 cm/3 in plain or fluted cutter. Cut out the centre of the round using a 2.5 cm/1 in plain cutter. Alternatively, use a garrette frill cutter, as here.*

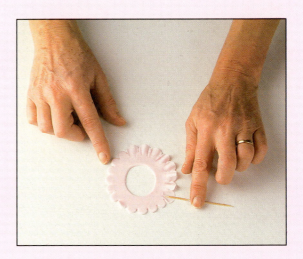

2 *Roll a cocktail stick or toothpick, sprinkled with cornflour (cornstarch), around the outer edge of the ring to frill. Cut the ring open with a sharp knife. Gently ease the frill open and attach to the cake, securing with royal icing.*

GOOD LUCK CAKE

This cake design would be ideal for a variety of occasions – a wedding, good luck, engagement or anniversary.

INGREDIENTS

Serves 70
- 25 cm/10 in horseshoe-shaped rich fruitcake (use quantities for a standard 20 cm/8 in round cake)
- 45 ml/3 tbsp/3 tbsp apricot glaze
- 900 g/2 lb/2 lb homemade or commercial white marzipan
- 1.1 kg/2½ lb/2½ lb champagne-coloured sugarpaste (fondant) icing
- 300 g/11 oz/11 oz petal paste
- yellow food colouring
- 15 ml/1 tbsp/1 tbsp royal icing

DECORATION

- 2 m/2 yd × 1 cm/½ in wide yellow ribbon
- 2 m/2 yd × 2 cm/¾ in wide white ribbon
- 2 m/2 yd × 2 mm/⅛ in wide yellow ribbon

MATERIALS AND EQUIPMENT

- 28 cm/11 in round silver cakeboard
- V-shaped crimping tool
- greaseproof (wax) paper
- scalpel
- flower cutter
- blossom plunger cutter
- yellow stamens
- flower wire and tape

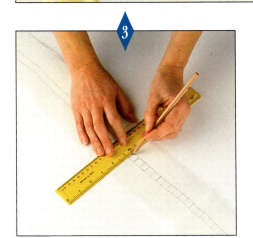

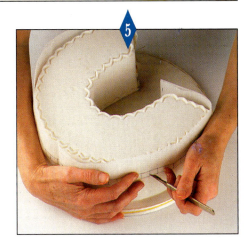

1 Bake the cake and allow to cool. Brush with apricot glaze, place on the cakeboard and cover with marzipan.

2 Using about two-thirds of the sugarpaste (fondant), cover the cake smoothly. Knead all the sugarpaste (fondant) trimmings together and use to cover the cakeboard. Carefully remove the cake, then replace it after the board has been covered. Using a V-shaped crimping tool, crimp the top edge and base of the horseshoe cake. Do not crimp inside the base of the horseshoe, as it is difficult to fit the crimper into the space.

3 Cut a band of greaseproof (wax) paper the height of the cake to fit around the outside curve and over the ends of the horseshoe as a template. Measure and mark 1 cm/½ in intervals in the centre of the template (see Template, overleaf).

4 Fit the band around the cake, securing with two pins.

5 Cut through the marked lines with a scalpel to make slits the width of the wider yellow ribbon. Remove the template.

6 Insert the lengths of ribbons into alternate pairs of slits. Measure and fit the white and narrow yellow ribbon around the cakeboard and secure with a pin. Store the cake in a cake box in a warm, dry place until required.

7 Make up the petal paste, cut into three pieces and colour pale, medium and deep yellow. Make 31 cut-out flowers, using all the icing shades, and add stamens. Make 17 sprays of plunger blossoms using the stamens, flower wire and tape. Leave to dry overnight.

8 Arrange the sugar flowers on top of the cake and secure with a little royal icing. Place a few flowers on the cakeboard in-between the horseshoe and secure with royal icing.

This represents one-quarter of the complete template band; reproduced at actual size.

SWEETHEART CAKE

This romantic cake would be ideal for St Valentine's Day, or to celebrate an engagement or anniversary. Change the icing colours to suit the particular occasion.

INGREDIENTS

Serves 70
- 20 cm/8 in heart-shaped, light fruit cake (make using quantities for standard 23 cm/9 in round cake)
- 30 ml/2 tbsp/2 tbsp apricot glaze
- 900 g/2 lb/2 lb homemade or commercial white marzipan
- 900 g/2 lb/2 lb sugarpaste (fondant) icing
- red food colouring
- 225 g/8 oz/³/₄ cup royal icing

DECORATION

- 1 m/1 yd × 2.5 cm/1 in wide red ribbon
- 1 m/1 yd × 1 cm/¹/₂ in wide looped red ribbon
- ¹/₂ m/¹/₂ yd × 5 mm/¹/₄ in wide red ribbon
- fresh red rosebuds

MATERIALS AND EQUIPMENT

- 25 cm/10 in silver heart-shaped cakeboard
- large and medium-sized heart-shaped plunger cutters
- greaseproof (wax) paper piping bag
- medium star nozzle

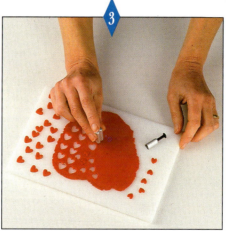

3 Colour the remaining sugarpaste (fondant) bright red with red food colouring. Roll out thinly and cut out 18 large and 21 medium-sized hearts. Leave flat to dry.

4 Measure and fit the wide ribbon around the cakeboard and secure with a pin. Fit a band of the looped ribbon around the side of the cake, securing with a bead of icing. Tie a bow with long tails and attach to the side of the cake with a bead of icing.

1 Bake the cake and allow to cool. Brush with apricot glaze, place on the cakeboard and cover with marzipan. Using about three-quarters of the sugarpaste (fondant), cover the cake smoothly.

2 Trim away the excess sugarpaste (fondant). Knead the trimmings together with the remaining sugarpaste (fondant) and use to cover the cakeboard. Return the cake to the cakeboard and leave in a cake box to dry overnight.

5 Using a greaseproof (wax) paper piping bag fitted with a medium-sized star nozzle, fill with royal icing. Pipe a row of stars around the base of the cake and attach a medium-sized heart to alternate stars. Arrange the large red hearts around the top of the cake, and pipe a star to secure each one.

6 Choose several tiny rosebuds or one large rose and tie a bow with the remaining ribbons. Place on top of the cake just before serving.

GOLDEN WEDDING CAKE

For fifty years of marriage, you must have a special cake. With a fine lace edging, embossed horseshoes, bells and flowers, this anniversary cake will be exactly right.

INGREDIENTS

Serves 80

- *23 cm/9 in hexagonal rich fruit cake (make using quantities for a standard 23 cm/9 in round cake)*
- *45 ml/3 tbsp/3 tbsp apricot glaze*
- *1.1 kg/2½ lb/2½ lb homemade or commercial white marzipan*
- *1.4 kg/3 lb/3 lb champagne-coloured sugarpaste (fondant) icing*
- *gold petal dust*
- *300 g/11 oz/11 oz petal paste*
- *old gold food colouring*
- *450 g/1 lb/1½ cups royal icing*

DECORATION

- *1½ m/1½ yd × 2.5 cm/1 in wide gold ribbon*
- *1½ m/1½ yd × 2 cm/¾ in wide gold ribbon*
- *30 gold dragées*
- *'50' gold emblem*
- *6 gold paper leaves*

MATERIALS AND EQUIPMENT

- *28 cm/11 in hexagonal gold cakeboard*
- *horseshoe-shaped embossing tool*
- *bell mould*
- *foam sponge*
- *blossom plunger cutter*
- *flower stamens*
- *wire and tape*
- *sheet of perspex or glass*
- *run-out silk or greaseproof (wax) paper*
- *greaseproof (wax) paper piping bag*
- *No. 0 plain writing nozzle*

1 Bake the cake and allow to cool. Brush with apricot glaze, place on the cakeboard and cover with marzipan. Using three-quarters of the sugarpaste (fondant), cover the cake smoothly.

2 Fit the wide ribbon around the base of the cake and secure with a pin. Measure and fit the narrower ribbon around the cakeboard, securing with a pin.

3 Using a horseshoe-shaped embossing tool and gold petal dust, emboss the sides of the cake with five horseshoes on each side and one on each corner. Place the cake in a box and leave in a warm place to dry.

4 Make up the petal paste and tint to a champagne colour using old gold food colouring. Using a well-cornfloured (cornstarched) bell mould, fill with a small piece of petal paste, pressing into the mould and rubbing the paste against the mould to make the shape. Trim the paste off at the edge and tap to release. Make three bells using two-thirds of the petal paste and leave to dry on a piece of foam sponge. Dust with gold petal dust when dry.

Reserve just a little petal paste. Using the remaining paste, blossom plunger and stamens, wire and tape, make up nine sprays of blossoms and leave to dry.

5 Make up the royal icing using double-strength egg albumen. Tint a champagne colour with old gold food colouring. Trace the lace design (see template) onto a sheet of paper and cover with a piece of perspex or glass. Cover this with a piece of run-out silk or greaseproof (wax) paper and secure with tape. Using a greaseproof (wax) paper piping bag fitted with a No. 0 plain writing nozzle, half-fill with icing. Follow the lace shapes, piping with fine threads of icing. Move the lace designs and continue to make 40 pieces, allowing for breakages.

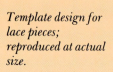

Template design for lace pieces; reproduced at actual size.

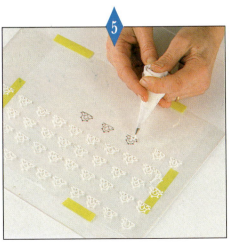

6 Attach the lace pieces to the top edge of the cake with a few beads of icing. Secure gold dragées in between, using icing to fix on. Press a small piece of petal paste into each bell shape and secure the sprays of blossoms just inside the bell openings. Arrange the bells in the centre of the cake, tilting the bells and supporting them on tiny pieces of petal paste.

7 Arrange the remaining ribbon in loops and secure in the centre of the bells, with the '50' emblem on top. Place the leaves in pairs in-between the bells and secure with royal icing. Leave to set.

SILVER WEDDING CAKE

This may look difficult, but it is really a simple cake to decorate once all the sugar pieces have been made.

INGREDIENTS	DECORATION	MATERIALS AND EQUIPMENT
Serves 80	• 50 large silver dragées	• 30 cm/12 in round silver cakeboard
• 25 cm/10 in round rich or light fruit cake	• 7 silver leaves	• club cocktail cutter
• 60 ml/4 tbsp/4 tbsp apricot glaze	• '25' silver emblem	• tiny round cutter
• 1.1 kg/2½ lb/2½ lb homemade or commercial white marzipan	• 1½ m/1½ yd × 2.5 cm/1 in wide white ribbon	• greaseproof (wax) piping bag
• 1.4 kg/3 lb/4½ cups royal icing	• 2 m/2 yd × 2.5 cm/1 in wide silver ribbon	• No. 1 plain writing nozzle
• 575 g/1¼ lb/1¼ lb petal paste	• 1½ m/1½ yd × 5 mm/¼ in wide silver ribbon	

1 Bake the rich or light fruit cake and allow to cool. Brush with apricot glaze and cover with marzipan. Place the cake on the cakeboard.

2 Flat ice the top and sides of the cake with three or four smooth layers of royal icing. Leave to dry overnight, then ice the cakeboard. Place the cake in a box and dry in a warm, dry place. Reserve the remaining royal icing for decorations.

3 Measure and fit the white ribbon around the cakeboard and the wider silver ribbon around the sides of the cake; secure with a bead of icing.

4 Roll out small pieces of petal paste one at a time very thinly and, using a club cocktail cutter, cut out the sugar pieces. Using tiny round cutters, cut four holes out of each sugar piece. Make about 65 cut-out sugar pieces, allowing for breakages, and leave flat to dry overnight.

5 Arrange 25 cut-out pieces around the top of the cake so that they fit evenly. Using a greaseproof (wax) paper piping bag fitted with a No. 1 plain writing nozzle, half-fill with royal icing. Pipe small beads of icing onto the top edge of the cake and fit the sugar pieces in position. Repeat at the base of the cake, tilting the pieces upwards slightly. Pipe beads of icing in between each sugar piece and press a silver dragée in position. Leave the cake in a box to dry overnight.

6 Measure the finer silver ribbon to fit around the top edge of the sugar pieces, allowing enough to join. Very carefully thread the ribbon in and out of the sugar pieces, joining the ribbon at the back underneath the sugar pieces.

7 Arrange a circle of seven sugar pieces in the centre of the cake and secure each one with a bead of icing with seven silver dragées in between. Place the silver leaves and '25' emblem in position and secure with icing.

EASTER SPONGE CAKE

This light lemon quick-mix sponge cake is decorated with lemon butter icing and cut-out marzipan flowers.

INGREDIENTS

Serves 10–12
- *3-egg quantity lemon-flavoured quick-mix sponge cake*
- *675 g/1½ lb/1½ lb lemon-flavoured butter icing*
- *50 g/2 oz/½ cup flaked almonds, toasted*
- *50 g/2 oz/2 oz homemade or commercial white marzipan*
- *green, orange and yellow food colouring*

DECORATION

- *10 green cut-out marzipan flowers*
- *8 orange cut-out marzipan flowers*
- *6 cut-out marzipan daffodils*

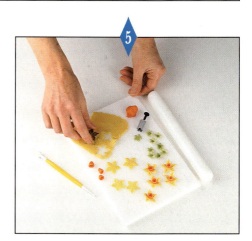

MATERIALS AND EQUIPMENT

- *greaseproof (wax) paper*
- *2 × 20 cm/8 in sandwich tins (shallow cake pans)*
- *nylon piping bag*
- *medium-sized gateau nozzle*
- *flower cutters*

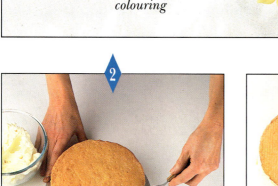

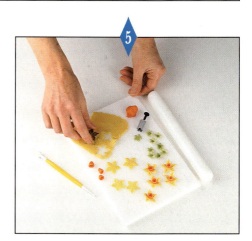

1 *Preheat the oven to 160°C/325°F/Gas 3 and bake the cakes in two lined and greased 20 cm/8 in round sandwich tins (shallow cake pans) for 35–40 minutes until golden brown and the cakes spring back when lightly pressed in the centre. Loosen the edges of the cakes with a palette knife (metal spatula), turn out, remove the lining paper and cool on a wire rack.*

2 *Sandwich the cakes together with one-quarter of the butter icing. Spread the side of the cake evenly with another one-quarter of icing.*

3 *Press the almonds onto the sides to cover evenly. Spread the top of the cake evenly with another one-quarter of icing and finish with a palette knife (metal spatula) dipped in hot water, spreading backwards and forwards to give an even lined effect.*

4 *Place the remaining icing into a nylon piping bag fitted with a medium-sized gateau nozzle and pipe a scroll edging.*

5 *Using the marzipan and food colourings, make the cut-out marzipan flowers.*

6 *Arrange the marzipan flowers on the cake and leave the icing to set.*

SIMNEL CAKE

This traditional Easter cake contains a layer of marzipan in the centre of a fruit cake mixture. A marzipan decoration also finishes the cake.

INGREDIENTS

Serves 10
- 450 g/1 lb/1 lb homemade or commercial white marzipan
- 225 g/8 oz/1½ cups raisins
- 175 g/6 oz/1 cup sultanas (golden raisins)
- 50 g/2 oz/⅓ cup glacé cherries, quartered
- 50 g/2 oz/⅓ cup cut mixed candied peel
- 175 g/6 oz/¾ cup butter, softened
- 175 g/6 oz/¾ cup caster (superfine) sugar
- 3 eggs
- 225 g/8 oz/2 cups plain (all-purpose) flour
- 5 ml/1 tsp/1 tsp baking powder
- 5 ml/1 tsp/1 tsp ground mixed spice
- 30 ml/2 tbsp/2 tbsp apricot glaze
- 1 egg, separated
- 175 g/6 oz/1 cup icing (confectioners) sugar, sifted

DECORATION

- 50 g/2 oz/2 oz homemade or commercial marzipan
- purple and green food colourings
- 3 purple marzipan cut-out flowers
- 11 green marzipan blossom flowers
- 1 m/1 yd × 2 cm/¾ in wide yellow ribbon
- 1½ m/1½ yd × 3 mm/⅛ in wide spotted yellow ribbon

MATERIALS AND EQUIPMENT

- 18 cm/7 in round deep cake tin
- flower cutter
- blossom plunger cutter

1 Cut the marzipan in half and roll out thinly on a surface lightly dusted with icing (confectioners) sugar. Using the base of an 18 cm/7 in round deep cake tin (pan), cut out the marzipan round.

2 Grease and double line the tin (pan) and preheat the oven to 170°C/325°F/Gas 3. Mix together in a bowl the raisins, sultanas (golden raisins), glacé cherries and mixed candied peel until evenly blended.

3 Place butter and sugar into a bowl, beat together until light and fluffy. Add in the eggs one at a time, beating well after each addition. Sift the flour, baking powder and mixed spice into the bowl and fold in gently, using a plastic spatula, until all the flour has been incorporated. Add the mixed fruit and fold in until evenly mixed.

4 Place half of the mixture in the tin (pan) and level. Place the marzipan round on top of the mixture, pressing down to level. Spoon the remaining cake mixture on top, smooth the top and make a slight depression in the centre. Bake in the oven for about 2¼–2½ hours until the cake is golden brown. Test with a skewer. Cool in the tin (pan), then turn the cake out, remove the paper and place on a wire rack.

5 Using two-thirds of the remaining marzipan, roll out and trim to an 18 cm/7 in circle. Brush the top of the cake with apricot glaze and cover with the marzipan round. Shape 11 small egg shapes, and form the remaining marzipan into a rope long enough to go around the top of the cake.

6 Secure the rope and eggs with apricot glaze.

7 Brush the marzipan evenly with egg yolk. Prepare a hot grill and sit the cake on a baking sheet. Grill (broil) the marzipan quickly until tinged with golden brown. Leave until cold.

8 Mix together the egg white and icing (confectioners) sugar and beat together until thick, glossy and white. Spread the icing in the centre of the cake and leave to set.

9 Using the marzipan and food colourings, make the flowers. Decorate the cake with flowers. Measure and fit the wide and spotted ribbons around the side of the cake. Tie a bow from the remaining spotted ribbon and secure the ribbons with a stainless steel pin.

CHOCOLATE FRUIT BIRTHDAY CAKE

A moist chocolate Madeira cake is covered in marzipan and chocolate fudge icing. The fruits are moulded from coloured marzipan and make an eye-catching decoration.

INGREDIENTS

Serves 30
- 18 cm/7 in square deep chocolate-flavoured Madeira cake
- 45 ml/3 tbsp/3 tbsp apricot glaze
- 450 g/1 lb/1 lb homemade or commercial white marzipan
- 450 g/1 lb/1 lb chocolate fudge icing
- red, yellow, orange, green and purple food colouring

DECORATION

- selection of marzipan fruits
- whole cloves
- angelica strips
- 0.75 m/³/4 yd × 1 cm/¹/2 in wide yellow ribbon

MATERIALS AND EQUIPMENT

- greaseproof (wax) paper
- 18 cm/7 in square deep cake tin (pan)
- 20 cm/8 in square silver cakeboard
- wire rack
- nylon piping bag
- medium-sized gateau nozzle

1 Bake the cake and allow to cool on a wire rack. Cut a slice off the top of the cake to level if necessary and invert on to the cakeboard. Brush evenly with apricot glaze.

2 Roll out two-thirds of the marzipan thinly to a 25 cm/10 in square. Place over the cake and smooth the top and down the sides. Trim off the excess marzipan around the base of the cake. Knead the trimmings together and reserve for making the marzipan fruits.

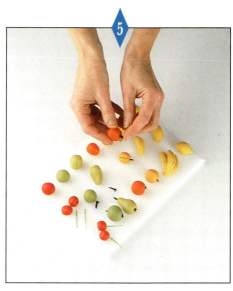

3 Place the cake on a wire rack over a tray and pour the freshly-made chocolate fudge icing over the cake, spreading quickly with a palette knife (metal spatula). Allow the excess icing to fall on the tray. Leave for 10 minutes, then place on to the cakeboard.

4 Using the remaining icing, place in a nylon piping bag fitted with a medium-sized gateau nozzle. Pipe a row of stars around the top edge and base of the cake. Leave to set.

5 Using the reserved marzipan, food colouring, cloves and angelica strips, model a selection of fruits.

6 Measure and fit the ribbon around the side of the cake and secure with a pin. Decorate the top with marzipan fruits.

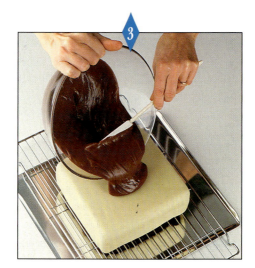

EIGHTEENTH BIRTHDAY CAKE

A really striking cake for a lucky someone celebrating their eighteenth birthday. Change the shape if you cannot hire the tin (pan).

INGREDIENTS

Serves 80
- 33.5 × 20 cm/13½ × 8 in diamond-shaped deep rich or light fruit cake (make using quantities for a standard 23 cm/9 in round cake)
- 45 ml/3 tbsp/3 tbsp apricot glaze
- 1.1 kg/2½ lb/2½ lb homemade or commercial white marzipan
- 1.6 kg/3½ lb/3½ lbs white sugarpaste (fondant)
- black food colouring
- 30 ml/2 tbsp/2 tbsp royal icing

DECORATION

- 2 m/2 yd × 2.5 cm/1 in wide white ribbon
- ½ m/½ yd × 2 mm/⅛ in wide black ribbon

MATERIALS AND EQUIPMENT

- '18' numeral cutter or template
- greaseproof (wax) paper piping bag
- No. 1 plain writing nozzle

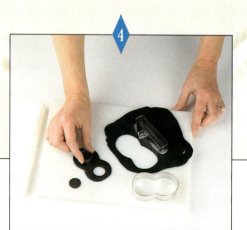

1 Bake the cake and allow to cool. Brush with apricot glaze and place on the cakeboard. Cover with marzipan.

2 Cover the cake using 1.1 kg/2½ lb/2½ lb sugarpaste (fondant). Knead the trimmings into the remaining sugarpaste (fondant) and colour using black food colouring.

3 Roll out two-thirds of the black sugarpaste (fondant) and cut into four strips the width and length of each section of the cakeboard. Brush the board with apricot glaze and place each strip in position; trim to fit neatly.

4 Roll-out one-quarter of the remaining sugarpaste (fondant) and cut out the number '18' using a special biscuit (cookie) cutter or by cutting round a template. Leave on a piece of foam sponge to dry.

5 Roll out some more icing thinly and cut out 40 triangles for the bow ties and 20 for the wine glasses.

6 Use a tiny round cutter or the end of a plain nozzle to cut out 20 music notes and 10 bases for the glasses, cut in half. Cut out thin strips of icing for the tails of the music notes and the stems of the glasses.

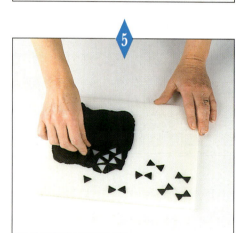

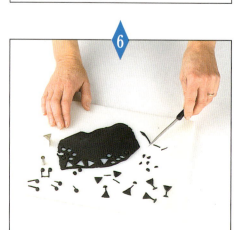

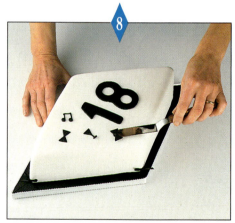

7 Using a greaseproof (wax) paper piping bag fitted with a No. 1 plain writing nozzle, half-fill with royal icing coloured black. Join the bow ties together with tiny beads of icing. Attach the music notes to their tails and the glasses to the stems and bases. Leave them all to dry.

8 Arrange the '18', music notes, wine glasses and bow ties over the top of the cake and attach each with a bead of icing. Continue to fix the decorations onto the sides of the cake.

TWENTY-FIRST BIRTHDAY CAKE

This cake looks good in any pale colour or simply white to suit the occasion. Add the colour with the ribbons and write your own personal message in the card.

INGREDIENTS

Serves 80
- 25 cm/10 in round rich fruit cake
- 45 ml/3 tbsp/3 tbsp apricot glaze
- 1.1 kg/2½ lb/2½ lb homemade or commercial white marzipan
- 1.4 kg/3 lb/4½ cups royal icing
- blue food colouring
- 575 g/1¼ lb/1¼ lb petal paste

DECORATION

- 1½ m/1½ yd × 2 cm/¾ in wide pale blue ribbon
- 1½ m/1½ yd × 1 cm/½ in wide royal blue ribbon
- 1¼ m/1¼ yd × 1.5 cm/⅝ in wide looped royal blue ribbon
- 1¼ m/1¼ yd × 5 mm/¼ in wide royal blue ribbon
- ¾ m/¾ yd × 2 mm/⅛ in wide royal blue ribbon

MATERIALS AND EQUIPMENT

- 30 cm/12 in round silver cakeboard
- 7.5 cm/3 in square fluted cutter
- 5 cm/2 in plain oval cutter
- No. 2 and 3 plain writing nozzle
- club-shaped cocktail cutter
- tiny petal cutter
- greaseproof (wax) paper piping bag
- blue food-colouring pen

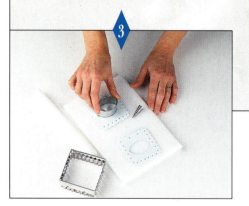

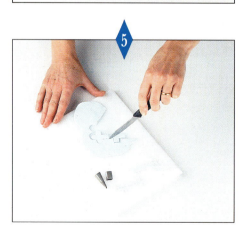

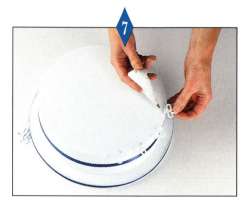

1 Bake the cake and allow to cool. Brush with apricot glaze, cover with marzipan and place on a cakeboard.

2 Make the royal icing and colour pale blue with a few drops of blue food colouring. Flat-ice the top and sides of the cake with three layers of smooth royal icing. Leave the cake to dry, then ice the cakeboard. Reserve the remaining royal icing for decorating.

3 Make the petal paste and colour pale blue with a few drops of blue food colouring. Roll out about one-third of the paste thinly on a surface sprinkled with cornflour (cornstarch). Cut out two squares using the square fluted cutter. Cut out an oval shape from one square using the plain oval cutter. Make 2 tiny holes using a No. 2 plain writing nozzle on the left-hand edge, and match these on the plain square so that the ribbons will meet to tie the card together. Continue to make a cut-out pattern all around the card for the ribbon to thread through. Leave on a piece of foam sponge to dry.

4 Roll out some more petal paste thinly and, using a club-shaped cocktail cutter, cut out 25 shapes, allowing for breakage. Use a tiny petal cutter to cut out three shapes on each piece. Leave to dry.

5 To make the keys, roll out the paste thinly and cut two end shapes with the club cutter. Then, using a sharp knife, cut out two key shapes. Pattern the keys by using tiny cutters to make a pattern. Leave to dry.

6 Measure and fit the pale blue and royal blue plain ribbons around the board, securing with a pin. Fit the looped ribbon around the side of the cake and secure with a bead of icing.

7 Fit a greaseproof (wax) paper piping bag with a No. 3 plain writing nozzle and fill with blue icing. Arrange the 18 cut-out sugar pieces around the top edge of the cake and secure each with a bead of icing. Leave to dry. Pipe a shell edging around the base of the cake, and beads of icing in between the cut-out pieces around the top edge.

8 Using the food-colouring pen, write the message on the plain card and decorate the keys.

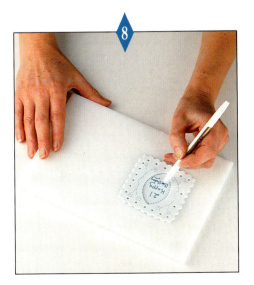

9 Thread the ribbon through the matching holes to join the card together – do not tie too tightly or the card will not open – and tie a small bow with long ends.

10 Thread the remaining blue ribbon in and out of the cut-out sugar pieces on the top edge of the cake and join the ends together with a bead of icing underneath. Tie a bow and attach it to the side of the cake with a bead of icing. Arrange the card and key on top of the cake and place the remaining key on the cakeboard. Secure each with a little icing. Leave the cake to dry.

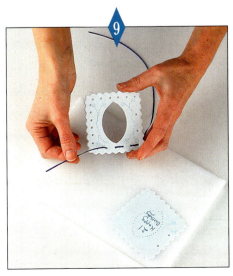

FLOWER
BIRTHDAY CAKE

A simple birthday cake decorated with piped sugar flowers and ribbons; use any mixture of flowers and ribbons, and finish the cake in royal icing or sugarpaste.

INGREDIENTS	DECORATION	MATERIALS AND EQUIPMENT
Serves 40	● *22 piped sugar flowers*	● *23 cm/9 in round silver cakeboard*
● *18 cm/7 in round light fruit cake*	● *1 m/1 yd × 2 cm/³⁄4 in wide white ribbon*	● *greaseproof (wax) paper piping bags*
● *30 ml/2 tbsp/2 tbsp apricot glaze*	● *2 m/2 yd × 1 cm/¹⁄2 in wide coral ribbon*	● *flower nail*
● *675 g/1¹⁄2 lb/1¹⁄2 lb homemade or commercial white marzipan*	● *¹⁄4 m/¹⁄4 yd × 5 mm/¹⁄4 in wide coral ribbon*	● *petal nozzle, No. 1 and 2 plain writing nozzle, and medium star nozzle*
● *1.1 kg/2¹⁄2 lb/3³⁄4 cups royal icing*		
● *yellow and orange food colouring*		

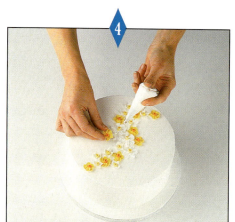

1 Bake the cake and allow to cool. Brush with apricot glaze and cover with marzipan. Place on the cakeboard.

2 Flat-ice the top and side of the cake with three layers of smooth royal icing. Leave the cake to dry, then ice the cakeboard. Reserve the remaining royal icing for decorating the cake. Store the cake in a box until required.

3 Make several greaseproof (wax) paper piping bags. Snip an inverted 'V' shape off the point of one bag. Fit one with a petal nozzle and one with a No. 1 plain writing nozzle, and another bag with a medium-sized star nozzle. Colour one-third of the icing yellow with yellow food colouring. Colour 15 ml/1 tbsp/1 tbsp of icing orange with orange food colouring. Pipe the narcissi using the petal nozzle for the petals and the plain writing nozzle for the centres: make four white narcissi with yellow centres and nine yellow narcissi with orange centres.

4 Pipe nine simple white flowers with the snipped bag and add yellow centres with the plain nozzle. Leave to dry overnight in a warm, dry place. Peel the paper off the back of the flowers and arrange them on the top of the cake. Secure each flower with a little icing.

5 Fill the star nozzle with white icing and pipe a shell edging around the top edge and base of the cake. Using the No. 2 plain writing nozzle and white icing, pipe the words 'HAPPY BIRTHDAY' on the right and left of the flower arrangement. Over-pipe the writing using a No. 1 nozzle and some orange icing.

6 Measure and fit the white ribbon around the cakeboard and secure with a pin. Fit the coral ribbon around the board and side of the cake, securing with a bead of royal icing. Tie a bow and attach to the front of the cake with a bead of royal icing. Leave the cake to dry.

HEXAGONAL RETIREMENT CAKE

An easily decorated cake for a happy retirement. It is probably more suitable for a man, since it sports plain lines and a smart appearance.

INGREDIENTS

Serves 80
- 26 cm/10½ in hexagonal deep rich fruit cake (make using quantities for a standard 25 cm/10 in round cake)
- 45 ml/3 tbsp/3 tbsp apricot glaze
- 1.1 kg/2½ lb/2½ lb homemade or commercial white marzipan
- 1.4 kg/3 lb/3 lb sugarpaste (fondant) icing
- ice-blue food colouring
- 30 ml/2 tbsp/2 tbsp royal icing

DECORATION

- 1 m/1 yd × 2 cm/¾ in wide light green looped ribbon
- 4 m/4 yd × 5 mm/¼ in wide dark green looped ribbon
- 3 m/3 yd × 5 mm/¼ in wide light green looped ribbon
- 1 m/1 yd × 2 mm/⅛ in wide light green ribbon
- 1 m/1 yd × 2 mm/⅛ in wide dark green ribbon

MATERIALS AND EQUIPMENT

- 28 cm/11 in hexagonal silver cakeboard
- 7.5 cm/3 in square fluted cutter
- No. 3 plain writing nozzle
- wooden dowel
- food-colouring pen

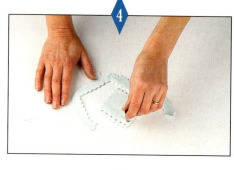

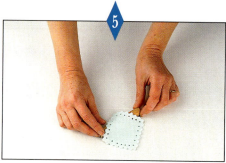

1 Bake the cake and allow to cool. Brush with apricot glaze and place on the cakeboard. Cover the cake with marzipan.

2 Add a few drops of blue food colouring to the sugarpaste (fondant).

3 Only partially knead in to create a marbled effect. Cover the cake with the marbled sugarpaste (fondant) and leave overnight to set.

4 Press the sugarpaste (fondant) trimmings together and use to cover the cakeboard. Replace the cake carefully onto the cakeboard and leave to dry. Roll out the remaining trimmings and cut out a square, using the fluted cutter. Make small holes around the border using a No. 3 plain writing nozzle.

5 Leave to dry over a small piece of wooden dowel to shape.

6 Measure and fit the 2 cm/¾ in wide light green looped ribbon around the cakeboard and secure with a pin. Measure and fit the 5 mm/¼ in wide dark green looped ribbon around the board, base and the top of the cake. Secure with a bead of royal icing. Cut six lengths of light and six lengths of dark green looped ribbon the depth of the cake. Fit one strip of each coloured ribbon 5 cm/2 in from each corner on each side of the cake. Secure with beads of icing behind the bands of ribbon. Attach bows to the side ribbon.

7 Cut two strips of each ribbon to fit parallel across the top of the cake, leaving a space in the centre. Secure with beads of royal icing.

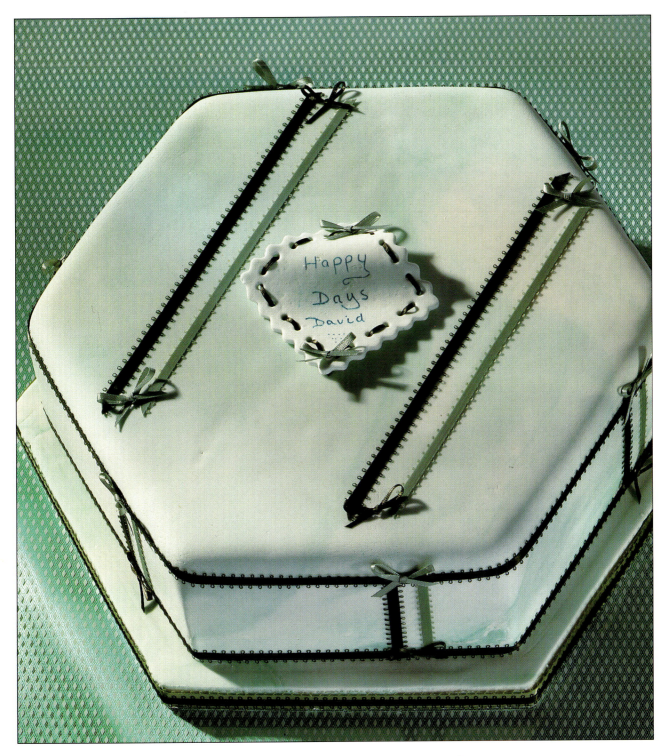

8 *Using a food-colouring pen, write the message or name on the plaque and place on the cake. Attach two bows onto the sugar plaque. Using the fine ribbon, thread the dark green ribbon in and out of the plaque, secure the ends underneath with icing. Tie the remaining ribbon into eight light and six dark bows.*

PETAL RETIREMENT CAKE

This cake is suitable for a special lady retiring from work. Choose any fresh flowers of your choice, such as lilies or freesias.

INGREDIENTS

Serves 50
- 20 cm/8 in petal-shaped deep light fruit cake (make using quantities for a standard 20 cm/8 in round cake)
- 45 ml/3 tbsp/3 tbsp apricot glaze
- 900 g/2 lb/2 lb homemade or commercial white marzipan
- 900 g/2 lb/2 lb sugarpaste (fondant) icing
- mulberry and pink food colouring
- 275 g/10 oz/10 oz petal paste
- 15 ml/1 tbsp/1 tbsp royal icing
- 1 egg white
- caster (superfine) sugar

DECORATION

- 2 m/2 yd × 2 cm/³/4 in wide white ribbon
- 2 m/2 yd × 1 cm/¹/2 in wide fuchsia ribbon
- 2 m/2 yd × 2 mm/¹/8 in wide fuchsia ribbon
- fresh flowers

MATERIALS AND EQUIPMENT

- 23 cm/9 in petal-shaped silver cakeboard
- foam sponge
- large and small blossom plunger cutters
- greaseproof (wax) paper piping bag
- No. 1 plain writing nozzle
- pink food colouring pen

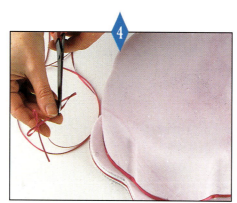

1 Bake the cake and allow to cool. Brush with apricot glaze and place on the cakeboard. Cover the cake with marzipan.

2 Add some mulberry food colouring to the sugarpaste (fondant) and only knead lightly to give a marbled effect. Cover the cake with three-quarters of the sugarpaste (fondant) and leave to dry overnight. Roll out the remaining sugarpaste (fondant) and cover the cakeboard. Replace the cake in the centre of the board.

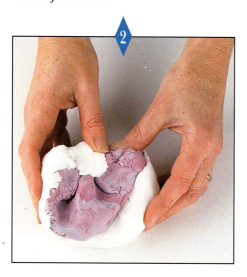

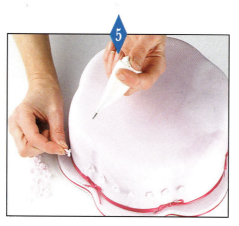

3 Make the petal paste and colour pink with food colouring. Roll out thinly and cut out an oblong 5 × 2.5 cm/2 × 1 in. Fold in half and dry over the end of a piece of foam sponge. Make four holes in the top edges of the fold to thread the ribbon through. Cut out 30 large and four small plunger blossom flowers and leave to dry.

4 Place the royal icing in a greaseproof (wax) paper piping bag fitted with a No. 1 plain writing nozzle. Measure and fit the white and fine fuchsia ribbon around the cakeboard, then the medium ribbon around the base of the cake. Secure all ribbons with beads of icing in the corner of the petal shapes. Tie six small bows from the fine ribbon and attach them to the base ribbon.

5 Attach the large blossom flowers around the side of the cake with beads of icing. Secure the remaining small blossom flowers to the card. Using the food colouring pen, write the message inside and draw a design. Thread some fine ribbon through the holes and tie a bow.

6 *Choose fresh flowers to match the ribbon on the cake, sugar-frost them with egg white and sugar and leave to dry. Arrange the flowers on the centre of the cake with the sugarpaste card.*

MOTHER'S DAY BASKET

Every mother would love to receive a cake like this on Mother's Day. Choose fresh flowers to decorate the top.

INGREDIENTS	DECORATION	MATERIALS AND EQUIPMENT
Serves 12 • 3-egg quantity of orange-flavoured quick-mix sponge cake • 900 g/2 lb/2 lb orange-flavoured butter icing	• 1 m/1 yd × 1 cm/½ in wide mauve ribbon • ½ m/½ yd × 2 mm/⅛ in wide spotted mauve ribbon • fresh flowers	• 1.1 l/2 pt/5 cup fluted ovenproof glass dish • 15 cm/6 in round silver cakecard • greaseproof (wax) paper piping bags • basket-weave nozzle • kitchen foil

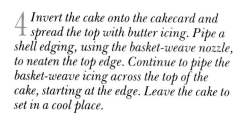

1 Lightly grease and line the base of a fluted ovenproof glass dish (or brioche mould). Make the cake without any baking powder and bake in the oven for 1 hour 15 minutes to 1 hour 25 minutes until well risen, golden brown and firm to the touch.

2 Spread the side of the cake with one-third of the orange-flavoured butter icing and place upside down on a board.

3 Make plenty of greaseproof (wax) paper piping bags and fit with a basket-weave nozzle. Half-fill with butter icing and pipe the sides with a basket-weave pattern (see Basket-weave Wedding Cake).

4 Invert the cake onto the cakecard and spread the top with butter icing. Pipe a shell edging, using the basket-weave nozzle, to neaten the top edge. Continue to pipe the basket-weave icing across the top of the cake, starting at the edge. Leave the cake to set in a cool place.

5 Fold a piece of foil in half, then half again and continue to fold until you have a strip several layers thick.

6 Using the ribbon, bind the strip to cover the foil; bend up the end to secure the ribbon. Bend the foil to make a handle, and press into the icing.

7 Choose some flowers and make a neat arrangement tied with ribbon on top of the cake just before serving. Tie a bow and pin it to the sides of the cake.

FATHER'S DAY CAKE

Coffee cakes are always a favourite with men. Ice this one in coffee frosting and decorate with piped chocolate and cut-out decorations.

INGREDIENTS	MATERIALS AND EQUIPMENT

Serves 12

- 3-egg quantity coffee-flavoured quick sponge cake mixture
- 675 g/1½ lb/1½ lb coffee-flavoured butterscotch frosting
- 125 g/4 oz/¾ cup plain chocolate chips
- 30 ml/2 tbsp/2 tbsp chocolate and hazelnut spread

- baking parchment
- 18 cm/7 in square deep cake tin (pan)
- 20 cm/8 in square silver cakeboard
- baking sheet (tray)
- greaseproof (wax) paper piping bags
- star and No. 2 plain writing nozzle

1 Prepare and line an 18 cm/7 in square deep cake tin (pan). Make the cake and bake for 45–50 minutes until well risen, golden brown and firm to the touch.

2 Place the cake on a rack over a baking sheet (tray) and pour the freshly-made frosting over to cover completely, allowing the excess frosting to fall. Leave to set. Place on the cakeboard.

3 Melt the chocolate, pour onto a sheet of baking parchment and spread evenly. As the chocolate begins to set, place another sheet of baking parchment on top and turn the chocolate 'sandwich' over. Peel off the baking paper and turn the chocolate sheet over.

4 Cut out seven 2.5 cm/1 in squares of chocolate with a sharp knife and cut into 14 triangles.

5 Using a greaseproof (wax) paper piping bag fitted with a star nozzle, half-fill with chocolate and hazelnut spread. Pipe a shell border around the base and on the top edge of the cake. Using a No. 2 plain writing nozzle, pipe 'HAPPY FATHER'S DAY' onto the cake.

6 Decorate the sides and top of the cake with the chocolate cut-outs. Leave until set.

FRILLS AND FLOWERS CHRISTENING CAKE

This pretty cake, decorated with flowers and frills, is perfect for a baby girl's Christening, and would be ideal for a little girl's birthday cake, too.

INGREDIENTS

Serves 50
- 20 cm/8 in round rich fruit cake
- 30 ml/2 tbsp/2 tbsp apricot glaze
- 800 g/1¾ lb/1¾ lb homemade or commercial white marzipan
- 1.1 kg/2½ lb/2½ lb sugarpaste (fondant) icing
- pink and red food colourings

DECORATION

- 2 m/2 yd × 1 cm/½ in wide deep pink ribbon
- 1½ m/1½ yd × 2 cm/¾ in wide deep pink ribbon
- 1 m/1 yd × 5 mm/¼ in wide deep pink ribbon

MATERIALS AND EQUIPMENT

- 23 cm/9 in round silver cakeboard
- scalloped crimping tool
- greaseproof (wax) paper
- greaseproof (wax) paper piping bag
- No. 1 plain writing nozzle
- frill cutter
- large and medium blossom plunger cutters
- food-colouring pen

1 Bake the cake and allow to cool. Brush with apricot glaze, place on the cakeboard and cover the cake with marzipan. Tint the sugarpaste (fondant) pale pink using a few drops of pink food colouring. Using two-thirds of the sugarpaste (fondant), cover the cake. Fit the widest ribbon around the cakeboard and the narrowest ribbon around the base of the cake. Secure with a bead of icing.

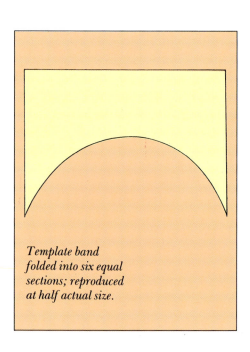

Template band folded into six equal sections; reproduced at half actual size.

2 Using a scalloped crimping tool, crimp the top edge of the cake by pressing the crimper into the icing but not squeezing it together.

3 Cut a strip of greaseproof (wax) paper to fit around the cake and of the same height. Fold the paper into six equal divisions and position a plate halfway over the template and draw around the shape. Cut out the shape to form the template and reserve the cut-out pieces. Fit the template around the cake and mark the shape with a scriber or pin. Remove the paper template.

4 Using a greaseproof (wax) paper piping bag fitted with a No. 1 plain writing nozzle, fill with royal icing. Using some of the remaining sugarpaste (fondant), roll and cut out a frill using a garrette frill cutter, but cut out a larger centre circle to make a thinner frill. Frill the edges (see Champagne Wedding Cake for general instructions). Make six frills, one at a time. Pipe a line of royal icing following the scalloped shape marked on the cake and attach the frill. Repeat to fit six frills.

5 Using a cut-out piece of the template, make a semi-circle shape to fit under the frill and mark ten 1 cm/½ in lines in a semi-circle for the ribbon insertion cuts. Transfer these marks to the side of the cake under each frill and cut the slits the same size as the ribbon. Cut the 1 cm/½ in wide ribbon into pieces to fit the gaps and insert five pieces under each frill.

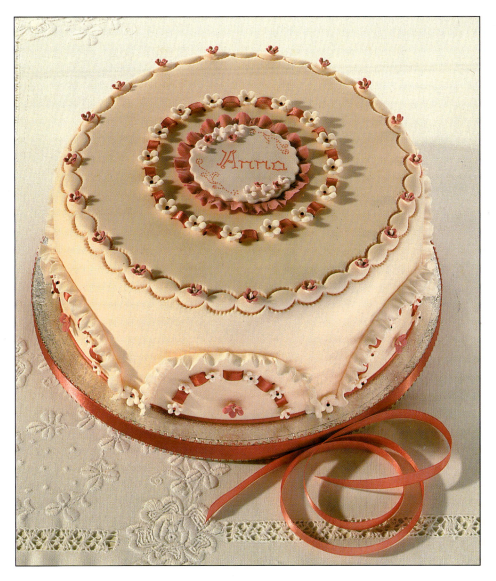

6 Mark a 10 cm/4 in circle on top of the cake and mark 34 ribbon insertion lines. Cut the slits and insert 17 pieces of ribbon.

7 Knead all the sugarpaste (fondant) trimmings together and tint half dark pink to match the ribbon, using pink and red food colouring. Cut out 22 large and 40 medium light plunger blossom flowers, and 24 medium and 6 large dark plunger blossom flowers. Pipe a bead of icing in the centre of each.

8 Roll out a piece of dark pink sugarpaste (fondant) thinly and cut out a round using the frill cutter. Frill the edges, as above. Roll out the pale pink sugarpaste (fondant) and cut out a 5 cm/2 in fluted circle and place on top of the dark pink frill. Leave to dry. Attach eight plunger blossom flowers at the opposite sides of the plaque and secure with royal icing.

9 Using a food-colouring pen, dot in the design and write the child's name across the centre. Place in position on top of the cake. Mark the dark centres on the blossom flowers with the food-colouring pen. Attach the medium-sized dark pink flowers to the top edge of the cake and the large ones in the centre of the frilled scallop. Secure the medium light-pink flowers in-between the ribbon circle on top of the cake, and the small flowers on the side of the cake in-between the ribbon. Secure the remaining light pink flowers between each frill. Leave the cake to dry.

BUNNY AND BIB CAKE

This delicate cake may be made for a girl or a boy, using any pastel shade of icing. Make the decorations in advance and store in a warm, dry place. The bib may be kept as a keepsake.

INGREDIENTS

Serves 50
- 25 cm × 20 cm/10 × 8 in oval deep rich or light fruit cake (make using quantities for a standard 25 cm/10 in round cake)
- 60 ml/4 tbsp/4 tbsp apricot glaze
- 1.1 kg/2½ lb/2½ lb homemade or commercial white marzipan
- 1.1 kg/2½ lb/3¾ cups royal icing
- 275 g/10 oz/10 oz petal paste
- blue food colouring

DECORATION

- 1¼ m/1¼ yd × 2 cm/¾ in wide pale blue ribbon
- 1¼ m/1¼ yd × 1 cm/½ in wide pale blue ribbon
- 1¼ m/1¼ yd × 5 mm/¼ in wide pale blue ribbon
- ¼ m/¼ yd × 2.5 mm/⅛ in wide pale blue ribbon

MATERIALS AND EQUIPMENT

- 30 × 23 cm/12 × 9 in oval silver cakeboard
- card for template
- small crimping tool
- No. 3 and No. 1 plain writing nozzle
- medium-sized heart-shaped plunger cutter
- greaseproof (wax) paper piping bag
- bunny-shaped cutter
- blue food-colouring pen

1 Bake the cake and allow to cool. Brush with apricot glaze, cover with marzipan and place on the cakeboard. Flat-ice the top and sides of the cake with three layers of smooth royal icing. Leave the cake until dry, then ice the cakeboard. Reserve the remaining royal icing for decorating the cake.

Template for 'bib'; reproduced at half actual size.

2 Tint the petal paste pale blue with a few drops of blue food colouring. Cut out a card template of the 'bib' (see above). Roll out a small piece of petal paste very thinly. Place the template on top and cut around the shape using a pointed knife.

3 Using a small crimping tool, crimp the edge to give a fluted finish. Using the medium-sized heart-shaped plunger cutter, cut out five heart shapes around the edge of the bib. Use the end of a No. 3 plain writing nozzle and cut out six small rounds in-between the heart shapes.

4 Half fill a greaseproof (wax) paper piping bag fitted with a No. 1 plain writing nozzle with royal icing. Pipe fine threads of icing following the outlines of the cut-out shapes. Pipe alternate scrolls and three beads of icing as a border design, following the shape of the bib.

5 Pipe the child's name across the centre. Leave overnight to dry.

6 Roll out another piece of blue petal paste thinly and cut out 32 hearts using the plunger cutter. Then roll out some more icing thinly and use a tiny bunny cutter to cut out 16 bunny shapes. Mark their eyes using a blue food-colouring pen. Leave all the cut-out shapes to dry overnight.

7 Measure and fit the wide blue ribbon around the cakeboard and secure with a pin. Measure and fit the 1 cm/½ in wide ribbon around the base and the 5 mm/¼ in wide ribbon around the top edge of the cake and secure with a bead of royal icing.

Secure alternate bunnies and hearts to the side of the cake between the ribbons with beads of royal icing. Secure 20 hearts on top of the cake with royal icing.

8 Place the bib in the centre of the cake and support it with a piece of petal paste; arrange the remaining five bunnies around it. Tie a tiny bow from the fine ribbon, leave the ends long and pull over the scissors to curl the ends. Place in position at the neck of the bib and the side of the cake.

NOEL CHRISTMAS CAKE

For those who prefer a traditional royal-iced cake, this is a simple design using only one icing and easy-to-pipe decorations.

INGREDIENTS	DECORATION	MATERIALS AND EQUIPMENT
Serves 50 • 20 cm/8 in round rich fruit cake • 30 ml/2 tbsp/2 tbsp apricot glaze • 800 g/1¾ lb/1¾ lb homemade or commercial white marzipan • 900 g/2 lb/3 cups royal icing • red and green food colouring	• 2½ m/2½ yd × 2 cm/¾ in wide gold ribbon • 2½ m/2½ yd × 5 mm/¼ in wide red ribbon • 44 large gold dragées	• greaseproof (wax) paper • 23 cm/9 in round silver cakeboard • greaseproof (wax) paper piping bag • No. 1 and 2 × No. 0 plain writing nozzles

1 Bake the cake and allow to cool. Brush with apricot glaze, cover with marzipan and place on the cakeboard.

2 Flat-ice the top of the cake with two layers of royal icing and leave until dry. Ice the sides of the cake and peak the royal icing, leaving a space around the centre of the side to fit the ribbon. Reserve the remaining royal icing for decorating.

3 Pipe beads of icing around the top edge of the cake and attach a gold dragée on every other bead of icing.

4 Using a greaseproof (wax) paper piping bag fitted with a No. 1 plain writing nozzle, half-fill with royal icing. Write NOEL across the cake and then pipe holly leaves, stems and berries around the cake.

5 Measure and fit the gold ribbon around the side of the cake, taking care not to break the peaks. Press into the icing. Measure and fit the red ribbon over the top of the gold, and secure with a bead of icing. Tie a neat red bow and attach it to the front of the cake. Use the remaining ribbon to fit around the cakeboard, securing with a pin. Leave overnight to dry.

6 Colour 30 ml/2 tbsp/2 tbsp of the royal icing bright green and 15 ml/1 tbsp/1 tbsp bright red with food colouring paste. Use a greaseproof (wax) paper piping bag and a No. 0 plain writing nozzle. Over-pipe NOEL in red.

7 Pipe alternate dots around the edge of the cake in red for the berries and overpipe the holly in green. Leave to dry.

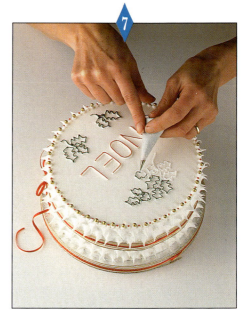

CHRISTMAS STOCKING CAKE

A bright and happy cake to make for Christmas. Make the stocking and parcels in advance to save time at Christmas.

INGREDIENTS

Serves 50
- 20 cm/8 in square rich fruit cake
- 45 ml/3 tbsp/3 tbsp apricot glaze
- 900 g/2 lb/2 lb homemade or commercial white marzipan
- 1.1 kg/2½ lb/2½ lb sugarpaste (fondant) icing
- 15 ml/1 tbsp/1 tbsp royal icing
- red and green food colouring

DECORATION

- 1¼ m/1¼ yd × 2 cm/¾ in wide red ribbon
- 1 m/1 yd × 2 cm/¾ in wide green ribbon

MATERIALS AND EQUIPMENT

- 25 cm/10 in square silver cakeboard
- card for template

1 Bake the cake and allow to cool. Brush with apricot glaze and place on the cakeboard. Cover the cake with marzipan.

2 Reserve 225 g/8 oz/½ lb sugarpaste (fondant) icing for decorations, and use the remainder to cover the cake smoothly. Place the cake in a box and leave to dry in a warm dry place. Measure and fit the red ribbon around the board, securing with a pin, and the green ribbon around the cake, securing with royal icing.

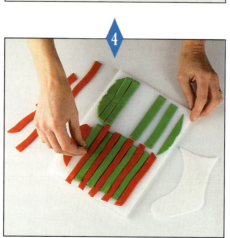

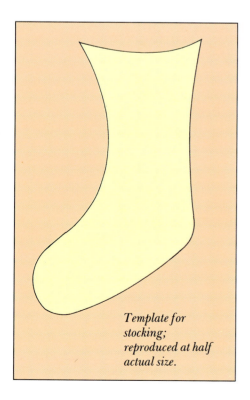

Template for stocking; reproduced at half actual size.

3 Knead the sugarpaste (fondant) trimmings together. Reserve 125 g/4 oz/¼ lb and cut the remainder in half; colour one half red and the other half green with food colouring. Trace the template of the stocking onto card and cut out. Roll out a piece of white sugarpaste (fondant) and cut out round the template.

4 Roll out the red and green sugarpaste (fondant) to 5 mm/¼ in thick and cut each into seven 1 cm/½ in strips. Remove alternate green strips and replace with red strips. Gently roll the stripey sugarpaste (fondant) together.

5 Use the template to cut out another stocking shape, allowing an extra 5 mm/¼ in all around.

6 Brush the white stocking with apricot glaze and, using a palette knife (metal spatula), lift the striped stocking and place over the white one. Press lightly together and leave to dry.

7 Shape the remaining white sugarpaste (fondant) into four parcel shapes and trim each with thin strips of red and green sugarpaste (fondant) ribbons.

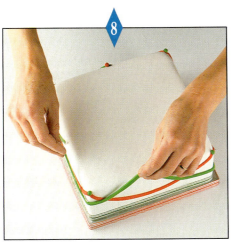

8 *Knead the remaining green and red sugarpaste (fondant) together, keeping the colours separate. Roll out each into a 20 cm/8 in strip, 1 cm/½ in wide. Cut each into two 5 mm/¼ in strips. Pipe a bead of royal icing on to each corner, press alternate green and red strips in position and trim to size. Shape four red and four green balls and press in position where the sugarpaste (fondant) strips join, securing with a little royal icing.*

9 *Arrange the stocking and parcels in position on the top of the cake. Leave to dry.*

MINI CHRISTMAS GIFT CAKES

These little cakes make a welcome gift, especially for friends or family on their own. Gift-wrap them in pretty boxes tied with ribbon.

INGREDIENTS

Makes 9

- 20 cm/8 in square rich fruit cake (make using quantities for a standard 18 cm/7 in round cake)
- 45 ml/3 tbsp/3 tbsp apricot glaze
- 675 g/1½ lb/1½ lb homemade or commercial white marzipan
- 450 g/1 lb/1 lb sugarpaste (fondant) icing
- 675 g/1½ lb/2¼ cups royal icing
- red, green and yellow food colouring

DECORATION

- 1 m/1 yd × 2 cm/¾ in wide green ribbon
- 1 m/1 yd × 5 mm/¼ in wide green ribbon
- 1 m/1 yd × 5 mm/¼ in wide red ribbon
- 1 m/1 yd × 2 cm/¾ in wide red ribbon
- 1 m/1 yd × 2 cm/¾ in wide gold ribbon
- 18 gold leaves
- 3 gold candles

MATERIALS AND EQUIPMENT

- 3 silver, 3 red and 3 gold 10 cm/4 in thin cakecards
- small crimping tool
- holly leaf cutter

1 Bake the cake and allow to cool. Cut the cake into three strips each way to make nine square cakes. Brush each with apricot glaze and place on a cakecard.

2 Cut the marzipan into nine pieces. Cut two-thirds off one piece and roll out a strip long enough and wide enough to cover the sides of one cake. Trim to size and wrap around the cake, keeping a good square shape. Roll out the remaining one-third of the marzipan large enough to fit the top. Invert the cake onto the square, trim to shape and replace on to the cakecard. Repeat to cover all the cakes with marzipan. Knead all the trimmings together and reserve for decorations.

3 Cut the sugarpaste (fondant) icing into three pieces. On a lightly sugared surface, roll out one piece at a time large enough to cover the top and sides of a cake. Cover the three cakes on the red cakecards. Crimp the top edges of each cake using a small crimping tool.

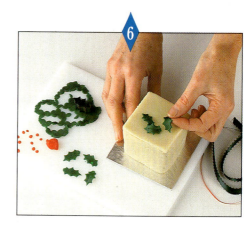

4 Cover the three cakes on the gold cards with royal icing and peak the surfaces to finish, working on one cake at a time. Leave a strip plain around the sides to fit the ribbons.

5 Cut the marzipan trimmings into three portions. Colour one red, one green and the other piece yellow. Roll out the green marzipan thinly and cut out 27 leaves, using a holly leaf cutter. Mark the veins with a knife and bend the leaves. Make lots of tiny red berries, and form the remaining red marzipan into nine candle shapes – three small, three medium and three large. Shape nine flames from the yellow marzipan. Arrange the candles, flames, holly leaves and berries on the sugarpaste cakes and tie each with a wide red ribbon and a bow. Secure all the decorations with a little royal icing.

6 *Arrange a holly garland on the plain marzipan cakes with a few berries. Tie each marzipan cake with wide green and fine red and green ribbon and a double bow.*

7 *Arrange the six gold leaves on each peaked royal icing cake. Position a gold candle in the centre and the gold ribbon around each cake with a bow. Leave all the cakes to set overnight before gift-wrapping them.*

189

MARZIPAN BELL CAKE

An unusual Christmas cake, this is decorated purely with marzipan which gives a Christmas feel without the sweetness of icing.

INGREDIENTS	DECORATION	MATERIALS AND EQUIPMENT
Serves 40	• 1 m/1 yd × 2 cm/³/4 in wide red ribbon	• 20 cm/8 in round silver cakeboard
• 18 cm/7 in round rich or light fruit cake	• 1 m/1 yd × 5 mm/¼ in wide green ribbon	• crimping tool
• 30 ml/2 tbsp/2 tbsp apricot glaze	• ¼ m/¼ yd × 5 mm/¼ in wide red ribbon	• bell cutter
• 900 g/2 lb/2 lb homemade or commercial white marzipan		• holly leaf cutter
• green, yellow and red food colouring		

1 Bake the cake and allow to cool. Brush with apricot glaze and place on the cakeboard.

2 Colour two-thirds of the marzipan pale green with a few drops of green food colouring. Knead until evenly coloured.

3 Roll out the marzipan to a 23 cm/9 in circle and place over the cake, smoothing across the top and down the side. Trim the excess marzipan away from the base of the cake. Using a crimping tool, crimp the top edge of the cake to make a scalloped pattern.

4 Colour a small piece of marzipan bright yellow, a small piece bright red and the remaining trimmings and marzipan bright green.
  Roll out the yellow marzipan and using a bell cutter, cut out two bells and mould two clappers.
  Using some green marzipan, cut two pencil-thin lengths and form into bell ropes, bending them into shape. Roll out the remaining green marzipan and using a holly cutter, cut out eleven holly leaves. Mark the veins with a knife and bend them to shape.
  Using the red marzipan, shape some tiny red berries and also two thin strips to wind around the end of the bell ropes. Leave the decorations to dry.

5 Measure and fit the wide red and fine green ribbon around the side of the cake, securing each with a pin. Tie a neat double bow from red and green fine ribbon and attach to the side with a bead of icing.

6 Arrange the bells, clappers, bell ropes, holly leaves and berries on top of the cake and secure each with a little apricot glaze.

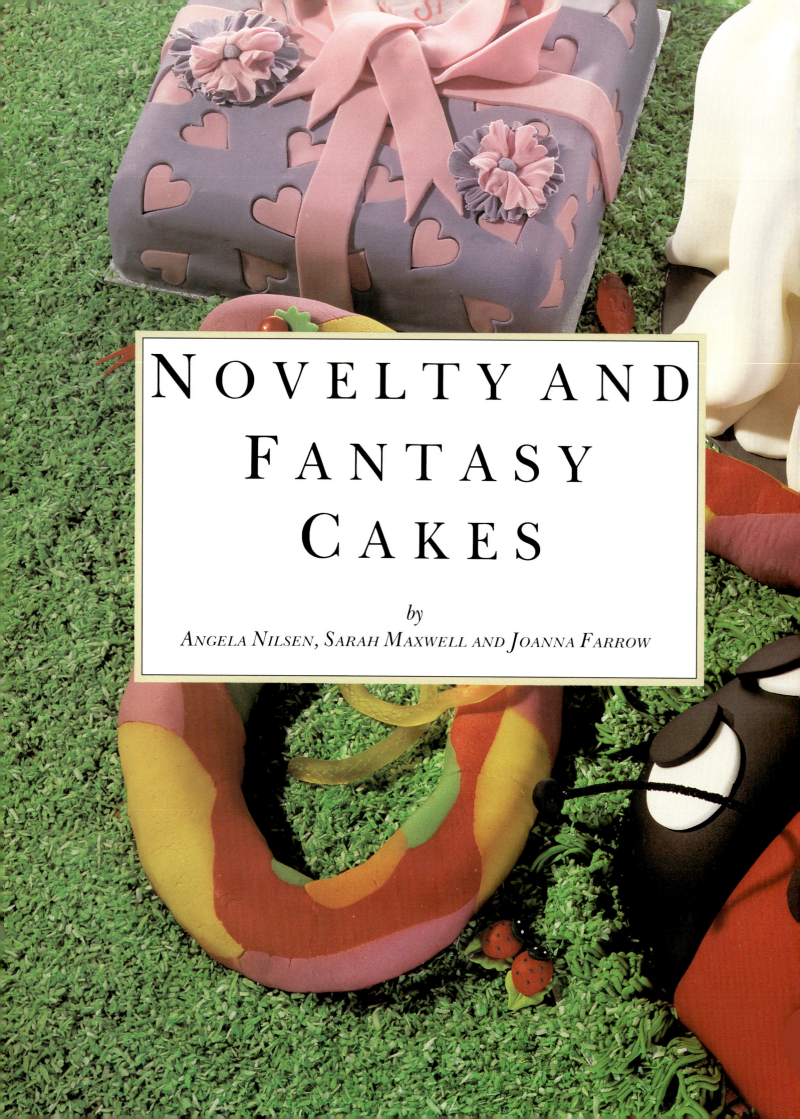

NOVELTY AND FANTASY CAKES

by

ANGELA NILSEN, SARAH MAXWELL AND JOANNA FARROW

INTRODUCTION

A NOVELTY CAKE is a wonderful way to celebrate a special event or birthday, and can provide an amusing twist to traditional occasions. In the following pages, there are original cake designs for recipients of all ages, as well as unusual cakes for anniversaries and seasonal celebrations. For the kids, for instance, there are birthday balloons, a merry-go-round, or a jolly coloured snake; for adults there are cakes to suit every special interest — a mobile phone, a sailing boat, even a terracotta flower pot. There is a sophisticated egg timbale for an Easter table, and a beautiful hand-painted festive cake for Christmas.

The cakes are all highly distinctive but not too difficult to achieve. There are creations using coloured sugarpaste or fondant, royal icing, butter icing, various frostings and flavoured icings. A whole range of special decorating techniques are described and explained step by step, so you can build up a whole repertoire of cake effects. A basket of strawberries is created from basketweave piping with chocolate butter icing; a candle cake shows how to marble coloured sugarpaste; a present-shaped cake uses inlaid sugarpaste in contrasting colours to spectacular effect. Follow the projects exactly or adapt the techniques to suit your own occasions.

A BASKET OF STRAWBERRIES

Quick and easy to make, a perfect surprise for a birthday or Valentine's day. And don't be put off by the icing technique – it's much easier than it looks!

INGREDIENTS

Serves 6–8

- 2-egg quantity quick-mix sponge cake
- 45 ml/3 tbsp/3 tbsp apricot glaze
- 675 g/1½ lb/1½ lb commercial or homemade marzipan
- icing (confectioners) sugar, for dusting
- 50 g/2 oz/4 tbsp caster (superfine) sugar
- 350 g/12 oz/¾ lb chocolate-flavoured butter icing
- red food colouring

MATERIALS AND EQUIPMENT

- 450 g/1 lb/3 cup loaf tin (bread pan)
- 18 cm/7 in oval cakeboard
- piping bag fitted with a small star nozzle
- 10 plastic strawberry stalks
- 30 × 7.5 cm/12 × 3 in strip kitchen foil
- 30 cm/12 in thin red ribbon

STORING

The cake can be made up to two days in advance, wrapped in foil and stored in an airtight container. The finished cake can be refrigerated for up to one week.

FREEZING

The un-iced cake can be frozen for up to three months.

VARIATION

For a Get Well cake, fill the basket with a selection of different shaped marzipan fruits. For a keen gardener, fill with marzipan vegetables.

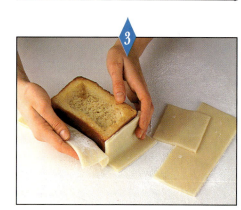

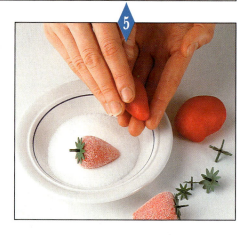

1 Preheat the oven to 180°C/350°F/Gas 4. Grease and line the base and sides of a 450 g/1 lb/3 cup loaf tin (bread pan). Spoon the cake mixture into the prepared tin (pan) and smooth the top with a plastic spatula. Bake in the preheated oven for 40–50 minutes, or until a skewer inserted into the middle of the cake comes out clean. Leave for 5 minutes before turning out on to a wire rack to cool.

2 Slice a thin layer off the top of the cake to make it perfectly flat. Score a 5 mm/¼ in border around the edge of the cake and scrape out the insides to make a shallow hollow.

3 Place the cake in the middle of the cakeboard and brush the sides and border edges with the apricot glaze. Roll out 275 g/10 oz/10 oz of the marzipan on a surface lightly dusted with icing (confectioners) sugar. Cut the marzipan into rectangles and use to cover the sides of the cake, overlapping the border edges. Gently press the edges of the marzipan together to seal.

4 Fill the piping bag with the butter icing. Pipe vertical lines about 2.5 cm/1 in apart all around the sides of the cake. Starting at the top of the cake pipe short horizontal lines alternately crossing over and then stopping at the vertical lines to give a basket-weave effect. Pipe a decorative line of icing around the top edge of the basket, to finish.

5 Colour the remaining marzipan with the red food colouring and mould into strawberry shapes. Roll in caster (superfine) sugar and press a plastic stalk into the top of each one. Carefully arrange the strawberries in the basket.

6 *To make the basket handle, fold the foil into a thin strip and wind the ribbon evenly around it to cover completely. Bend into a curve and push the ends into the sides of the cake. Decorate with ribbon bows.*

MERMAID

This mermaid cake would make a splash at any little girl's birthday party! The scales can be cut out using a 2.5 cm/1 in plain round cutter, then cut in half, if you don't have a crescent-shaped one. Use seashells, starfish or any other sea objects of your choice to decorate the sand.

INGREDIENTS

Serves 6–8

- 2-egg quantity quick-mix sponge cake
- 175 g/6 oz/6 oz butter icing
- 25 g/1 oz/1 oz plain popcorn
- 450 g/1 lb/1 lb milk chocolate, melted
- icing (confectioners) sugar, for dusting
- 225 g/8 oz/¹/₂ lb homemade or commercial marzipan
- 225 g/8 oz/¹/₂ lb sugarpaste (fondant) icing
- pink food colouring
- 1 egg white, lightly beaten
- a little sunflower oil
- 75 g/3 oz/6 tbsp demerara sugar (granulated brown sugar) for the sand

MATERIALS AND EQUIPMENT

- 1.1 l/2 pt/5 cup pudding basin (bowl)
- 25 cm/10 in fluted cakeboard
- 1 × doll, similar in dimensions to a 'Barbie' or 'Sindy' doll
- 1 small crescent-shaped cutter
- small scallop shell or shell-shaped chocolate mould

STORING

The cake can be made up to two days in advance, wrapped in foil and stored in an airtight container. The finished cake can be stored for three to four days in a cool, dry place.

FREEZING

The un-iced cake can be frozen for up to three months.

VARIATION

Flavour the sponge cake and butter icing with chocolate to make this an ideal choice for chocoholic children.

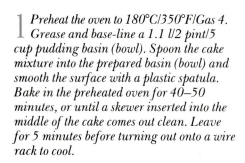

1 Preheat the oven to 180°C/350°F/Gas 4. Grease and base-line a 1.1 l/2 pint/5 cup pudding basin (bowl). Spoon the cake mixture into the prepared basin (bowl) and smooth the surface with a plastic spatula. Bake in the preheated oven for 40–50 minutes, or until a skewer inserted into the middle of the cake comes out clean. Leave for 5 minutes before turning out onto a wire rack to cool.

2 Place the cake flat side down on the work surface and cut across into 3 layers of equal thickness. Spread the bottom layer with two-thirds of the butter icing. Place the second layer of sponge cake on top and spread with the remaining butter icing. Top with the remaining piece of sponge cake. Position slightly off-centre on the cakeboard and set aside.

3 Mix the popcorn with about one-third of the melted chocolate and spoon around the base and up the sides of the cake. Pour the remaining melted chocolate over the top of the cake to cover completely. Leave to set at room temperature.

4 Lightly dust the work surface with icing (confectioners) sugar and roll out half of the marzipan to an oblong shape, wide enough to wrap around the doll's legs and 5 cm/2 in longer. Use to surround her legs, starting at the waist and working downwards. Mould the bottom section into a fin-shaped tail. Position the doll so she is sitting on the cake.

5 Divide the sugarpaste (fondant) in half; colour one half dark pink and the other half light pink with pink food colouring. Thinly roll out the dark pink sugarpaste (fondant) on a work surface lightly dusted with icing (confectioners) sugar. Reserve a small piece of the sugarpaste (fondant) to make the mermaid's top. Cut out 'scales' with a small crescent-shaped cutter, keeping the cut scales covered with a sheet of cling film (plastic wrap) to stop them drying out. Thinly roll out the light pink sugarpaste (fondant) icing and continue to cut out the scales in the same way.

6 *To make the bodice, press the reserved piece of dark pink sugarpaste (fondant) icing over an oiled tiny scallop shell, or into an oiled shell-shaped chocolate mould. Gently remove the sugarpaste (fondant) from the mould and trim the edges. Brush with a little egg white and stick in place for the mermaid's top.*

Brush each scale with a little egg white and, starting at the fin end, stick on to the tail in overlapping rows, until the marzipan is completely covered.

7 *Sprinkle the cakeboard with demerara (granulated brown) sugar for the sand and decorate with seashells, starfish or any other sea objects of your choice.*

LADYBIRD

Create a little animal magic and make this cake for a nature lover or gardener.

INGREDIENTS

Serves 10–12
- 3-egg quantity lemon-flavoured quick mix sponge cake
- 175 g/6 oz/6 oz lemon-flavoured butter icing
- 60 ml/4 tbsp/4 tbsp lemon curd, warmed
- icing (confectioners) sugar, for dusting
- good 1 kg/2 lb 6 oz/2 lb 6 oz sugarpaste (fondant) icing
- red, black and green food colourings
- 5 marshmallows
- 50 g/2 oz/2 oz golden commercial or homemade marzipan
- edible ladybird icing decorations (optional)

MATERIALS AND EQUIPMENT

- 1.1 l/2 pt/5 cup ovenproof mixing bowl
- greaseproof (wax) paper
- wooden skewer
- 28 cm/11 in round cakeboard
- 4 cm/1½ in plain round biscuit (cookie) cutter
- 5 cm/2 in plain round biscuit (cookie) cutter
- garlic press
- 2 pipe cleaners

STORING

The cake can be made up to two days in advance, wrapped in foil and stored in an airtight container. The finished cake, covered in sugarpaste (fondant), can be stored for three to four days in a cool, dry place.

FREEZING

The un-iced cake can be frozen for up to three months.

VARIATION

Marzipan works just as well as a covering for this cake.

1 *Preheat the oven to 180°C/350°F/Gas 4. Grease and line the base of a 1.1 l/2 pt/5 cup ovenproof mixing bowl. Spoon the mixture into the prepared bowl and smooth the surface with a plastic spatula. Bake in the preheated oven for 55–60 minutes, or until a skewer inserted into the centre of the cake comes out clean. Leave for 5 minutes before turning out on to a wire rack to cool.*

2 *Cut the cake across in half and sandwich together with the butter icing. Cut vertically through the cake, about a third of the way in. Brush both pieces of cake with the lemon curd.*

3 *Colour 450 g/1 lb/1 lb sugarpaste (fondant) icing red, with red food colouring. Lightly dust the work surface with icing (confectioners) sugar and roll out the red sugarpaste (fondant) to about 5 mm/¼ in thick. Use to cover the larger piece of cake to make the ladybird's body. Use a wooden skewer or the back of a knife to make an indentation down the centre of the cake for the wings.*

4 *Colour 350 g/12 oz/¾ lb sugarpaste (fondant) icing black, with black food colouring. Roll out three-quarters of the black sugarpaste (fondant) and use to cover the smaller piece of cake for the ladybird's head. Place the cakes on the cakeboard, assembling the ladybird and lightly pressing the head and body together to shape.*

5 *Roll out 50 g/2 oz/2 oz sugarpaste (fondant) icing and cut out two circles with a 5 cm/2 in round biscuit (cookie) cutter for the eyes. Brush with a little water and stick in position on the head.*

6 *Roll out the remaining black sugarpaste (fondant) icing thinly. Use to cut out eight circles with a 4 cm/1½ in round biscuit (cookie) cutter. Use two of these rounds for the eyes and stick the others on to the body with a little water. Reserve the trimmings.*

7 *Colour 225 g/8 oz/½ lb sugarpaste (fondant) icing green. To make the grass, break off pieces of green sugarpaste (fondant) and squeeze through a garlic press. Trim off with a knife. Brush the board around the ladybird with a little water and gently stick down the grass.*

8 To make the marshmallow flowers, roll the marzipan into a 2 cm/³/₄ in long sausage shape and cut into slices to make rounds. Set aside. Dust the work surface with a little icing (confectioners) sugar and flatten each marshmallow with a rolling pin, sprinkling with more icing (confectioners) sugar to prevent sticking. Using scissors, snip from the outside edge towards the middle of each marshmallow to make the petals. Press a marzipan round into the middle of each flower and use to decorate the cake.

9 To make the antennae, paint the pipe cleaners with black food colouring and press a small ball of the remaining black sugarpaste (fondant) on to the end of each one. Bend each pipe cleaner slightly and insert it into the cake between the head and the body. Arrange the decorations around the cake, if using.

PIZZA CAKE

Quick, easy and impressive – a definite winner for pizza fanatics everywhere.

INGREDIENTS

Serves 8–10
- 2-egg quantity quick-mix sponge cake
- 350 g/12 oz/³/4 lb butter icing, coloured red
- 175 g/6 oz/6 oz yellow commercial or homemade marzipan
- 15 ml/1 tbsp/1 tbsp desiccated (shredded) coconut
- red and green food colouring
- icing (confectioners) sugar, for dredging
- 25 g/1 oz/1 oz sugarpaste (fondant) icing

MATERIALS AND EQUIPMENT

- 23 cm/9 in shallow cake tin (pan)
- greaseproof (wax) paper
- 25 cm/10 in pizza plate
- cheese grater
- a leaf cutter or stencil

STORING

The cake can be made up to two days in advance, wrapped in foil and stored in an airtight container. The finished cake can be refrigerated for up to one week.

FREEZING

The un-iced cake can be frozen for up to three months.

1 Preheat the oven to 180°C/350°F/Gas 4. Grease and line the base of a 23 cm/9 in shallow cake tin (pan). Spoon the mixture into the prepared tin (pan) and smooth the surface with a plastic spatula. Bake in the preheated oven for 40–50 minutes, or until a skewer inserted into the centre of the cake comes out clean. Leave for 5 minutes before turning out onto a wire rack to cool.

2 Place the cake on the pizza plate and spread evenly with the red butter icing, leaving a 1 cm/1/2 in border around the edge.

3 Knead the marzipan for a few minutes, to soften slightly, then grate it in the same way as grating cheese. Use to sprinkle over the red butter icing.

4 Colour the sugarpaste (fondant) icing green with green food colouring. For the leaf garnish, lightly dust the work surface with icing (confectioners) sugar and roll out the green sugarpaste (fondant) to about 5 mm/1/4 in thick. Use the leaf cutter or stencil to cut out two leaf shapes. Garnish the pizza cake with the sugarpaste (fondant) leaves.

5 To make the chopped herbs, place the desiccated (shredded) coconut in a small bowl and add enough green food colouring to make it dark green, stirring after each addition of colouring.

6 Scatter the coconut herbs over the pizza cake.

THE BEAUTIFUL PRESENT CAKE

For a best friend, mother, aunt, grandmother or sister, this beautiful cake is fitting for any occasion.

INGREDIENTS

Serves 15–20
- 4-egg quantity vanilla-flavoured quick-mix sponge cake
- 350 g/12 oz/³/4 lb vanilla-flavoured butter icing
- 60 ml/4 tbsp/4 tbsp apricot glaze
- icing (confectioners) sugar, for dusting
- 575 g/1¹/4 lb/1¹/4 lb homemade or commercial marzipan
- 850 g/1 lb 14 oz/1 lb 14 oz sugarpaste (fondant) icing
- purple and pink food colouring
- cold water, for brushing

MATERIALS AND EQUIPMENT

- 23 cm/9 in square cake tin (pan)
- 25 cm/10 in square cakeboard
- heart-shaped biscuit (cookie) cutter
- small brush
- small fluted carnation cutter
- cocktail stick
- pink food-colouring pen

STORING

The cake can be made up to two days in advance, wrapped in foil and stored in an airtight container. The finished cake, covered in sugarpaste (fondant), can be stored for three to four days in a cool, dry place.

FREEZING

The un-iced cake can be frozen for up to three months.

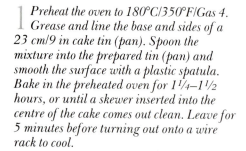

1 Preheat the oven to 180°C/350°F/Gas 4. Grease and line the base and sides of a 23 cm/9 in cake tin (pan). Spoon the mixture into the prepared tin (pan) and smooth the surface with a plastic spatula. Bake in the preheated oven for 1¹/4–1¹/2 hours, or until a skewer inserted into the centre of the cake comes out clean. Leave for 5 minutes before turning out onto a wire rack to cool.

2 Cut the cake in half horizontally and spread with the vanilla butter icing. Sandwich with the top sponge cake and place the cake in the centre of the cakeboard. Brush the cake with apricot glaze. Lightly dust the work surface with icing (confectioners) sugar and roll out the marzipan to about ¹/2 cm/¹/4 in thick. Use to cover the cake.

3 Colour 575 g/1¹/4 lb/1¹/4 lb sugarpaste (fondant) icing purple. Roll out the purple sugarpaste (fondant) on the work surface, lightly dusted with icing (confectioners) sugar. Use to cover the cake, smoothing down the sides gently and trimming away any excess sugarpaste (fondant).

4 Using the heart-shaped cutter, stamp out hearts all over the cake to make an even pattern. Remove the purple hearts with a small, sharp knife, taking care not to damage the surrounding sugarpaste (fondant). Knead the hearts together and keep this reserved purple sugarpaste (fondant) in a plastic bag to use later.

5 Colour 275 g/10 oz/10 oz sugarpaste (fondant) icing pink. Roll out to about ¹/2 cm/¹/4 in thick on a work surface, lightly dusted with icing (confectioners) sugar. Use the heart-shaped cutter to cut out as many hearts as you need to fill the spaces left by the purple ones on the cake, re-rolling the pink sugarpaste (fondant), as necessary. Reserve the excess. Carefully insert the pink hearts into the spaces.

6 Roll out the reserved pink sugarpaste (fondant) to about ¹/2 cm/¹/4 in thick on a work surface, lightly dusted with icing (confectioners) sugar and cut into three strips about 2 cm/³/4 in wide and 30 cm/12 in long. Lay one strip across the centre of the cake and another at right angles across the centre, brushing the strips with a little water to secure. Trim away any excess sugarpaste (fondant) at the edges, if necessary. Reserve all the trimmings.

7 To make the bow, divide the remaining strip of pink sugarpaste (fondant) icing into quarters. Loop two of the quarters and seal the joins with a little water. Position at the centre of the cake, where the strips cross. Trim the ends of the remaining quarters to look like the ends of bows and overlap them across the joining of the loops; secure with a little water. Reserve the trimmings.

8 To make the flowers, roll out the remaining purple and pink sugarpaste (fondant) on a work surface, lightly dusted with icing (confectioners) sugar. Cut out two ½ cm/¼ in thick fluted rounds from each colour, using the carnation cutter.

9 With a cocktail stick or toothpick, carefully roll out the edges of each fluted round to make the frilled petals. Use a little of the purple sugarpaste (fondant) to make two tiny balls for the centres of the flowers. Then, using a little water, place a pink flower on top of a purple one and the tiny ball in the centre. Carefully lift and pinch behind the flower to secure. Repeat with the other flower and position them both on the cake. Mould together any remaining sugarpaste (fondant), roll out and cut into a pretty tag. Write a name or short message using the food-colouring pen and position on the cake.

SAILING BOAT

Make this cake for someone who loves sailing or is going on a journey – you can even personalize the cake with a rice paper nametag flag, written with a food-colouring pen.

INGREDIENTS

Serves 10–12

- 3-egg quantity quick-mix sponge cake
- 60 ml/4 tbsp/4 tbsp apricot glaze
- 450 g/1 lb/1 lb sugarpaste (fondant) icing
- 1 grissini (bread stick)
- 1 sheet of rice paper
- 9 short candy sticks
- 4 Polo (Lifesaver) mints
- 1 thin red 'bootlace' liquorice strip
- 1 thin black 'bootlace' liquorice strip
- 1 black liquorice Catherine wheel, with an orange sweet in the centre
- 1 blue sherbet 'flying saucer'
- 350 g/12 oz/3/4 lb butter icing coloured blue
- blue food colouring

MATERIALS AND EQUIPMENT

- 900 g/2 lb/5 cup loaf tin (bread pan)
- greaseproof (wax) paper
- 33 × 18 cm/13 × 7 in cakeboard
- 1 cocktail stick or toothpick
- black food-colouring pen

STORING

The cake can be made up to two days in advance, wrapped in foil and stored in an airtight container. The finished cake, covered in sugarpaste (fondant), can be stored for three to four days in a cool, dry place.

FREEZING

The un-iced cake can be frozen for up to three months.

VARIATION

To make this boat even more colourful, draw an attractive design on the sails using coloured pens. Remember that only the special cake decorating pens contain edible inks, so if you use another type of pen, don't eat the sails.

1 Preheat the oven to 180°C/350°F/Gas 4. Grease and line the base and sides of a 900 g/2 lb/5 cup loaf tin (bread pan). Spoon the cake mixture into the prepared tin (pan) and smooth the top with a plastic spatula. Bake in the preheated oven for 55–60 minutes, or until a skewer inserted into the centre of the cake comes out clean. Leave for 5 minutes before turning out on to a wire rack to cool.

2 Slice a thin layer off the top of the cake to make it perfectly flat. Trim one end to make a pointed bow. Using a small sharp knife, cut a shallow hollow from the centre of the cake, leaving a 1 cm/1/2 in border.

3 Brush the cake all over with the apricot glaze. Roll out the sugarpaste (fondant) icing to 35 × 23 cm/14 × 9 in rectangle and lay over the cake. Gently ease the sugarpaste (fondant) into the hollow middle and down the sides of the cake, until completely and evenly covered. Trim the edges at the base.

4 Cover the cakeboard with the blue butter icing, peaking it to resemble a rough sea. Position the cake on the iced board. Cut the rice paper into two tall triangular sails. Using a small brush, apply a little water along the length of the grissini (bread) stick and secure the rice paper sails to it. Insert the mast into the front of the hollowed compartment at the bow of the boat, pushing through the cake to the board.

5 Insert seven of the short candy sticks around the bow of the boat, leaving a little space between each one and allowing them to stand about 2.5 cm/1 in above the surface of the cake. Insert the remaining two short candy sticks at either side of the stern of the boat and hang two Polo (Lifesaver) mints on each, for the life belts. Use the bootlace liquorice strips to tie loosely in and out of the candy sticks at the bow of the boat for the guard rail. Trim away any excess, if necessary.

6 Cut a small flag shape from the
remaining rice paper and personalize it
using the food colour pen. Stick onto the
cocktail stick using a little water and
position the flag at the stern of the boat.

7 Uncoil the liquorice Catherine wheel
and remove the sweet from the centre.
Use the liquorice to make a fender all
around the outside of the boat, securing it
with a little water. Trim the excess and use
the remainder to line the seating area in the
same way. Position the sweet from the centre
of the Catherine wheel to one side of the boat
for the searchlight. Place the sherbet flying
saucer in the seating area for the cushion.

SHIRT AND TIE CAKE

Instead of buying the man in your life yet another shirt and tie for his birthday, make him a cake for a deliciously novel surprise!

INGREDIENTS

Serves 20–30

- 4-egg quantity coffee-flavoured quick-mix sponge cake
- 350 g/12 oz/³/₄ lb coffee-flavoured butter icing
- 90 ml/6 tbsp/6 tbsp apricot glaze
- icing (confectioners) sugar, for dusting
- good 1 kg/2 lb 6 oz/2 lb 6 oz sugarpaste (fondant) icing
- blue food colouring
- 125 g/4 oz/1 cup icing (confectioners) sugar, sifted
- 45–60 ml/3–4 tbsp/3–4 tbsp water

MATERIALS AND EQUIPMENT

- 19 × 26.5 cm/7¹/₂ × 10¹/₂ in roasting tin (pan)
- greaseproof (wax) paper
- 30 × 32.5 cm/12 × 13 in cakeboard
- steel ruler
- wooden skewer
- piping bag fitted with a small round nozzle
- 40 × 5 cm/16 × 2 in piece of flexible card, the short ends cut at an angle, for the collar
- small brush
- 'Happy Birthday' cake decoration (optional)
- blue tissue paper (optional)

STORING

The cake can be made up to two days in advance, wrapped in foil and stored in an airtight container. The finished cake, covered in sugarpaste (fondant), can be stored for three to four days in a cool, dry place.

FREEZING

The un-iced cake can be frozen for up to three months.

VARIATION

Choose your own colour contrasts for the shirt and the tie to suit the man; for example, a blue or red collar on a white or red shirt with a zany yellow tie!

1 Preheat the oven to 180°C/350°F/Gas 4. Grease and line the base and sides of a 19 × 26.5 cm/7¹/₂ × 10¹/₂ in roasting tin (pan). Spoon the mixture into the prepared tin (pan) and smooth the surface with a plastic spatula. Bake in the preheated oven for 1¹/₄–1¹/₂ hours, or until a skewer inserted into the centre of the cake comes out clean. Leave for 5 minutes before turning out on to a wire rack to cool.

2 Cut the cake in half horizontally and spread with the coffee-flavoured butter icing. Sandwich together with the top half of the sponge cake. Brush the cake evenly with the apricot glaze and lightly dust the work surface with icing (confectioners) sugar. Colour 675 g/1¹/₂ lb/1¹/₂ lb sugarpaste (fondant) icing light blue. Roll out the light blue sugarpaste (fondant) to about 5 mm/¹/₄ in thick and use to cover the cake, gently easing the sugarpaste (fondant) down the sides and corners. Trim away any excess icing. Place the cake on the cakeboard.

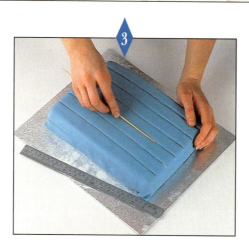

3 Using a steel ruler, make grooves down the length and sides of the cake, in straight lines, about 2.5 cm/1 in apart. Use a wooden skewer to re-indent the grooves, rolling the skewer slightly from side to side to make the channels deeper and slightly wider.

4 Mix the icing (confectioners) sugar and water together in a small bowl to make a just thick glacé icing and use to fill the piping bag fitted with the small, round nozzle. Pipe lines of glacé icing into the grooves on the top and sides of the cake, moving slowly and evenly for the best results.

5 To make the collar, roll out 225 g/ 8 oz/½ lb sugarpaste (fondant) icing, on a work surface lightly dusted with icing (confectioners) sugar, to a 40.5 × 10 cm/ 16½ × 4 in rectangle. Lay the piece of card for the collar on top, placing it along one edge of the sugarpaste (fondant). Brush a little water around the edges of the sugarpaste (fondant), then carefully lift the other edge of the sugarpaste (fondant) and fold over the card to encase it completely. Trim the two short ends to match the angles of the card. Carefully lift the collar and gently bend it round and position on the cake, applying a little water to help secure it in place.

6 Colour 175 g/6 oz/6 oz sugarpaste (fondant) icing dark blue. To make the tie, cut off one-third of the dark blue sugarpaste (fondant) and shape into a pyramid for the tie knot. Position the knot. Lightly dust the work surface with icing (confectioners) sugar and roll out the remaining dark blue sugarpaste (fondant) icing to about 5 mm/¼ in thick. Cut out a tie piece to fit under the knot and long enough to hang over the edge of the cake, making it slightly wider at the end where you cut a point. Position the tie piece, tucking it under the knot and applying a little water to secure it in place. Finish the cake with the 'Happy Birthday' decoration and tissue paper, if using.

MERRY-GO-ROUND CAKE

Choose your own figures to sit on the merry-go-round, from chocolate animals to jelly bears.

Remember to position the top of the merry-go-round at the last minute for the best results.

INGREDIENTS

Serves 16–20
- 3-egg quantity lemon-flavoured quick-mix sponge cake
- 60 ml/4 tbsp/4 tbsp apricot glaze
- icing (confectioners) sugar, to dust
- 575 g/1¼ lb/1¼ lb sugarpaste (fondant) icing
- orange and yellow food colouring
- 8 × 18 cm/7 in long candy sticks
- sweet (candy) figures

MATERIALS AND EQUIPMENT

- 2 × 20 cm/8 in round sandwich cake tins (pans)
- greaseproof (wax) paper
- 23 cm/9 in round fluted cakeboard
- 18 cm/7 in round piece of stiff card
- cocktail stick or toothpick
- 2 different sizes of star-shaped biscuit (cookie) cutters

STORING

The cake can be made up to two days in advance, wrapped in foil and stored in an airtight container. The finished cake, covered in sugarpaste (fondant), can be stored for three to four days in a cool, dry place.

FREEZING

The un-iced cake can be frozen for up to three months.

1 Preheat the oven to 180°C/350°F/Gas 4. Grease and line the bases of two 20 cm/8 in round sandwich tins (pans). Spoon two-thirds of the mixture into one tin (pan) and the other third into the other tin (pan). Smooth the surfaces with a plastic spatula. Bake for 55–60 minutes, or until a skewer inserted into the centre of each cake comes out clean. Leave for 5 minutes before turning out onto a wire rack to cool.

2 Place the larger cake, upside-down, on the fluted cakeboard to make the base of the merry-go-round, and place the smaller cake, right-side up, on the piece of card. Brush both cakes evenly with the apricot glaze and set aside. Lightly dust the work surface with icing (confectioners) sugar and place 450 g/1 lb/1 lb sugarpaste (fondant) icing on it. Using the cocktail stick or toothpick, apply a few spots of the orange food colouring to the sugarpaste (fondant).

3 To achieve the marbled effect in the sugarpaste (fondant) icing, roll into a sausage shape on the work surface. Fold the sausage shape in half and continue to roll out until it reaches its original length. Fold over again and roll out again into a sausage shape. Continue this process until the fondant is streaked with the orange colour.

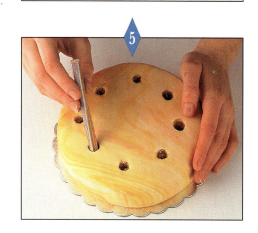

4 Divide the marbled sugarpaste (fondant) into two-thirds and one third. Roll out the larger portion on the work surface lightly dusted with icing (confectioners) sugar and use to cover the larger cake. Repeat with the smaller portion of marbled sugarpaste (fondant) and use to cover the smaller cake. Trim away any excess sugarpaste (fondant) and reserve, wrapped in cling film (plastic wrap).

5 Using one of the candy sticks, make eight holes at even distances around the edge of the larger cake, leaving about a 2 cm/¾ in border. Press the upright stick right through the cake to the board. Knead the reserved marbled sugarpaste (fondant) until the orange colour is evenly blended, then roll out on the work surface lightly dusted with icing (confectioners) sugar. Using the smaller star cutter, cut out nine stars. Cover with cling film (plastic wrap) and set aside. Colour 125 g/4 oz/¼ lb sugarpaste (fondant) icing yellow. Roll out on a surface lightly dusted with icing (confectioners) sugar and cut out nine stars with the larger star cutter. Sit the smaller cake on an upturned bowl and stick eight larger and eight smaller stars around the edge of the cake, using a little water to secure. Stick the remaining stars on top of the cake.

6 *To secure the sweet figures to the candy sticks, stick tiny balls of the excess sugarpaste (fondant) behind the figures and then lightly press onto the sticks. Leave to set for about 30 minutes. Place the candy sticks in the holes on the larger cake.*

7 *To assemble the cake, carefully lift the smaller cake, with its card base, onto the candy sticks, making sure it balances before letting go!*

MOBILE PHONE CAKE

For the upwardly mobile man, this novel cake is the business!

INGREDIENTS

Serves 8–10

- 2-egg quantity *vanilla-flavoured quick-mix sponge cake*
- 30 ml/2 tbsp/2 tbsp apricot glaze
- *icing (confectioners) sugar, for dusting*
- 375 g/13 oz/13 oz sugarpaste (fondant) icing
- *black food colouring*
- 10 small square sweets (candies)
- 1–2 stripey liquorice sweets (candies)
- 30–45 ml/2–3 tbsp/2–3 tbsp icing (confectioners) sugar
- 2.5–5 ml/$^1\!/_2$–1 tsp/$^1\!/_2$–1 tsp water

MATERIALS AND EQUIPMENT

- 900 g/2 lb/5 cup loaf tin (bread pan)
- 23 × 18 cm/9 × 7 in cakeboard
- diamond-shaped biscuit (cookie) cutter
- small brush
- small strip of kitchen foil
- piping bag fitted with a small round nozzle

STORING

The cake can be made up to two days in advance, wrapped in foil and stored in an airtight container. The finished cake, covered in sugarpaste (fondant), can be stored for three to four days in a cool, dry place.

FREEZING

The un-iced cake can be frozen for up to three months.

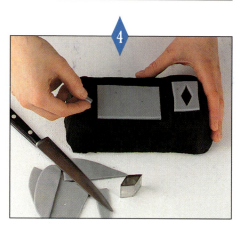

1 Preheat the oven to 180°C/350°F/Gas 4. Grease and line the base and sides of a 900 g/2 lb/5 cup loaf tin (bread pan). Spoon the mixture into the prepared tin (pan) and smooth the surface with a plastic spatula. Bake in the preheated oven for 40–50 minutes, or until a skewer inserted into the centre of the cake comes out clean. Leave for 5 minutes before turning out on to a wire rack to cool.

2 Turn the cake upside-down and starting about 2.5 cm/1 in along the cake, slice into it, across and at an angle, about 1 cm/$^1\!/_2$ in deep. Cut out this wedge, then slice horizontally along the length of the cake, stopping about 2.5 cm/1 in away from the end. Withdraw the knife and re-insert it at the end of the cake and slice into the cake to meet up with the horizontal cut. Remove the inner piece of cake and discard.

3 Place the cake on the cakeboard. Brush the cake evenly with the apricot glaze. Colour 275 g/10 oz/10 oz sugarpaste (fondant) icing black. Lightly dust the work surface with icing (confectioners) sugar and roll out the black sugarpaste (fondant) to about 5 mm/$^1\!/_4$ in thick. Use to cover the cake, carefully smoothing the sugarpaste (fondant) into the carved shape of the cake and down the sides and corners. Trim away any excess sugarpaste (fondant) and reserve, wrapped in cling film (plastic wrap).

4 Colour 75 g/3 oz/3 oz sugarpaste (fondant) icing grey, with a little black food colouring. Roll out the grey sugarpaste (fondant) to about 5 mm/$^1\!/_4$ in thick on a work surface lightly dusted with icing (confectioners) sugar. Cut out one piece of sugarpaste (fondant) to fit the centre of the cake, leaving a 1 cm/$^1\!/_2$ in border and another piece, about 2.5 cm/1 in square. Using the diamond-shaped biscuit (cookie) cutter, stamp out the centre of the square. Place the diamond at the bottom of the phone, and the square at the top. Position the piece of sugarpaste (fondant) for the centre, securing all the grey pieces with a small brush dipped in a little water.

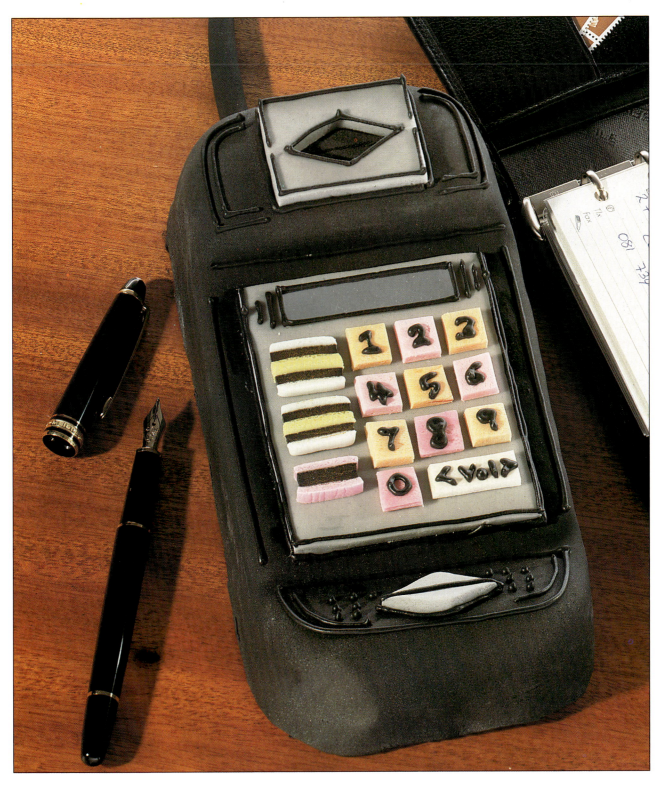

5 *Position the sweets (candies) and the strip of kitchen foil for the dial pad. To make the glacé icing, mix the icing (confectioners) sugar with the water and black food colouring, until of piping consistency. Fill the piping bag fitted with the small, round nozzle and pipe border lines around the edges of the phone, including the grey pieces of sugarpaste (fondant). Pipe the numbers on the keys.*

6 *Knead the reserved black sugarpaste (fondant) and use to roll into a sausage shape for the aerial. Indent the top with a knife and position at the top of the phone, to one side. Secure with a little water.*

RAINBOW SNAKE CAKE

This wild cake needs no cooking. It uses leftover sponge-cake crumbs – or you can buy a sponge cake and grind it yourself. Its heavy texture and sweet flavour make it an excellent party cake, for kids or adults. You only need serve a little, so it goes a long way. For a large party, double the ingredients to make an extra big snake. Use rubber gloves to protect your hands when colouring the marzipan and remember to wash them between colours.

INGREDIENTS

Serves 10–15

- 175 g/6 oz/3 cups plain sponge-cake crumbs
- 175 g/6 oz/1½ cups ground almonds
- 75 g/3 oz/6 tbsp light brown muscovado (molasses) sugar
- 5 ml/1 tsp/1 tsp ground mixed spice
- 2.5 ml/½ tsp/½ tsp ground cinnamon
- 45 ml/3 tbsp/3 tbsp fresh orange juice
- finely grated zest of 1 orange
- 75 ml/5 tbsp/5 tbsp clear runny honey or golden syrup (light corn syrup)
- 675 g/1½ lb/1½ lb white commercial or homemade marzipan
- icing (confectioners) sugar, for dusting
- red, yellow, orange, violet and green food colouring
- 2 red sugar-coated chocolate Smarties (M&Ms)
- 125 g/4 oz/2 cups desiccated (shredded) coconut
- wine-gum (chewy) snake sweets (optional)

MATERIALS AND EQUIPMENT

- 5 cocktail sticks
- rolling pin
- 25 cm/10 in round cakeboard
- small piece of thin red card cut into a tongue shape
- small star-shaped cutter
- small brush

STORING

The marzipan-iced cake can be made up to four days in advance and stored in an airtight container in a cool, dry place.

FREEZING

Not recommended.

1 In a large mixing bowl, combine the cake crumbs, almonds, sugar, spices, orange juice and zest and the honey. Stir well until all the ingredients hold together in a moist, thick paste. Set aside.

2 To colour the marzipan, divide it into five equal portions. Lightly dust the work surface with icing (confectioners) sugar and apply one of the food colourings to one of the portions of marzipan, using a cocktail stick or toothpick. Knead the colour into the marzipan, until evenly blended. Clean the work surface and lightly dust again with icing (confectioners) sugar. Take another piece of marzipan and apply another of the colourings. Repeat this process, until all five portions of marzipan are different colours, using a new cocktail stick (toothpick) each time. Remove a tiny ball from the green portion and reserve, covered in cling film (plastic wrap).

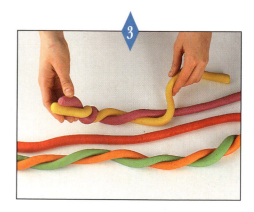

3 Using your hands, roll each piece of marzipan out on a work surface lightly dusted with icing (confectioners) sugar, to a sausage shape, about 1 cm/½ in in diameter. Line up the sausage shapes next to each other on the work surface and twist together the two outside sausages, leaving only the centre sausage untouched. Push the two outside twists together to squeeze against the middle sausage firmly.

4 Use a little icing (confectioners) sugar to dust the rolling pin and make short, sharp downward movements starting at one end, rolling the marzipan out a little at a time to about 15 cm/6 in wide. Keep the rolled width even all along the snake. Carefully slide a heavy, sharp knife underneath the rolled out marzipan to unstick it from the work surface. Flip the rolled out marzipan over, taking care not to tear it.

5 Spoon the cake-crumb mixture evenly down the centre of the marzipan, using your hands to form it into a firm sausage shape. Starting at one end, gather up the sides of the marzipan around the cake mixture, pinching the sides together firmly to seal, until the cake mixture is completely encased. Shape the head by flattening the marzipan slightly, and the tail by squeezing it into a tapered end. Roll the snake over so the seal lies underneath.

6 Carefully slide the snake on to the cakeboard, tail-end first, coiling it round as you go. The head can either be propped up on an extra lump of marzipan or left to flop over the rest of the snake. Both methods look very effective. Make a small incision where the mouth would be and insert the red tongue. Roll the reserved green marzipan out on a work surface lightly dusted with icing (confectioners) sugar and cut out two eyes, using the small star cutter. Position the eyes, securing them with a small brush dipped in a little water. Press the small Smarties or M&Ms on top.

7 Place the desiccated (shredded) coconut in a bowl and add a few spots of green food colouring with a little water. Stir until the coconut is flecked green. Scatter around the snake on the board to make the grass. Decorate with the wine-gum (chewy candy) snakes, if using.

EASTER CAKE

An unusual presentation for a spicy Easter fruit cake. The cake is covered with marzipan and chocolate moulding icing, then finished with ribbons and eggs made from chocolate modelling paste. The cake can be completed up to four weeks in advance.

INGREDIENTS

Serves 16

- 125 g/4 oz/¹/₂ cup softened butter or margarine
- 125 g/4 oz/¹/₂ cup light brown sugar
- 3 eggs
- 175 g/6 oz/1¹/₂ cups plain (all-purpose) flour
- 10 ml/2 tsp/2 tsp ground mixed spice
- 400 g/14 oz/3¹/₂ cups mixed dried fruit
- 50 g/2 oz/¹/₄ cup glacé cherries, chopped
- 50 g/2 oz/¹/₄ cup hazelnuts
- 45 ml/3 tbsp/3 tbsp apricot glaze
- 450 g/1 lb/1 lb homemade or commercial marzipan
- brown food colouring

MATERIALS AND EQUIPMENT

- 1.5 l/2¹/₂ pt/3 pt pudding basin (bowl)
- greaseproof (wax) paper
- 25 cm/10 in round gold cakeboard
- clean piece sponge
- several squares of gold foil, about 6.5 cm/2¹/₂ in in diameter
- paintbrush

STORING

The iced cake can be covered loosely in foil and stored in a cool dry place for up to four weeks.

FREEZING

The fruit cake can be frozen for up to six months.

CHOCOLATE MOULDING ICING

- 100 g/4 oz/4 squares plain (semisweet) or milk chocolate
- 30 ml/2 tbsp/2 tbsp liquid glucose
- 1 egg white
- 450 g/1 lb/3¹/₂ cups icing (confectioners) sugar
- cornflour (cornstarch) for dusting

CHOCOLATE MODELLING PASTE

- 50 g/2 oz/2 squares plain chocolate
- 50 g/2 oz/2 squares white chocolate
- 30 ml/2 tbsp/2 tbsp liquid glucose
- pink paste food colouring

1 Preheat the oven to 150°C/300°F/Gas 2. Grease and line the base of the pudding basin (bowl) with a circle of greaseproof (wax) paper. Cream together the butter or margarine and brown sugar. Gradually add the eggs with a little of the flour to prevent curdling. Sieve (sift) the remaining flour and spice and add to the bowl. Stir in the mixed fruit and nuts and turn into the prepared basin or bowl. Level the surface and bake for 1¹/₂ hours or until a skewer inserted into the centre of the cake comes out clean. Allow to cool completely.

2 To make the chocolate moulding icing, break up the chocolate and place in a bowl with the glucose over a pan of hot water. Leave until melted, cool slightly then add the egg white. Gradually add the icing (confectioners) sugar, beating well after each addition, until too stiff to manage. Turn out onto a flat surface and knead in the remaining sugar until stiff.

3 To make the modelling paste, melt the plain (semisweet) and white chocolate in separate bowls. Add half the glucose to the plain chocolate and stir until a stiff paste is formed. Wrap tightly. Add some pink food colouring and the remaining glucose to the white chocolate and mix to a paste. Chill both pastes until firm.

4 Cut a triangular wedge out of the cake, place the cake on the board and brush all over with apricot glaze. Roll out the marzipan on a surface dusted with icing (confectioners) sugar and cover the cake, tucking the paste into the cut section to maintain the cut-out shape. Trim off the excess marzipan around the base.

5 Roll out the chocolate moulding icing on a surface dusted with cornflour (cornstarch) and use to cover the cake in the same way. Cut two thin strips from the marzipan trimmings. Dampen the undersides with water and position inside the cut-out wedge to resemble marzipan layer.

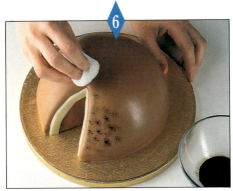

6 *Thin a little brown food colouring with water. Dip the sponge in the colour and stipple the surface of the icing. Leave to dry.*

7 *Lightly knead two-thirds of the modelling paste and shape into 18 small eggs. Cover some with gold foil. Position the eggs inside the cut-out wedge.*

Thinly roll out the remaining modelling paste and cut 2 cm/¾ in wide strips from the dark paste and 5 mm/¼ in wide strips from the pink paste. Dampen the undersides of the pink paste and lay over the dark. Cut two 13 cm/5 in strips, press the ends together to make loops and secure to the cake. Secure two 7.5 cm/3 in strips for ribbon ends and cover the centre with another small strip. (Place a piece of crumpled foil under each strip until hardened.)

GHOST

This children's cake is really simple to make yet very effective. Use an 18 cm/7 in square cake of your choice, such as a citrus- or chocolate-flavoured Madeira, or a light fruit cake.

INGREDIENTS

Serves 14

- 4-egg quantity orange-flavoured quick-mix sponge cake
- 900 g/2 lb/2 lb sugarpaste (fondant) icing
- black food colouring
- 350 g/12 oz/³/₄ lb butter icing
- cornflour (cornstarch) for dusting

MATERIALS AND EQUIPMENT

- 18 cm/7 in square cake tin (pan)
- greaseproof (wax) paper
- 300 ml/¹/₂ pt/1¹/₄ cup pudding basin (bowl)
- 23 cm/9 in round cakeboard
- palette knife (spatula)
- fine paintbrush

STORING

The iced cake can be covered loosely in foil and stored in a cool, dry place for up to two weeks.

FREEZING

The sponge can be frozen for up to two months.

1 Preheat the oven to 150°C/300°F/Gas 2. Grease and line the base of cake tin with greased greaseproof (wax) paper. Grease and line the base of pudding basin (bowl) with greaseproof (wax) paper. Half-fill the basin with cake mixture and turn the remainder into the cake tin (pan). Bake the basin for 25 minutes and the tin for 1¹/₂ hours. Allow to cool.

2 Knead a little black food colouring into 125 g/4 oz/¹/₄ lb of the sugarpaste (fondant) icing and use to cover the cakeboard. Trim off the excess.

3 Cut two small corners off the large cake. Cut two larger wedges off the other two corners. Stand the large cake on the iced board. Halve the larger cake trimmings and wedge around the base of cake.

4 Secure the small cake to the top of the larger cake with a little of the butter icing. Use the remaining butter icing to completely cover the cake.

5 Roll out the remaining sugarpaste (fondant) on a surface dusted with cornflour (cornstarch) to an oval shape about 51 cm/20 in long and 30 cm/12 in wide. Lay over the cake, letting the icing fall into folds around sides. Gently smooth the icing over the top half of the cake and trim off any excess around the base.

6 Using black food colouring and a fine paintbrush, paint two oval eyes onto the head.

BIRTHDAY BALLOONS

A colourful cake for a child's birthday party, made using either a round sponge cake or fruit cake base.

INGREDIENTS

Serves 18–20

- 20 cm/8 in round sponge or fruit cake, covered with 800 g/1¾ lb/ 1¾ lb marzipan, if liked
- 900 g/2 lb/2 lb sugarpaste (fondant) icing
- red, green and yellow food colourings
- cornflour (cornstarch), for dusting
- 3 eggs
- 2 egg whites
- 450 g/1 lb/4 cups icing (confectioners) sugar

MATERIALS AND EQUIPMENT

- 25 cm/10 in round silver cakecard
- 3 bamboo skewers, 25 cm/10 in, 24 cm/9½ in and 23 cm/9 in long
- small star cutter
- baking parchment
- greaseproof (wax) paper piping bags
- fine writing nozzle
- 1 m/1 yd fine coloured ribbon
- birthday candles

STORING

The iced cake will keep well in a cool place for up to three weeks.

FREEZING

A fruit cake base can be frozen for up to six months, and a sponge base for up to two months.

Template for the balloon-shaped run-outs; reproduced at actual size.

1 Place the cake on the cakecard. Colour 50 g/2 oz/2 oz of the sugarpaste (fondant) red, 50 g/2 oz/2 oz green and 125 g/4 oz/¼ lb yellow. Roll out the remaining icing on a surface dusted with cornflour (cornstarch) and use to cover the cake. Use 50 g/2 oz/2 oz of the yellow icing to cover the cakecard.

2 Using the tip of a skewer or the end of a paintbrush, make a small hole in the pointed end of one egg. Stir the egg lightly inside then tip out into a bowl. Repeat with the remaining eggs. Carefully wash and dry the shells. (The eggs should be strained before using.)

3 Roll out the red sugarpaste (fondant) icing to about 11 cm/4½ in. diameter circle and use to cover one of the egg shells, smoothing to fit around sides and trimming off any excess around the pointed ends. Keep smoothing the icing in the palms of the hands. Push a bamboo skewer up through hole and rest in a tall glass to harden. Repeat on other egg shells with the green and yellow sugarpaste (fondant).

4 Roll out the red, green and yellow trimmings and cut out a small star shape from each. Dampen lightly then thread onto the skewers and secure to the bases of balloons, matching the colours, for the balloon knots.

5 Trace 16 balloon shapes onto a large sheet of baking parchment. Beat the egg whites with the icing (confectioners) sugar until smooth and divide among 4 bowls. Add red colouring to one bowl, green to the second and yellow to the third, leaving the last white. Cover each tightly with cling film (plastic wrap) to prevent a crust forming.

6 Place the white icing in a piping bag fitted with a plain writing nozzle and use to pipe over the traced outlines. Leave to harden slightly. Thin the green icing with a little water until the consistency of pouring cream. Place in a greaseproof (wax) paper piping bag and snip off end. Use to fill a third of the balloon shapes. Repeat with the red and yellow icings. Leave the run-outs for at least 24 hours to harden.

7 Carefully peel the balloons off the baking parchment and secure around the sides of the cake. Pipe strings for the balloons with white icing.

8 Press the large balloons into the top of cake and decorate with the ribbon. Press the candles into the icing around the top edge.

FISH

A very easy, but colourful cake, perfect for a small child's birthday party. Candles can be pressed into the icing covering the board.

INGREDIENTS

Serves 8
- 2-egg quantity quick-mix sponge cake
- 450 g/1 lb/1 lb sugarpaste (fondant) icing
- blue, orange, red, mauve and green food colourings
- cornflour (cornstarch), for dusting
- 350 g/12 oz/¾ lb butter icing
- 1 blue Smartie (M&M)

MATERIALS AND EQUIPMENT

- 3.4 l/6 pt/7½ pt ovenproof mixing bowl
- large oval cakecard or board
- palette knife (spatula)
- 2.5 cm/1 in plain biscuit (cookie) cutter
- greaseproof (wax) paper piping bag

STORING

The iced cake can be covered loosely in foil and stored for up to one week.

FREEZING

The sponge cake can be frozen for up to two months.

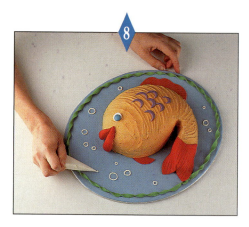

1 Preheat the oven to 170°C/325°F/Gas 3. Grease and line base of the mixing bowl with a circle of greaseproof (wax) paper. Spoon the cake mixture into the prepared bowl, level the surface and bake for 40–50 minutes until just firm, or until a skewer inserted into the middle of the cake comes out clean. Allow to cool.

2 Colour two-thirds of the sugarpaste (fondant) icing blue and roll out very thinly on a surface dusted with cornflour (cornstarch). Lightly dampen the cakecard or board and cover with the sugarpaste (fondant) icing. Trim off excess icing.

3 Invert the cake onto a flat surface and trim to create a fish shape with a curved tail. Using a small knife, trim the edges to give sloping sides. Place on the icing-covered board.

4 Colour all but 15 ml/1 tbsp/1 tbsp of the butter icing orange. Cover the cake completely with the orange butter icing and smooth down with a palette knife (spatula). Score curved lines for scales with the palette knife (spatula), starting from the tail-end and working up towards head.

5 Colour half the remaining sugarpaste (fondant) red. Shape and position two lips. Thinly roll the remainder and cut out the tail and fins. Mark with lines using a knife and position on the fish.

6 Roll a small ball of white sugarpaste (fondant) icing, flatten slightly and position for the eye. Press the blue Smartie (M&M) into centre.

7 Colour a small ball of sugarpaste (fondant) mauve, cut out crescent-shaped scales using a biscuit (cookie) cutter and place on the fish. Colour the remaining sugarpaste (fondant) icing green, roll out and cut long thin strips. Twist each strip and arrange them around board.

8 Place the reserved butter icing in a piping bag and snip off the end. Pipe small circles on the cakeboard around fish for bubbles.

CHRISTMAS CAKE

An unusual Christmas cake which is thoroughly enjoyable to make, provided that you like painting and have a reasonably steady hand.

INGREDIENTS

Serves 35

- 25 cm/10 in round rich fruit cake, covered with 1.1 kg/2½ lb/2½ lb marzipan
- 1.4 kg/3 lb/3 lb sugarpaste (fondant) icing
- cornflour (cornstarch), for dusting
- red, yellow, green and mauve food colourings

MATERIALS AND EQUIPMENT

- 33 cm/13 in round gold cakeboard
- baking parchment
- dressmakers' pins
- fine paintbrush
- 1 m/1 yd × 2.5 cm/1 in wide red ribbon
- red candle

STORING

The iced cake can be wrapped loosely in foil and stored in a cool place for up to one month.

FREEZING

The fruit cake base can be frozen for up to six months.

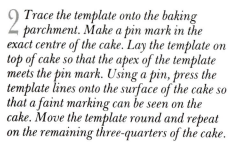

1 Place the cake on the board. Reserve 125 g/4 oz/¼ lb of the sugarpaste (fondant) icing and use the remainder to cover the cake. Colour the reserved sugarpaste (fondant) red and roll out thinly on a surface dusted with cornflour (cornstarch). Dampen the surface of the cakeboard and cover with strips of icing. Smooth down gently and trim off the excess around edge of board. Leave for at least 24 hours to harden.

2 Trace the template onto the baking parchment. Make a pin mark in the exact centre of the cake. Lay the template on top of cake so that the apex of the template meets the pin mark. Using a pin, press the template lines onto the surface of the cake so that a faint marking can be seen on the cake. Move the template round and repeat on the remaining three-quarters of the cake.

3 Cut another piece of baking parchment to fit around the circumference of cake and 6.5 cm/2½ in wide. Lay around the sides of the cake so that the base of the template rests on the cakeboard, securing the ends with a pin. Using a pin, mark a line onto the icing around the top edge of the template. Cut the template in half lengthways and reposition around the cake as before. Mark another line around the top edge of the template, halfway down the sides of the cake. Remove the template.

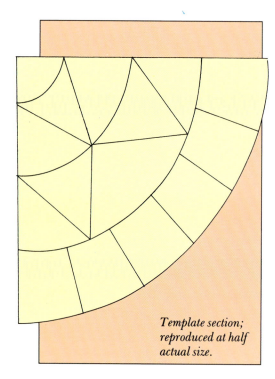

Template section; reproduced at half actual size.

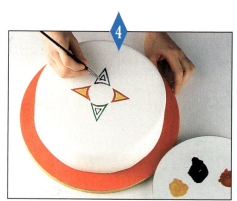

4 Place a little red, yellow, green and mauve food colourings onto a large flat plate and thin each with a little water, as if on a painter's palette. Paint a red triangle of icing onto the cake next to the central circle to within 1 mm/$^1/_{16}$ in of the template markings. Paint another triangle opposite the first. Fill in the centres with yellow. Use the green and mauve colours to fill the remaining triangles around the central circle.

5 Using a clean paintbrush dampened with water, lightly 'smudge' the red and yellow colours together. Repeat on the green and mauve triangles.

6 Using this technique, build up a design over the top and sides of the cake, creating a random design or following the photographed cake. Leave the area between the two marked lines around the cake blank for the ribbon. Incorporate a holly leaf at intervals around the cake, first painting an outline and then filling in with colour. Finish the leaves with red berries.

7 Secure the ribbon around cake and place a candle in the centre, using a little icing (confectioners) sugar mixed to a paste with water as glue.

ARTIST'S BOX AND PALETTE

Making cakes is an art in itself, and this cake proves it. It is the perfect celebration cake for any artist of any age.

INGREDIENTS

Serves 30
- 20 cm/8 in square rich fruit cake
- 45 ml/3 tbsp/3 tbsp apricot glaze
- 450 g/1 lb/1 lb marzipan
- 800 g/1¾ lb/1¾ lb sugarpaste (fondant) icing
- 125 g/4 oz/⅓ cup royal icing, for fixing
- chestnut, blue, mulberry, yellow, green, black, silver and paprika food colourings

MATERIALS AND EQUIPMENT
- stiff paper for template
- greaseproof (wax) paper
- 25–26 cm/10 in square cakeboard
- fine paintbrush

STORING
The iced cake can be stored in an airtight container for up to three weeks.

FREEZING
Not recommended.

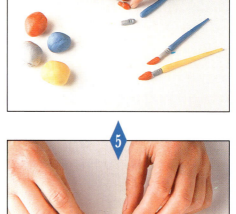

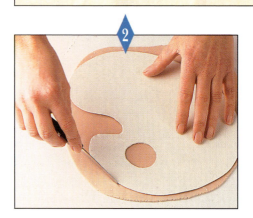

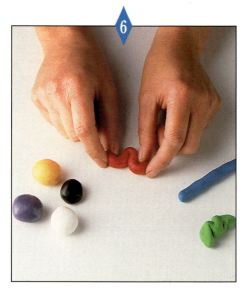

1 Brush the cake with the apricot glaze. Roll out the marzipan, cover the cake and leave to dry for 12 hours.

2 Make a template out of stiff paper in the shape of a painter's palette that will fit on top of the cake. Take 175 g/6 oz/6 oz sugarpaste (fondant) and colour a very pale chestnut. Roll out and cut out the palette shape using the template. Place on a sheet of greaseproof (wax) paper and leave to dry for 12 hours.

3 Take 450 g/1 lb/1 lb sugarpaste (fondant) icing and colour brown with the chestnut colouring. Roll this out, brush the marzipanned cake with a little water to slightly dampen, and cover the cake with the brown-coloured sugarpaste (fondant) icing, cutting away any surplus. Position the cake on the cakeboard, securing underneath with a dab of royal icing. Leave to dry for several hours.

4 Take the remaining 175 g/6 oz/6 oz of the sugarpaste (fondant) icing. Leave half white, divide the remainder into seven equal parts and colour yellow, blue, black, silver, paprika, green and mulberry. Shape the box handle and clips with black and silver and leave to dry on greaseproof (wax) paper for several hours. Shape the paintbrush bristles from paprika-coloured sugarpaste and mark the hairs of the bristles with a knife. Shape the paintbrush handles in various colours and attach the handles, silver metal parts and bristles with a little royal icing. Leave to dry on greaseproof (wax) paper for several hours.

5 Shape the paint tubes from small oblongs of white rolled-out sugarpaste (fondant) icing, sealing the edges with a little water.

6 Paint on markings with a fine paintbrush. Shape squeezed-out paint in various colours and attach two to the paint tubes with a little royal icing. Leave all to dry on greaseproof (wax) paper for several hours.

7 Roll out two small rectangles of any remaining white sugarpaste (fondant) icing to represent sheets of paper, and with a paintbrush and watered down food colours, brush on patterns. Leave to dry on greaseproof (wax) paper for several hours.

8 *Using a fine paintbrush, paint wood markings onto the box.*

9 *To assemble, using a little royal icing, attach the handle and clips onto the front side of the box, and the palette to the top of the cake. Position the paintbrushes, paint tubes, squeezed-out paint and painted paper on the cake and around the board.*

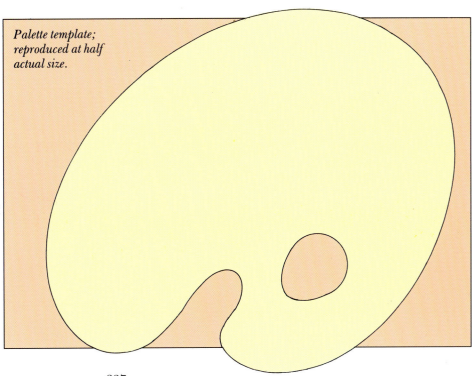

Palette template; reproduced at half actual size.

LIQUORICE SWEET (CANDY) CAKE

If liquorice sweets (candies) are a favourite, this is a cake to fantasize over. Larger than lifesize, its base is a square Madeira cake filled with butter icing, and topped with a pile of smaller look-alike liquorice sweets (candies).

INGREDIENTS

Serves 15–20
- 20 cm/8 in square Madeira cake
- 15 cm/6 in square Madeira cake
- 675 g/1½ lb/1½ lb butter icing
- 45 ml/3 tbsp/3 tbsp apricot glaze
- 350 g/12 oz/¾ lb marzipan
- 800 g/1¾ lb/1¾ lb sugarpaste (fondant) icing
- egg-yellow, black, blue, mulberry food colourings

MATERIALS AND EQUIPMENT

- 25 cm/10 in square cakeboard
- 4.5 cm/1¾ in round cutter

STORING

Kept in an airtight container, the cake will stay fresh for up to three days.

FREEZING

Not recommended.

1 Cut both the cakes horizontally into three. Fill with the butter icing, reserving a little to coat the outsides of the smaller cake. Wrap and set aside the smaller cake.

2 Brush the 20 cm/8 in cake with the apricot glaze. Roll out the marzipan and cover the cake. Position the cake on the cakeboard, securing underneath with a little butter icing. Leave to dry for 12 hours.

3 Take 350 g/12 oz/¾ lb of the sugarpaste (fondant) and colour yellow. Take 125 g/4 oz/¼ lb of the sugarpaste (fondant) and colour half black and leave the other half white. Brush the marzipanned cake lightly with water. Roll out the yellow icing; cover the top and down one third of the sides of the cake.

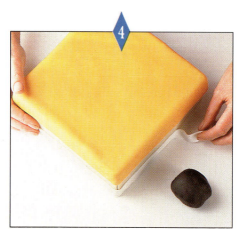

4 Roll out the white icing to a strip wide and long enough to cover the sides of the bottom one-third of the cake. Position onto the cake, securing the join with a little water. Roll out the black icing to a strip wide enough and long enough to fill the central third strip, between the yellow and white strips. Position onto the cake.

5 Take the 15 cm/6 in cake. Cut into three equal strips. Divide two of the strips each into three squares. From the remaining strip cut out two circles (about 4.5 cm/1¾ in), using a cutter as a guide.

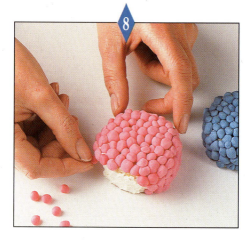

6 Take another 100 g/4 oz/¼ lb sugarpaste (fondant) and colour it black. Take the remaining 225 g/8 oz/½ lb sugarpaste (fondant) and divide into four equal amounts: colour blue, pink, yellow and leave one portion white.

7 Coat the outsides of the cut-out cake pieces with the reserved butter icing. Make the square liquorice sweets (candies) for the top of the cake using the coloured icings, rolling out strips for the sides and squares to coat the tops. Secure any of the strip joins with a little water.

8 Make small balls of pink and blue icing for the round sweets (candies), attaching them by lightly pressing into the butter icing.

9 To make the small rolls for the edges of the cake, roll out any black sugarpaste (fondant) trimmings into a strip about 18 × 13 cm/7 × 5 in. With your fingers, roll out 18 cm/7 in long sausage shapes of yellow, pink, white and blue icing. Position one of the colours down the length of the black strip, roll over to form a filled roll, securing the join underneath with water. Slice into three across. Repeat with the remaining colours.

10 Arrange the smaller liquorice allsorts in a pile on top and around the edges of the large cake.

CANDLE CAKE

Marbled icing is so effective that little other decoration is required. This design combines blue and orange but any other strong colour combination is equally effective.

| INGREDIENTS | MATERIALS AND EQUIPMENT | STORING |

INGREDIENTS

Serves 20
- 20 cm/8 in round rich fruit cake, covered with 800 g/1¾ lb/1¾ lb marzipan
- 900 g/2 lb/2 lb sugarpaste (fondant) icing
- blue, green and orange food colourings
- cornflour (cornstarch), for dusting

MATERIALS AND EQUIPMENT

- 25 cm/10 in round silver cakecard
- 1 bamboo skewer
- 2 household candles
- cling film (plastic wrap)

STORING

The iced cake can be wrapped loosely in foil and stored in a cool place for up to four weeks.

FREEZING

The fruit cake base can be frozen for up to six months.

1 Place the cake on the card. Colour 125 g/4 oz/¼ lb of the sugarpaste (fondant) icing orange and reserve. Reserve another 125 g/4 oz/¼ lb of white sugarpaste (fondant). Divide the remaining icing into three parts. Knead the orange colouring into one piece until deep orange but still streaked with colour. Knead a mixture of blue and green colour into another piece until streaky. Leave the remaining piece white.

2 Lightly dust the work surface with the cornflour (cornstarch). Roll long sausages of icing in the three colours and lay on the work surface.

3 Twist the colours together and knead for several seconds until the strips of colour are secured together but retain their individual colours.

4 Roll out the marbled icing and use to cover the cake, trimming off the excess around the base.

5 Take a small piece of the reserved orange sugarpaste (fondant), about the size of a large grape, and shape into a candle flame. Thread onto the end of the bamboo skewer. Thinly roll the remaining orange sugarpaste (fondant) and use to cover the card around cake. Re-roll the trimmings and cut another strip, 1 cm/½ in wide. Secure over the orange icing around the cake. Cut another strip, 5 mm/¼ in wide, and use to complete the border.

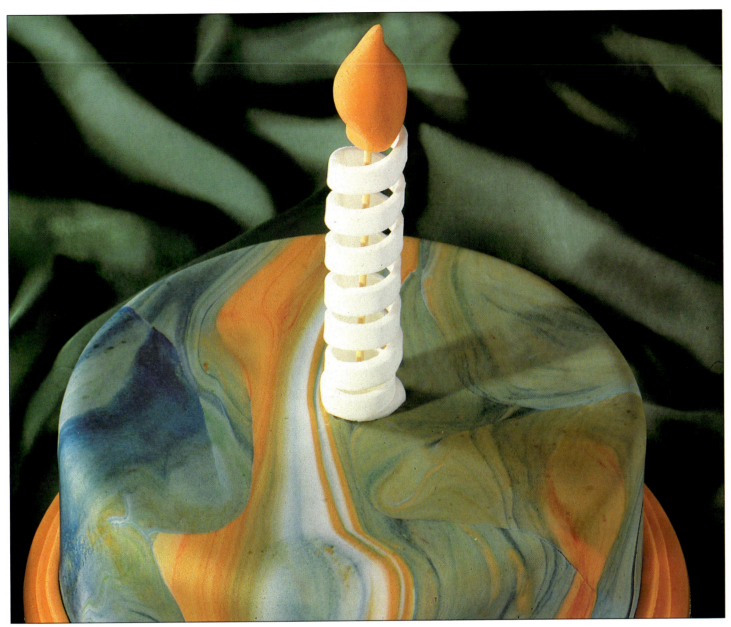

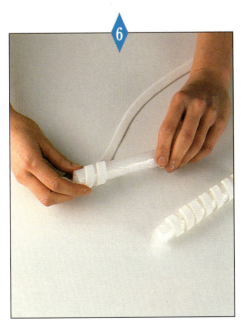

6 *Wrap the candles in cling film (plastic wrap), twisting ends together. (One candle is prepared as a spare.) Roll the reserved white sugarpaste (fondant) to a long thin strip cut vertically into two sections, each about 5 mm/¼ in wide. Starting from one end of a covered candle, coil the icing around the candle, trimming off any excess icing at end. Leave for at least 48 hours to harden.*

7 *To release the icing, untwist the cling film (plastic wrap) and gently push out the candle inside. Carefully peel away the cling film (plastic wrap).*

8 *Place a dot of white icing in the centre of the cake and use to secure the icing candle. Push the bamboo skewer down through the centre to finish.*

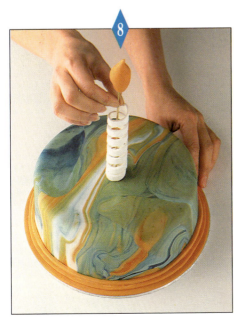

INDIAN ELEPHANT

This is a cake to say happy birthday to children and adults alike. Be as colourful as you like when decorating the elephant – dress it up for a very special occasion.

INGREDIENTS

Serves 30
- 30 cm/12 in square Madeira cake
- 675 g/1½ lb/1½ lb butter icing
- 225 g/8 oz/½ lb marzipan
- black, holly green, mint green, yellow, mulberry food colourings
- chocolate coins, silver balls, coloured chocolate buttons, white chocolate buttons, liquorice allsorts (candy), Smartie (M&M)
- 125 g/4 oz/¼ lb desiccated (shredded) coconut
- 30 ml/2 tbsp/2 tbsp apricot glaze

MATERIALS AND EQUIPMENT

- stiff paper for template
- 36 cm/14 in square cakeboard
- cocktail stick (or toothpick)

STORING

Kept in an airtight container, the cake will stay fresh for up to three days.

FREEZING

Not recommended.

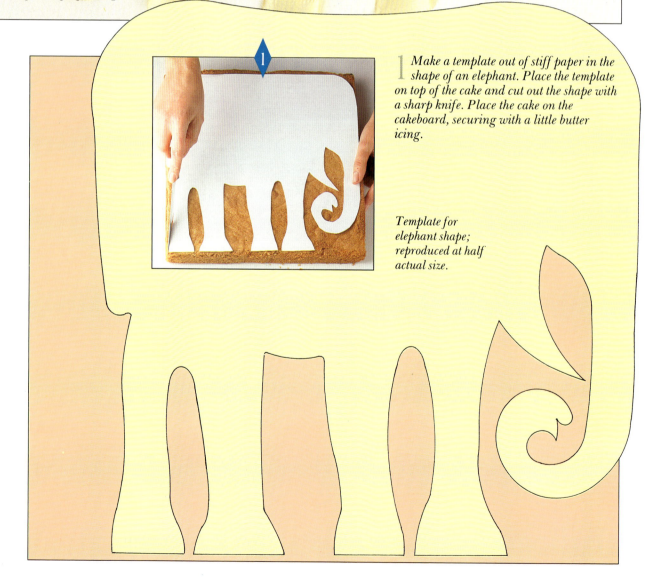

1 Make a template out of stiff paper in the shape of an elephant. Place the template on top of the cake and cut out the shape with a sharp knife. Place the cake on the cakeboard, securing with a little butter icing.

Template for elephant shape; reproduced at half actual size.

2 *Colour the remaining butter icing pale grey, using the black food colour. Cover the top and sides of the cake with the icing carefully, so as not to loosen the cake crumbs. Swirl with a palette knife (spatula).*

3 *Using a cocktail stick dipped in black food colour, swirl in black highlights.*

4 *Taking half of the marzipan, roll out and cut out shapes for the elephant's tusk, headpiece and blanket. Place them in position on the cake. Colour the remaining marzipan pink, yellow and holly green. Roll out and cut out patterns for the blanket, headpiece, trunk and tail. Roll small balls of yellow and pink to make the ankle bracelets.*

5 *Place all in position to decorate the elephant, along with the coins, silver balls, chocolate buttons (using the white ones, halved for the toe nails) and a liquorice allsort and Smartie (M&M) for the eye.*

6 *Rub a little mint green food colour into the coconut with your fingers until well mixed, to represent grass. Brush any uncovered cakeboard with a little apricot glaze and sprinkle the coconut over, in and around the elephant, carefully so as not to touch the icing.*

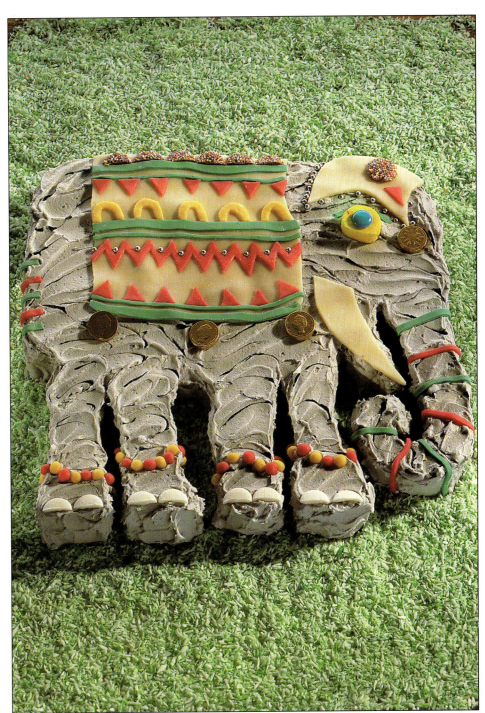

CHRISTMAS CRACKER

A festive cake that is fun to make and fun to eat. To make sure it is really fresh for your Christmas party, the cake can be made and decorated a day or two ahead of time, then simply cut it in half and arrange on the cakeboard with the colourful decorations to serve.

INGREDIENTS

Serves 8
- 4-egg quantity whisked sponge cake
- 225 g/8 oz/½ lb jam, for filling
- 30 ml/2 tbsp/2 tbsp apricot glaze
- 625 g/1 lb 6 oz/1 lb 6 oz sugarpaste (fondant) icing
- Christmas red, mint green, yellow, black, blue food colouring
- red, gold and green foil-wrapped chocolate eggs, coins and bars

MATERIALS AND EQUIPMENT

- 33 × 23 cm/13 × 9 in Swiss (jelly) roll tin (pan)
- 2 small red candles
- 32–36 cm/13–14 in cakeboard

STORING

Kept in an airtight container, the cake will stay fresh for up to three days.

FREEZING

Not recommended.

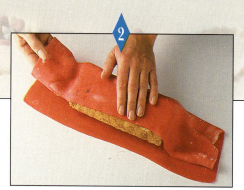

1 Preheat the oven to 180°C/350°F/Gas 4. Grease and line a 33 × 23 cm/13 × 9 in Swiss (jelly) roll tin (pan). Spoon the cake mixture into the prepared tin (pan) and bake in the preheated oven for 20–25 minutes. Allow to cool, spread with the jam and make into a roll. Cut 2.5 cm/1 in off each end of the Swiss (jelly) roll. Cut each piece in half. Set aside. Brush the outside of the roll with the apricot glaze.

2 Take 450 g/1 lb sugarpaste (fondant) and colour it red. Roll it out so it is 15 cm/6 in longer than the length of the trimmed cake, and wide enough to wrap around it. Position the cake in the centre of the red sugarpaste (fondant) icing and wrap around to cover, keeping the join underneath. Secure with water and trim where necessary.

3 Pinch the icing slightly where it meets the ends of the cake to resemble a cracker, and place the reserved pieces of cake inside each end of the icing to support them. Using any red icing trimmings, cut out two circles the same diameter as the ends of the cracker. Dampen the edges and position one at each end of the cracker, pressing together to seal.

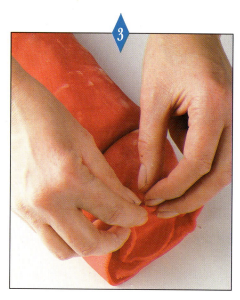

4 Use the remaining icing as follows: colour most of it green and yellow for the decorations, leave a little white for the snowman, and colour a very small amount black and blue. Roll out the green and yellow icing. Cut strips with a knife and small circles with a small cutter or end of a large piping nozzle to decorate the cracker. Arrange the decorations on the cracker, securing with a little water.

5 Make the snowman with the white icing. Shape the body, head, arms and legs separately, then attach to the body, securing with a little water. Shape the hat, eyes and mouth from the black icing, the bow tie from the green, buttons from the red, and a nose from the blue. Position these on the snowman, securing with a little water. Press two small red candles into his arms to hold. Leave to set.

6 When ready to serve, cut the cake in half, making jagged edges, and position on the cakeboard. Sit the snowman on top of one half and arrange the wrapped sweets around the board.

TERRACOTTA FLOWERPOT

A cake ideal for celebrating a gardener's birthday, Mother's Day or a Happy Retirement. The cake is baked in a pudding basin (deep bowl) for the flowerpot shape and filled with a colourful arrangement of icing flowers and foliage.

INGREDIENTS

Serves 15
- 3-egg quantity Madeira cake mixture
- 175 g/6 oz/6 oz jam
- 175 g/6 oz/6 oz butter icing
- 30 ml/2 tbsp/2 tbsp apricot glaze
- 575 g/1¼ lb/1¼ lb sugarpaste (fondant) icing
- 125 g/4 oz/⅓ cup royal icing, for fixing
- dark orange-red, black, red, silver, green, purple, yellow food colouring
- 2 chocolate-flake bars, coarsely crushed

MATERIALS AND EQUIPMENT

- 1.1 l/2 pt/5 cup pudding basin (deep bowl)
- greaseproof (wax) paper
- string
- fine paintbrush
- thin green wire
- 23 cm/9 in round cakeboard

STORING

Kept in an airtight container, the cake will stay fresh for up to three days.

FREEZING

Not recommended.

1 Preheat the oven to 160°C/325°F/Gas 3. Grease and line the bottom of a 1.1 l/2 pt/5 cup pudding basin (deep bowl). Spoon in the cake mixture and bake for 1¼ hours. Cover with foil for last 10 minutes if the top begins to brown. Turn out and cool on a wire rack.

2 When cold trim the top of the cake flat if it has domed. Cut the cake horizontally into three, and fill with the jam and butter icing.

3 Cut out a shallow circle from the top of the cake, leaving a 1 cm/½ in rim round the edge.

4 Brush the outside of the cake and the rim with the apricot glaze. Take 400 g/14 oz/scant 1 lb of the sugarpaste (fondant) icing and colour deep orange-red. Measure round the cake at its widest part and its height, with string. Roll out the deep orange-red-coloured icing to this measurement, remembering to add the width of the rim to the height. Wrap the icing round the cake and over the rim, moulding gently with your hands to fit. Reserve the trimmings, wrapped. Leave the cake to dry for several hours.

5 Using the trimmings, shape the decorations and handles for the flowerpot. Leave to dry on greaseproof (wax) paper. Sprinkle the flake into the top of the cake to represent soil.

6 Colour a small piece of the remaining sugarpaste (fondant) icing a very pale orange-red, roll out into an oblong and fold over to form a seed bag. Leave to dry then paint on a pattern with a fine paintbrush. Colour a very small piece of icing black and make the seeds. Leave to dry on greaseproof (wax) paper. Colour two more small pieces of icing red and silver and shape the trowel, leaving it to dry over a wooden spoon handle. Colour the remaining icing green, purple and a very small amount yellow.

7 Shape the flowers with the purple icing by moulding the petals individually and attaching together with royal icing. Roll out the yellow icing and cut out the flower centres with a small knife. Position in the middle of each flower with a small ball of yellow icing, securing with royal icing. Leave to dry on greaseproof (wax) paper.

8 Shape the leaves and short stems with the green icing using your fingers and mark the veins with the back of a knife. Insert short pieces of thin green wire up some of the stems, so you can create different heights when they go into the flowerpot. Leave to dry over the handle of a wooden spoon. Roll out any remaining green icing and cut to represent grass.

9 Attach the deep orange-red decorations on the flowerpot with royal icing. Arrange the leaves and flowers in the pot. Place on the cakeboard and place the trowel, seed packet and grass around the outside.

GLITTERING STAR

With a quick flick of a paintbrush you can give a sparkling effect to this glittering cake. Add some shimmering stars and moons and you have a cake ready to celebrate a birthday, Christmas, Halloween or silver wedding anniversary – all for the stars in your life.

INGREDIENTS

Serves 20–25

- 20 cm/8 in round rich fruit cake
- 40 ml/2½ tbsp/2½ tbsp apricot glaze
- 675 g/1½ lb/1½ lb marzipan
- 450 g/1 lb/1 lb sugarpaste (fondant) icing
- 125 g/4 oz/⅓ cup royal icing for fixing
- silver, gold, lilac shimmer, red sparkle, glitter green, primrose sparkle food colourings

MATERIALS AND EQUIPMENT

- greaseproof (wax) paper
- paintbrush
- stiff paper for templates
- 25 cm/10 in round cakeboard or plate

STORING

Kept in an airtight container, the cake will keep for up to three weeks.

FREEZING

Not recommended.

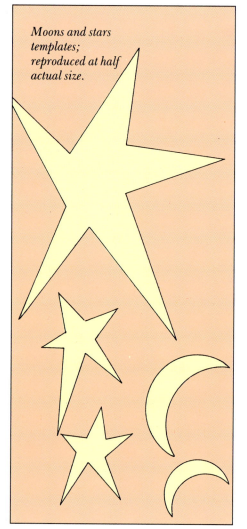

Moons and stars templates; reproduced at half actual size.

1 Brush the cake with the apricot glaze. Roll out two-thirds of the marzipan and cover the cake. Leave to dry for 12 hours.

2 Roll out the sugarpaste (fondant) icing. Brush the marzipanned cake with a little water to slightly dampen and cover the cake with the sugarpaste (fondant) icing. Leave to dry for several hours.

3 Place the cake on a large sheet of greaseproof (wax) paper. Water down a little powdered silver food colouring and, using a paintbrush loaded with the colour, flick this all over the cake to give a spattered effect. Allow to dry.

4 Make templates out of stiff paper in two or three different-sized moon shapes and three or four irregular star shapes. Take the remaining marzipan, divide into five pieces and colour silver, gold, lilac, pink, green and yellow. Roll out each colour and cut into stars and moons using the templates as a guide, cutting some of the stars in half.

5 Place the cut-out shapes on the greaseproof (wax) paper, brush each with its own colour in powdered form to add more glitter. Allow to dry for several hours.

6 Position the cake on the cakeboard, securing underneath with a dab of royal icing, or place on a plate. Arrange the stars and moons at different angles all over the cake, attaching with royal icing, and position the halved stars upright as though coming out of the cake. Allow to set.

PORCUPINE

Melt-in-the-mouth strips of flaky chocolate bars give this porcupine its spiky coating, and a quick-mix moist chocolate cake makes the base. It's a fun cake for a children's or adults' party.

INGREDIENTS

Serves 15

- 3-egg quantity chocolate-flavoured quick-mix sponge cake
- 575 g/1¼ lb/1¼ lb chocolate-flavoured butter icing
- 50 g/2 oz/2 oz white marzipan
- cream, black, green, red, brown food colourings
- 5–6 chocolate flake bars

MATERIALS AND EQUIPMENT

- greaseproof (wax) paper
- 1.1 l/2 pt/5 cup pudding basin (deep bowl)
- 600 ml/1 pt/2½ cup pudding basin (deep bowl)
- 36 cm/14 in long rectangular cakeboard
- cocktail stick (or toothpick)
- fine paintbrush

STORING

Kept in a container in the refrigerator, the cake will stay fresh for up to three days.

FREEZING

Not recommended.

1 Preheat the oven to 160°C/325°F/Gas 3. Grease and line the bottoms of a 1.1 l/2 pt/5 cup and a 600 ml/1 pt/2½ cup pudding basin (deep bowl). Spoon the cake mixture into both basins (bowls) to two-thirds full. Bake in the preheated oven, allowing 55 mins–1 hr for the larger basin (bowl) and 35–40 mins for the smaller basin (bowl). Turn out and allow to cool on a wire rack.

2 Place both cakes on a surface so the widest ends are underneath. Take the smaller cake and, holding a sharp knife at an angle, slice off a piece from either side to create a pointed nose at one end.

3 Place the larger cake on the cakeboard behind the smaller one. Cut one of the cut-off slices in half and position either side, between the larger and small cake, to fill in the side gaps. Place the other cut-off piece on top to fill in the top gap, securing all with a little butter icing.

4 Spread the remaining butter icing all over the cake. On the pointed face part, make markings with a cocktail stick.

5 Break or cut the flake bars into thin strips and stick into the butter icing over the body of the porcupine to represent spikes.

6 Reserve a small portion of marzipan. Divide the remainder into three and colour one portion black, one green and one cream. Colour a tiny portion of the reserved, white marzipan brown for the apple stems. With the cream marzipan shape the ears and feet, using black and white make the eyes, and with the rest of the black shape the nose and the claws for the feet. With the green marzipan make the apples, painting on red markings with a fine paintbrush. Position the stems. Place everything except the apples in its proper place on the porcupine cake. Finally, place the apples on the board by the front of the porcupine.

TROPICAL PARROT

Create a tropical feel to any celebration with this colourful, exotic cake, whether for a Bon Voyage to faraway places or a simple birthday. The cake is made from one round Madeira cake, cutting out three easy shapes to give the parrot's body, tail and the branch it sits on. You can then be as decorative as you like with the markings and foliage.

INGREDIENTS

Serves 15
- 20 cm/8 in round Madeira cake
- 500 g/1 lb 2 oz/1 lb 2 oz butter icing
- 450 g/1 lb/1 lb sugarpaste (fondant) icing
- red, brown, green, yellow, orange, blue, purple, pink, black food colouring

MATERIALS AND EQUIPMENT

- 20 cm/8 in round cake tin (pan)
- greaseproof (wax) paper
- stiff paper for templates
- 36 cm/14 in square cakeboard

STORING

Kept in an airtight container, the cake will stay fresh for up to three days.

FREEZING

Not recommended.

1 Make templates out of stiff paper for the parrot's body, tail and branch. Place the templates on top of the cake and cut out the shapes with a sharp knife.

2 Take the sugarpaste (fondant) icing and colour about one-third red. Colour a quarter of the remaining piece brown and the rest yellow, pink, orange, blue, purple, black, green and light green. Leave a small amount white.

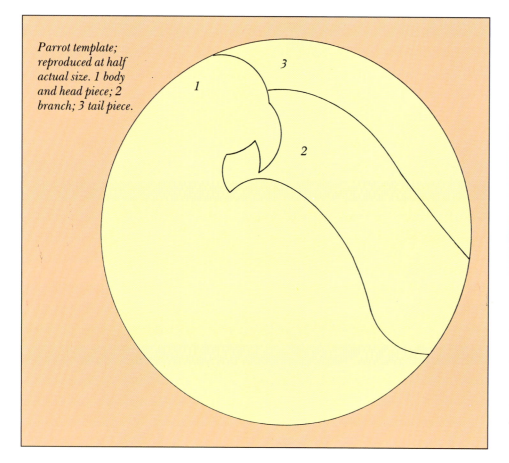

Parrot template; reproduced at half actual size. 1 body and head piece; 2 branch; 3 tail piece.

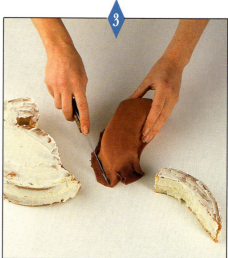

3 Slice each piece of cake (body, tail and branch) in half horizontally and fill with some of the butter icing. Use the remaining butter icing to coat the outsides of the cake. Measure the length and depth of the cake which forms the branch. Roll out the brown icing in one piece large enough to cover it. Position over the cake branch and trim to fit.

4 Measure the length and depth of the
sides of the parrot's body. Roll out some
of the red icing and cut strips to match the
measurements. Press onto the butter icing to
fix in position. Roll out a piece of red icing
for the top of the parrot's body, using the
template as a guide. Leave out the face,
beak and blue body parts. Position the red
sugarpaste (fondant) on the butter icing,
reserving the trimmings. Roll out a piece of
white and some black icing for the face and
beak, cut to fit and ease into position with
your fingers. Do the same with a piece of
blue icing to finish off the body, and with
the tailpiece, using the rest of the reserved
red icing.

5 Roll out the other coloured pieces of
icing. Cut out pieces in the shape of
feathers, some with jagged edges. Press these
into position on the body and tail, easing to
fit with your fingers. Secure with a little
water, bending and twisting some of the
'feathers' to create different angles and
heights. Cut out leaf and flower shapes for
the branch out of the green and pink icings.
Use templates as a guide, if wished.

6 Place the iced parrot pieces in position
on the cakeboard. Make the eye for the
parrot. Secure the eye onto the head with
water, and use water to fix leaves and
flower on the branch. If wished, colour an
additional 125 g/4 oz/¼ lb sugarpaste
(fondant) icing green. Roll and cut out more
leaves to decorate the base of the parrot.

HALLOWEEN PUMPKIN

Halloween is a time for spooky cakes – witches may even burst out of them. This one is made in two pudding basins (deep bowls), making it easy to create a pumpkin effect. Make the cake and icing with your favourite flavour – and you are all set for a party full of eerie surprises.

INGREDIENTS

Serves 15
- *3-egg quantity orange-flavoured Madeira cake mixture*
- *250 g/9 oz/9 oz orange-flavoured butter icing*
- *450 g/1 lb/1 lb sugarpaste (fondant) icing*
- *125 g/4 oz/¼ lb royal icing for fixing*
- *orange, black, yellow food colourings*

MATERIALS AND EQUIPMENT

- *greaseproof (wax) paper*
- *2 × 1.1 l/2 pt/5 cup pudding basins (deep bowls)*
- *thin wooden skewer*
- *thin paintbrush*
- *23 cm/9 in round cakeboard*

STORING

Kept in an airtight container, the cake will stay fresh for up to three days.

FREEZING

Not recommended.

1 Preheat the oven to 160°C/325°F/Gas 3. Grease and line the bottoms of two 1.1 l/2 pt/5 cup pudding basins (deep bowls). Divide the cake mixture equally between them and bake for 1¼ hours. Turn out and cool on a wire rack.

2 Trim the widest ends of each cake so they will fit flat against one another to make a round shape. Split each cake in half horizontally and fill with some of the butter icing, then stick the two cakes together with butter icing to form a pumpkin. Trim one of the narrow ends off slightly, to give a better shape. Let this end be the bottom of the pumpkin. Cover the outside of the cake with the remaining butter icing.

3 Take 350 g/12 oz/¾ lb of the sugarpaste (fondant) icing and colour it orange. Roll out to cover the cake, trimming to fit where necessary. Mould it gently with your hands to give a smooth surface. Reserve the trimmings.

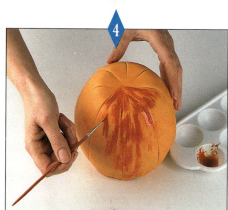

4 With a thin wooden skewer, mark the segments onto the pumpkin. With a fine paintbrush and watered-down orange food colouring, paint on the markings for the pumpkin flesh. Use orange sugarpaste (fondant) trimmings for the top of the cake where the witch bursts out, by cutting and tearing rolled out pieces to create jagged edges. Attach to the top of the cake with a little water.

5 Take the remaining sugarpaste (fondant) icing and colour three-quarters black. Of the remainder, colour a little yellow and leave the rest white. Use some of the black and white to make the witch, moulding the head, arms and body separately and securing with royal icing. When set, roll out some black icing and cut jagged edges to form a cape. Drape over the arms and body, securing with a little water. Make the hat in two pieces – a circle and a cone – and secure with royal icing. Leave to dry on greaseproof (wax) paper. Shape the cauldron, broomstick and cat's head out of more of the black and yellow icing, securing the handle of the cauldron with royal icing when dry. Leave all to dry completely on greaseproof (wax) paper.

6 Use the remaining black icing for the pumpkin features. Roll out and cut out the eyes, nose and mouth with a sharp knife. Attach to the pumpkin with a little water. Place the cake on the cakeboard, secure the witch on top of the cake with royal icing and arrange the cat, cauldron and broomstick around the base.

CHRISTENING SAMPLER

Instead of embroidering a sampler to welcome a newly-born baby, why not make a sampler cake to celebrate?

INGREDIENTS

Serves 30
- 20 cm/8 in square rich fruit cake
- 45 ml/3 tbsp/3 tbsp apricot glaze
- 450 g/1 lb/1 lb marzipan
- 675 g/1½ lb/1½ lb sugarpaste (fondant) icing
- brown, blue, pink, yellow, orange, green, cream, purple food colourings

MATERIALS AND EQUIPMENT

- 25 cm/10 in square cakeboard
- fine paintbrush
- small heart-shaped biscuit (cookie) cutter

STORING

Kept in an airtight container, the cake will stay fresh for up to three weeks.

FREEZING

Not recommended.

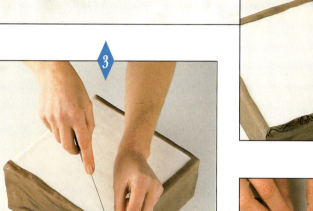

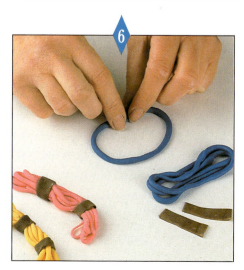

1 Brush the cake with apricot glaze. Roll out the marzipan, cover the cake and leave to dry for 12 hours.

2 Cut 450 g/1 lb/1 lb of the sugarpaste (fondant) icing into three. Take one-third and roll out to the size of the top of the cake. Brush the top of the cake with a little water and cover with the icing.

3 Take the other two-thirds of the icing for the sides and colour brown. Roll out in four separate pieces to the measured length and about 1 cm/½ in wider than the width of each side. Brush each side with a little water, then press each piece of brown icing on, folding over the extra width at the top to represent the edges of a picture frame. Cut off each corner at an angle to represent the mitred join of the frame. Reserve any brown trimmings. Place the cake on the cakeboard.

4 With a fine paintbrush, paint over the sides with watered-down brown food colouring to represent wood grain.

5 Take the remaining sugarpaste (fondant) icing and colour small amounts yellow, orange, brown, purple, cream, two shades of blue, green and pink. Leave a little white. Use these colours to shape the ducks, teddy bear, bulrushes, water, apple-blossom branch and leaves. Roll out a small piece of pink icing and cut out a heart with a small heart-shaped biscuit (cookie) cutter (or use a template).-Roll out a small piece of white icing and cut out the baby's initial with a small sharp knife.

For the border, roll out strips of blue and yellow icing and cut into oblongs and squares; make small balls and small squares out of the purple icing. For the apple blossom, gently work together the pale pink, deep pink and white sugarpaste (fondant) to give a marbled effect. Shape the flowers from this, placing a small white ball in the centre. Attach all the decorations onto the cake with a little water as you make them.

6 With any leftover colours, roll out long strips of icing with your hands to make 'threads'. Form them into loops, attaching the joins with water. Use small strips of brown icing trimmings to hold the threads together. Arrange around the base of the cake on the board.

MARKET STALL

An open-air market stall is the theme for this cake, bursting with colourful produce. Vary this design if you wish, adding as wide a variety of fruit and vegetables as you wish.

INGREDIENTS

Serves 30
- 20 cm/8 in square rich fruit cake
- 45 ml/3 tbsp/3 tbsp apricot glaze
- 900 g/2 lb/2 lb marzipan
- 450 g/1 lb/1 lb sugarpaste (fondant) icing
- 125 g/4 oz/1/4 lb royal icing, for fixing
- brown, green, red, orange, yellow, peach, purple, pink, black food colourings

MATERIALS AND EQUIPMENT

- greaseproof (wax) paper
- 25 cm/10 in square cakeboard
- fine paintbrush

STORING

Kept in an airtight container, the cake will stay fresh for up to three weeks.

FREEZING

Not recommended.

1 Slice 4 cm/1½ in off one side of the cake. Brush the cake with apricot glaze. Take half of the marzipan (reserve the other half for shaping the fruits and vegetables). Roll out three-quarters of it and cover the large piece of cake with it. With the other quarter of marzipan, cover one long side, the top and the two short sides of the cake slice. Leave to dry for 12 hours.

2 Colour half of the sugarpaste (fondant) icing brown and the other half green. Using three-quarters of the brown icing, cover three sides of the large cake (not the cut side), brushing the marzipan first with a little water to secure the icing. With the other quarter of brown icing, cover the marzipanned sides of the smaller piece of cake, measuring first to fit and brushing the marzipan with a little water to stick. Reserve any brown icing trimmings. With these trimmings, roll out and cut narrow dividers to fit the top of the cake. Leave the dividers on greaseproof (wax) paper to dry for several hours.

3 Place the large piece of cake on the cakeboard, with the smaller one in front to create a different level. Attach the cakes together with royal icing and use icing to attach to the board.

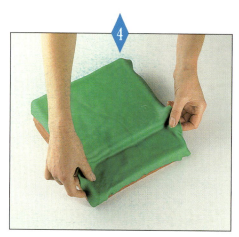

4 Measure the length and width of the cake, including the lower level. Roll out the green icing about 4 cm/1½ in wider and longer than the measured length and width. Brush the marzipan on the tops of the cakes with a little water and cover the cakes with the green icing. Allow it to fall naturally in folds over the edges. Leave the cake to dry for several hours.

5 Take the remaining 450 g/1 lb/1 lb marzipan, reserve a little for the stall holder and colour the rest red, orange, yellow, green, brown, peach and purple. Use these colours to shape the fruits and vegetables. Add markings with a fine paintbrush onto the melons, peaches and potatoes. For the front of the stall, shape baskets and a potato sack out of different shades of brown. For the stallholder, colour the reserved marzipan pink, purple, black and flesh-coloured and shape the head, body and arms separately, attaching with a little royal icing. Make the hands and face features and the hair, and press on with a little water. Place a melon in her arms to hold. Leave all to dry on greaseproof (wax) paper for several hours.

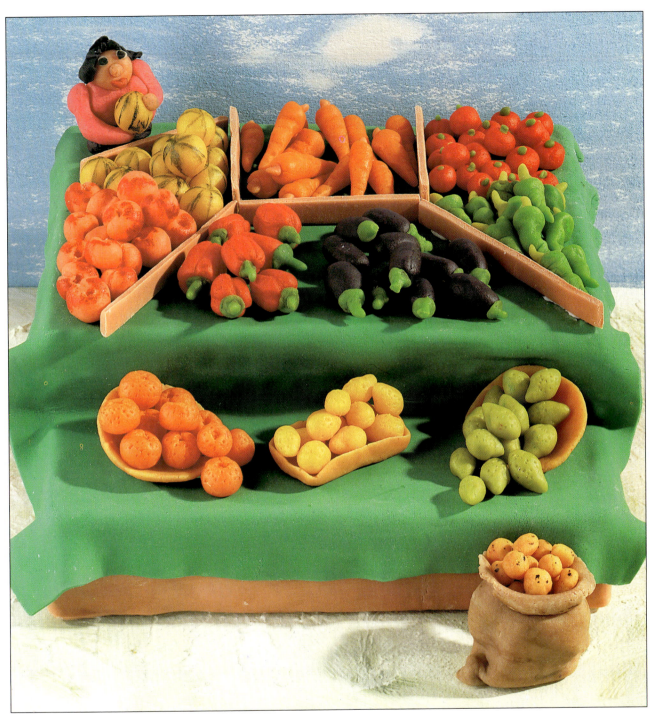

6 *Attach the dividers, the baskets and the stallholder onto the cake with royal icing. Arrange the produce in piles on the stall between the dividers and in the baskets, and the sack of potatoes in the front.*

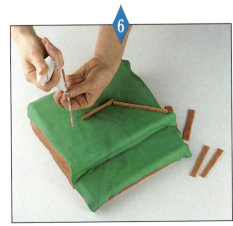

RACING RING

A simple ring cake makes the perfect base for this teddy-bear racing track. Choose the flattest and widest end of the cake for the top (this will depend on the shape of your ring mould), so there's plenty of room for the icing cars to race around on.

INGREDIENTS

Serves 12
- 2-egg quantity quick-mix sponge cake mixture
- 350 g/12 oz/³/₄ lb butter icing
- 500 g/1 lb 2 oz/1 lb 2 oz sugarpaste (fondant) icing
- 125 g/4 oz/¹/₄ lb royal icing, for fixing
- black, blue, yellow, green, orange, red, purple food colourings
- selection of miniature liquorice sweets (candies), dolly mixtures and teddy bears
- 113 g/4¹/₂ oz packet liquorice Catherine wheels

MATERIALS AND EQUIPMENT

- 22 cm/8¹/₂ in ring mould
- 25 cm/10 in round cakeboard
- 1 thin wooden kebab skewer
- fine paintbrush
- greaseproof (wax) paper

STORING

Kept in an airtight container, the cake will stay fresh for up to three days.

FREEZING

Not recommended.

1 Preheat the oven to 160°C/325°F/Gas 3. Spoon the cake mixture into a greased ring mould. Bake for 35–40 minutes. Turn out and cool on a wire rack.

2 Cut the cake in half horizontally and fill with some of the butter icing. Cover the outside of the cake with the remaining butter icing, having the widest part of the cake on top.

3 Cut 350 g/12 oz/³/₄ lb of the sugarpaste (fondant) icing in half. Use half for coating the top and inside ring of the cake and half for coating the outside. To coat the inside of the ring, cut one half of the icing in half again and roll out to the measured diameter and width, (reserve the other piece for the top). Press in position over the butter icing. Roll out the reserved piece for the top to the measured diameter and width (you may find this easier to do in two halves), pressing in position and easing into shape over the butter icing.

4 Take the half piece of icing reserved for coating the outside and roll out to the measured width and diameter. Press in position round the outside of the cake, reserving the white icing trimmings to make the flag. Place the cake on the cakeboard.

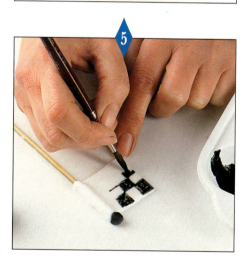

5 Take the reserved white icing trimmings and roll out to an oblong for the flag. Cut the wooden kebab skewer to a height of about 12.5 cm/5 in and fold one end of the flag round it, securing with a little water. With black food colouring and a fine paintbrush paint on a chequered pattern. Colour a small piece of icing black, make into a ball and stick on top of the skewer. Create a few folds in the flag and leave to dry on greaseproof (wax) paper.

6 Colour the remaining sugarpaste (fondant) icing blue, yellow, green, orange, red and a very small amount purple. Shape each car in two pieces, attaching in the centre with royal icing where the seat joins the body of the car. Add decorations and headlights and attach dolly mixture wheels with royal icing. Place a candy teddy bear in each car and leave to set.

7 *Take the liquorice Catherine wheels and unwind them, removing the centre sweets. Lay the liquorice over the top of the cake to represent the track, leaving a gap in the middle and securing onto the cake with royal icing. Secure one strip round the bottom of the cake also.*

8 *Cut some of the liquorice into small strips and attach round the middle of the outside of the cake with royal icing. Arrange small liquorice sweets around the bottom of the cake. Position the cars on top of the cake on the tracks and attach the flag to the outside with royal icing.*

Great Britain

THE BRITISH SUGARCRAFT GUILD
Wellington House, Messeter Place, Eltham, London SE9 5DP.

CAKE ART LTD
Wholesale suppliers of icings and equipment. Unit 16, Crown Close, Crown Industrial Estate, Priors Wood, Taunton, Somerset TA2 8RX.

SUGARCRAFT SUPPLIERS PME (HARROW) LTD
Suppliers of decorating equipment. Brember Road, South Harrow, Middlesex HA2 8UN.

JF RENSHAW LTD
Suppliers of icings. Locks Lane, Mitcham, Surrey CR4 2XG.

ESSEX ICING CENTRE
Suppliers of materials and equipment. 20 Western Road, Billericay, Essex CM12 9DZ.

INVICTA BAKEWARE LTD
Manufacturers and suppliers of bakery equipment. Westgate Business Park, Westgate Carr Road, Pickering, North Yorkshire YO18 8LX.

CRANHAM CATERING
Suppliers of materials and equipment. 95 Front Lane, Cranham, Upminster, Essex RM14 1XN.

CRAIGMILLAR
Suppliers of icings. Stadium Road, Bromborough, Wirral, Merseyside LO2 3NU.

PROMODEM LTD
Technical consultancy and suppliers of cake tilters. 141 Grange Road, Great Burstead, Billericay, Essex CM11 2SA.

SQUIRES KITCHEN
Squire House, 3 Waverley Lane, Farnham, Surrey GU9 8BB.

E RUSSUM & SONS
Edward House, Tenter Street, Rotherham.

THE HOUSE OF SUGARCRAFT
Suppliers of flower cutters, powder and paste colours and piping tubes. Unit 10, Broxhead Industrial Estate, Lindford Road, Bordon, Hampshire GU35 0NY.

CEL CAKES
Suppliers of modelling tools, containers and display cabinets. Springfield House, Gate Helmsley, York, North Yorkshire YO4 1NF.

JENNY CAMPBELL TRADING/B R MATTHEWS AND SON
12 Gypsy Hill, Upper Norwood, London SE19 1NN.

CYNTHIA VENN
3 Anker Lane, Stubbington, Fareham, Hampshire PO14 3HF.

KNIGHTSBRIDGE BUSINESS CENTRE (WILTON UK)
Knightsbridge, Cheltenham, Gloucestershire GL51 9TA.

RAINBOW RIBBONS
Unit D5, Romford Seedbed Centre, Davidson Way, Romford, Essex RM7 0AZ.

North America

ICES (INTERNATIONAL CAKE EXPLORATION SOCIETY)
*Membership enquiries: 3087–30th St. S.W., Ste.101, Grandville,
MI 49418.*

MAID OF SCANDINAVIA
Equipment, supplies, courses, magazine Mailbox News. *3244
Raleigh Avenue, Minneapolis, MN 55416.*

WILTON ENTERPRISES INC
2240 West 75th Street, Woodridge, Illinois 60517.

HOME CAKE ARTISTRY INC
1002 North Central, Suite 511, Richardson, Texas 75080.

LORRAINE'S INC
148 Broadway, Hanover, MA 02339.

CREATIVE TOOLS LTD
3 Tannery Court, Richmond Hill, Ontario, Canada L4C 7V5.

MCCALL'S SCHOOL OF CAKE DECORATING INC
3810 Bloor Street, Islington, Ontario, Canada M9B 6C2.

Australia

**AUSTRALIAN NATIONAL CAKE DECORATORS'
ASSOCIATION**
PO Box 321, Plympton, SA 5038.

CAKE DECORATING ASSOCIATION OF VICTORIA
*President, Shirley Vaas, 4 Northcote Road, Ocean Grove, Victoria
3226.*

CAKE DECORATING GUILD OF NEW SOUTH WALES
President, Fay Gardiner, 4 Horsley Cres, Melba, Act, 2615.

CAKE DECORATING ASSOCIATION OF TASMANIA
*Secretary, Jenny Davis, 29 Honolulu Street, Midway Point,
Tasmania 7171.*

**CAKE DECORATORS' ASSOCIATION OF SOUTH
AUSTRALIA**
*Secretary, Lorraine Joliffe, Pindari, 12 Sussex Crescent, Morphet
Vale, SA 5162.*

CAKE ORNAMENT CO
156 Alfred Street, Fortitude Valley, Brisbane 4006.

South Africa

SOUTH AFRICAN SUGARCRAFT GUILD
National Office, 1 Tuzla Mews, 187 Smit Street, Fairlan 2195.

JEM CUTTERS
PO Box 115, Kloof, 3 Nisbett Road, Pinetown 3600.

New Zealand

NEW ZEALAND CAKE DECORATORS' GUILD
Secretary, Morag Scott, 17 Ranui Terrace, Tawa, Wellington.

DECOR CAKES
RSA Arcade, 435 Great South Road, Otahaha.

INDEX

ACKNOWLEDGEMENTS

Janice Murfitt would like to thank the following: Mavis Giles for her unfailing ability to type illegible copy at a minute's notice; Jean Ainger for supplying equipment and sugarcraft props for photography; Cake Fayre, 11 Saddlers Walk, 44 East Street, Chichester, W Sussex, PO19 1HQ (Tel. 0243 771857).

Louise Pickford and Sarah Maxwell would like to thank Teresa Goldfinch for her assistance with home economy.